# The Hidden Realm of God

The Historical Jesus and His Healing Philosophy

**James Gaither, ThD**

*Angel !*
*So your name*
*suits you!*
*James Gaith*

Decad Publications

Book and Cover design by Joanna Carrell

ISBN: 9781508645818

First Edition: March 2015


10 9 8 7 6 5 4 3 2 1

# The Hidden Realm of God

## Contents

Acknowledgements ........................................................................................ iv

Introduction: Philosophy, Healing, and Jesus ....................................... 1

**Chapter One:  The Quest for the Historical Jesus** .......................... 5

*Brief History of the Four Canonical Gospels* ................................... 5

*A Fifth Gospel* .......................................................................................... 5

*Adventures in New Testament Scholarship* ................................... 7

*The Jesus Seminar* ................................................................................ 10

*Methodology for Identifying the Historical Jesus* ....................... 14

**Chapter Two:  About 30 Years** .............................................................. 16

*Jesus' Healing Work* ............................................................................. 22

*Was Jesus an "Exorcist"?* .................................................................. 23

*Healings* ................................................................................................ 28

*Entering the Healing "Christ-consciousness"* ............................ 30

**Chapter Three:  God, Faith, and Healing** ......................................... 33

*The First Century Idea of God* ......................................................... 33

*Jesus on God* .......................................................................................... 35

*God First* ............................................................................................... 35

*A Case for Faith in God* ..................................................................... 37

*The Unconditional Love of God* ...................................................... 48

**Chapter Four: Optimistic Thinking, Health and Healing** ............. 53

*The Presence of God's Realm and Rule* ......................................... 54

*Principle of Expansion* ....................................................................... 56

*A Friendly Universe: Ask and Receive* ........................................... 63

*Optimism and Health* ......................................................................... 70

*Practical Applications* ......................................................................... 72

**Chapter Five: Ethics, Love, and Healing** .......................................... 77

*On Love and Justice* ............................................................................. 78

*The Love Ethic* ....................................................................................... 82

*Generosity and Inclusivity* ............................................................... 83

*How to Love Your Enemies* ............................................................... 86

*Forgiveness and Non-Judgment* ..................................................... 90

*Love, Forgiveness, Health & Healing*..........................97

*A Practical Application* ..........................99

**Chapter Six: Jesus on the Laws of Moses** ..........................**100**

*Hate Your Family and Your Life?*..........................*104*

*Reason, Intuition, and the Ten Commandments* ..........................*107*

**Chapter Seven: Meditation Induction and Prayer** ..........................**114**

*Catalytic Aphorisms* ..........................*116*

*Jesus: An Early "Hypnotherapist"?* ..........................*117*

*Catalytic Aphorisms of Jesus* ..........................*123*

**Chapter Eight: Prayer, Meditation, and Hypnosis Research** ..........................**138**

*Jesus on Prayer* ..........................*138*

*Prayer Studies*..........................*142*

*Anxiety Reduction and Health* ..........................*145*

*Therapeutic Effects of Hypnosis and Meditation*..........................*146*

*The Practice of Meditation*..........................*150*

**Chapter Nine: Self Knowledge and Transformation** ..........................**154**

*Five Keys to Transformation* ..........................*157*

**Chapter Ten: Jesus on Human Potential and On Himself**..........................**173**

*Jesus on Human Potential* ..........................*173*

*What Jesus Said about Himself* ..........................*178*

**Chapter Eleven: Jesus as Philosopher, Humorist, and Healer** ..........................**183**

*The Cynic Jesus* ..........................*185*

*The Stoic Jesus* ..........................*190*

*The Pythagorean Jesus* ..........................*193*

*The Taoist Jesus* ..........................*195*

*The Moist Jesus* ..........................*197*

*Jesus as Humorist* ..........................*198*

*Context and Form of Jesus' Humorous Sayings* ..........................*201*

*The Therapeutic Effects of Humor and Laughter*..........................*204*

**Chapter Twelve: A Philosopher-Healer Goes to Jerusalem** ..........................**206**

*The Aftermath* ..........................*215*

**Chapter Thirteen: The Experiment** ..........................**221**

*Recovering the Unique Voice of Jesus* ..........................*221*

*Mark*..................................................................................................*223*

*Matthew*.............................................................................................*226*

*Luke* ...................................................................................................*228*

*John* ....................................................................................................*229*

*Thomas* ..............................................................................................*230*

*A 21st Century Study of Jesus' Philosophy and Altered States of*
*Consciousness* ....................................................................................*231*

*A Brief Digression on History, Mythology & Reality* ...................................*235*

**Chapter Fourteen: Conclusion** ...........................................................**238**

*Jesus the Therapist* ....................................................................................*239*

*The Original Philosophy of Jesus*...............................................................*240*

**APPENDIX A – ABSTRACT** ........................................................................**242**

*The Therapeutic Psychosomatic Effects of The Philosophy of the Historical*
*Jesus of Nazareth*.................................................................................*242*

**APPENDIX B – Study of Effects of Sayings of Jesus** ...............................**243**

*HYPOTHESES*................................................................................................*243*

**APPENDIX C – RESEARCH & METHODOLOGY** .......................................**246**

**BIBLIOGRAPHY** ......................................................................................**260**

**Endnotes**..................................................................................................**270**

# Acknowledgements

This work could not have been done without many years of guidance and many helpful people. Here I can only mention a few.

I greatly appreciate Holos University and the Holos professors who aided and encouraged me as I began to prepare this book. Special thanks to: Professor Berney Williams, my advisor at Holos, whose knowledge, teaching skills, guidance and understanding were invaluable for completing this project; Professor Bob Nunley, whose encouragement moved me to enter the Holos program and whose many helpful suggestions during my coursework aided me in completing this work; Professor Patricia Norris, who freely and enthusiastically offered assistance in the physiological and psychological measurement aspect of this research; Professor Paul Thomlinson, whose guidance and instruction in statistical analysis gave me the confidence and knowledge necessary for analyzing the results of this research; Professors Oliver London, Ann Nunley and Gary Simmons, all of whom offered helpful suggestions and encouragement along the way.

I could not have completed my research without the aid of Dr. Peter Parks, who loaned me equipment for measuring PST and taught me how to use it. I greatly appreciate the time, assistance and expertise he provided.

I am deeply grateful for the rigorous instruction of the faculty of the philosophy departments of Southern Illinois University-Edwardsville and the University of Kansas.

I owe a debt of gratitude to all New Testament scholars past and present who have provided groundwork for the selection and analysis of the sayings of Jesus used in this book, especially to the scholarly work of the Jesus Seminar.

I am also grateful to the Ministers of the Unity movement for their insights into the practical spiritual message of Jesus.

I wish to express appreciation especially to the Unity ministers and churches who made my research possible: the Unity Institute and Unity of Overland Park staffs who graciously provided office space, equipment and personal assistance; Rev. Erin McCabe of Unity Village Chapel and Rev. Patricia Bass of Unity of Overland Park, Kansas who allowed me to solicit volunteers for my research at their ministries; and finally all those who participated in the research as volunteers.

Special thanks to: my friend Neal Vahle, who made many helpful editorial suggestions; my daughter Joanna, who designed the cover and helped in the production of the book; and my wonderful wife Christine, for her many hours of meticulous proof reading.

My thanks and blessings go to all who made this work possible. It is my hope that together we have made a meaningful contribution to understanding the historical Jesus and to knowledge of practical spirituality and health.

# Introduction: Philosophy, Healing, and Jesus

A 42 year old woman entered a holistic research clinic in Copenhagen. She had been diagnosed with cancer but she did not want to rely entirely upon surgery, radiotherapy and chemotherapy. She wanted to do something herself to battle her illness. In the course of her holistic treatment her physician helped her work through some of her forgiveness issues. In conversation with her physician she revealed that she felt hopelessness and powerlessness. Her physician then had a conversation with her about Jesus' metaphor of the lilies of the field and the birds of the air. They talked about surrendering to God. They talked about the idea that life is good and will "carry" us. As they continued their discussion on philosophy of life suddenly, much to the physician's surprise, the cancer lump began to get measurably smaller.[1]

This incident, recorded in a paper published in the *Scientific World Journal*, indicates a relationship between philosophy and healing. The physician who reported the above incident of "spontaneous remission" was part of a research team which discovered that working with cancer patients on "life philosophy" significantly lengthened the patients' lives. While the patients in a control group all died within four years, some patients participating in the "life philosophy" intervention were still alive after 10 years and in complete remission.[2]

The authors of the article wrote:

> *"We know that spontaneous remission of cancer is seen with almost all kinds of cancer and we know that it often happens after a spiritual breakthrough. The spiritual breakthrough is almost always about being more alive, knowing oneself and the purpose of life better, stepping fully into personal character, realizing talents and how to use them."*[3]

The holistic physicians were not teaching religion but truly discussing philosophy; not philosophy as abstract theorizing but rather philosophy of life. Their discussion and conclusions indicate that spiritual breakthroughs can be enhanced by thinking about life – by "philosophizing." Philosophy of life is concerned with happiness, self-knowledge, purpose, and ethics.

At the same time, any philosophy of life has metaphysical

subtexts and is sometimes explicitly tied to a metaphysical perspective. In their article on "inducing spontaneous remission" the physician authors ventured briefly into how their own metaphysical subtext was related to cancer treatment. After acknowledging the role of biochemical theory in medicine, the authors stated: *"we believe that cancer is caused from our consciousness, when we repress emotions and place them in the tissues of the body. We therefore also believe a cure of cancer to come from fundamental shifts in our consciousness and state of being."*[4] The statement suggests that existence is not entirely material; there is an element of existence called "consciousness" which is not reducible to body chemistry.

It is striking that in the paper cited above the elements of "life philosophy" in the treatments were elements present in the teachings of Jesus: faith, "surrender to God," forgiveness, "considering the birds of the air and lilies of the field" and "realizing talents." The fact that elements of holistic therapy are also in the teachings of Jesus suggests that Jesus taught a therapeutic "life philosophy." He influenced people to change their minds and hearts – to shift their consciousness. Those shifts in consciousness might well have induced spontaneous remissions in some listeners.

The physicians' notion that working with forgiveness and surrendering to God are *philosophical* suggests that our ideas today of what is "philosophical" can be associated with the teachings of Jesus. Recently historians and biblical scholars have noted the similarities between sayings of Jesus and sayings of Cynic philosophers. Not as widely known as the New Testament healing stories are accounts from before New Testament times of healings produced by philosophers. The Pythagorean[5] and Therapeutae philosophers[6] were regarded as healers. The philosophers Empedocles[7] and Apollonius of Tyana[8] were reputed to have healing powers.

The Gospels in the Christian Bible tell us that Jesus was a teacher and healer. The assumption has long been that Jesus was a teacher of religion, yet there are clearly similarities between Jesus and teachers of philosophy. The assumption has long been that Jesus healed by supernatural power, yet there are elements in Jesus' philosophy that can be seen as therapeutic in light of modern health research.

There are practical reasons to seek a better understanding of Jesus as a historical figure. A better understanding of Jesus' philosophy will help us better understand how he became such a pervasively influential historical figure. A better understanding of the historical

Jesus could have a unifying and beneficial effect within Christianity and between Christians and non-Christians. A better understanding of therapeutic elements in Jesus' philosophy can give us a better understanding of how to cure human ailments.

The religion that began in his name has focused on his death and the "afterlife." However while he was alive he taught, among other things, about God, faith, wisdom, and love in the here and now. This work focuses on those "here and now" teachings and how they are related to health and healing.

The words of Jesus are not arranged into a system of thought in any of the Gospels written about him. The "Sermon on the Mount" in *Matthew* and the "Sermon on the Plain" in *Luke* appear to be summaries of Jesus' teachings, but there is a good deal more and a good deal less to Jesus' teachings than is found in either "sermon" or in both together.

When the words attributed to Jesus in the Gospel are examined in light of history, biblical scholarship, ancient philosophy, and modern science, what he actually said begins to come into focus. When the words of the historical Jesus are arranged thematically, a philosophy emerges which is distinct from Christian theology and religion. Jesus' philosophy and Christian religion do not stand in direct opposition to each other, but Jesus' philosophy and Christian religion are not identical either. If his philosophy contains elements that can be shown to be therapeutic, then his philosophy supports the claim that he was a healer.

The idea that Jesus was a philosopher is not opposed to believing in Jesus as a religious figure. There is no inherent contradiction between thinking of an individual as a philosopher and also as a religious figure. Augustine of Hippo and Thomas Aquinas were declared to be Catholic saints, but they were also philosophers in the traditions of Plato and Aristotle. Historically some individuals who were philosophers also came to be seen as "divine beings," e.g. Pythagoras, Confucius, and Lao-Tzu.

In the discussion of Jesus' philosophy I will relate his sayings to his reputation as a healer from a modern holistic and scientific perspective. Various elements found in Jesus' philosophy are now associated with health and healing. Healing elements in Jesus' philosophy include: faith, optimism, prayer, compassion and forgiveness. In this work we will examine an intriguing connection between Jesus' style of expression and meditation and hypnosis induction methods. Research supporting the therapeutic value of these and other elements of Jesus' philosophy will also be discussed.

Jesus' philosophy is consistent with what Dr. Bernie Siegel, a respected physician and medical professor at Yale, discovered in "exceptional patients." "Exceptional patients" are those who overcame medical odds and experienced seemingly "miraculous" healings. Dr. Siegel found that: *"Acceptance, faith, forgiveness, peace, and love are the traits that define spirituality for me. These characteristics always appear in those who achieve unexpected healing of serious illness."*[9]

Even though I believe that Jesus' therapeutic effect was the result of the organic whole of his philosophy and consciousness, in terms of scientific research it is necessary to examine *parts* of that whole separately. What follows then is an exploration of what medical research can tell us about the therapeutic value of the elements of Jesus' philosophy, including an experiment on "listening to Jesus' sayings," which I did for my doctoral dissertation.

Additional technical aspects of my research are included in the Appendices. The appendices are included to provide a fuller explanation of the methodologies used in my experimental research. Though the appendices are intended for technical and academic information, I hope the general reader will find points of some interest there too.

I collected the sayings of Jesus which a group of historians and bible scholars regard as most probably originating with the historical Jesus. I then attempted to identify a few basic themes into which the sayings could be categorized. The interpretations of his sayings along with scientific research provide the basis for my belief that Jesus was a philosopher and healer.

Before exploring Jesus' healing philosophy it is necessary to consider the issue of the historical Jesus, for we cannot understand his actual philosophy without some knowledge of what he actually said.

# Chapter One: The Quest for the Historical Jesus

Around 180 C.E. Irenaeus, a Christian bishop in Gaul (France), wrote a polemic against groups of Christians he referred to as "Gnostics" and the books they used for study and worship. Irenaeus asserted the importance of the developing church hierarchy and the authority of its bishops and contended against all Christians who rejected that hierarchy and authority. There were in fact in Europe at that time a wide variety of religious beliefs, texts and practices associated with Jesus; Irenaeus categorized the diverse groups with whom he disagreed as "Gnostic heresies."

He had a strong desire for Christians to be unified, especially during times of persecution. That desire undoubtedly motivated Irenaeus to attempt to suppress views with which he disagreed and especially to exalt books that exalted the authority of bishops. He emphasized the importance of the bishop of Rome, which was not yet established as the "Pope."

Irenaeus also contended that there were only four reliable Gospels: Matthew, Mark, Luke, and John. Irenaeus argued that there had to be exactly four pillars of the church as there were four corners of the earth. Viewed today, his logic is clearly problematic, since the earth does not have corners. In any case, in that time different Christian communities preferred different Gospels and different numbers of Gospels. The four named by Irenaeus were probably the most popular and widely used, at least in the churches Irenaeus approved of.

Irenaeus' view of the official canon of Christianity was not generally accepted in his time, but his view became influential and was officially adopted by church counsels some 200 years later. Other gospels were suppressed by the church, but some were hidden and rediscovered, many in a cave in Egypt in 1945.

*A Fifth Gospel*

The four canonical gospels are the primary information we have about the life and words of Jesus. However a strong case can be made for the value of a fifth gospel, one of the lost Gospels rediscovered in Egypt. The earliest version of the *Gospel of Thomas* was probably written before Paul's letters and the four canonical gospels, thus preserving one of the earliest records of sayings of Jesus. Early church writers from Origen to Jerome occasionally quoted from *Thomas*. As with other Gospels, caution must be used when drawing upon *Thomas* because in addition to containing authentic sayings of Jesus, it also undoubtedly contains sayings added by later copyist-editors. Those editorial sayings were probably already added by the time the church became concerned with declaring official canon.

Many books were written not long after Jesus' death featuring him as the central personality. The book *The Complete Gospels*[10] contains 21 books written about Jesus within 200 years after he lived. After that book was published, another gospel was rediscovered: *The Gospel of Judas*. In addition to known gospels there is strong evidence for at least two "sayings gospels" written *before* the canonical narrative Gospels: *The Gospel of Thomas* and "*Q*," which is a source of sayings in *Matthew* and *Luke* according to most biblical scholars.

Some 300 years after Jesus lived, Christian Church councils decided upon four official approved Gospels. However, religious organizations tend not to be the most objective and reliable sources of information about their founders. Religious organizations have a stake in presenting information in ways that support organizational agendas.

The Church sought to systematically destroy all unsanctioned works about Jesus. The works in *The Complete Gospels* and the *Gospel of Judas* were eventually rediscovered, but many only in fragmentary form. Because many lost books about Jesus have been recovered, we know that the church suppressed *most* of the books written about Jesus.

The suppression of books is intended to control information, not to preserve truth. In the search for historical truth, the "unofficial" lost books about Jesus should not be dismissed out of hand, nor can they be automatically considered more accurate than institutionally sanctioned documents. To attain historical truth, all information must be considered, compared, and critiqued.

The evidence regarding Jesus points to one historical person who became legendary. Some of the sayings attributed to him and stories told about him were undoubtedly products of legends and "mythological thinking," but some sayings clearly originated from him. Evidence for the existence of "the historical Jesus" is also found in the letters of Paul who knew and made reference to some of Jesus' original disciples, including James the brother of Jesus. There is at least as much evidence for the existence of Jesus as for the existence of Socrates and more than for Moses, Buddha, or Aesop.

The stories about Jesus' works were, at the very least, derived from what he meant to those who followed him. Assuming that Jesus was a healer, some of the healing stories probably were derived from the nature of what he actually did.

Today there are many different theories about Jesus, indicating that there is considerable uncertainty among experts regarding the historical reliability of the Gospels. The uncertainty regarding Jesus' life stems from the Christian Gospels themselves. The four canonical Gospels significantly diverge from each other regarding the details of Jesus' life, his sayings and his ancestry. The many other gospels written about Jesus portray him and his words in even more divergent terms.

## *Adventures in New Testament Scholarship*

In my description of Jesus' life and philosophy I am drawing upon a long tradition of New Testament scholarship, especially what is commonly referred to as "the quest for the historical Jesus."

The scholarly quest for the historical Jesus goes back to at least the 18th century when Hermann Samuel Reimarus (1694-1768) contended that what gospel authors said about Jesus could be distinguished from what Jesus himself said.[11] Thomas Jefferson (1743-1826) was one of many distinguished minds to explore the "quest for the historical Jesus."[12] Jefferson put together his own version of Jesus' life and sayings, eliminating sayings he believed did not originate with Jesus. David Friedrich Strauss (1808-1874) had a powerful influence on the development of New Testament scholarship through his book *The Life of Jesus Critically Examined* (1835), in which he distinguished between "myth" and the history in the gospels.[13]

In 1838, Christian Hermann Weisse concluded that *Mark* was the earliest Gospel. That same year, a more thorough argument for *Mark's* priority was published in "The Earliest Gospel" by Christian Gottlob Wilke.[14] The theory that the *Gospel of Mark* was a source for *Matthew* and *Luke* has been widely accepted among scholars since the beginning of the 20th century.

The theory of "sayings Gospels" upon which the canonical Gospels were based was suggested in the early 19<sup>th</sup> century. That theory of the "*Q*" gospel (from the German "quelle" meaning "source") was substantially supported by H. J. Holtzman's extensive analysis in 1863. Burnett Hillman Streeter demonstrated that the theory that *Matthew* and *Luke* independently used *Mark* and *Q* as sources best accounted for both the agreements and the variations in *Matthew* and *Luke*.[15] Streeter's theory is accepted by practically all mainstream Bible scholars today.

Albert Schweitzer's classic work *The Quest of the Historical Jesus*[16] has been very influential on New Testament scholars. Schweitzer (1875-1965) contended that a choice had to be made between viewing Jesus as an eschatological prophet or as non-eschatological. "Eschatological prophet" just means "one who predicts the imminent arrival of the resurrection and final judgment." Schweitzer attributed the discovery of that choice to Johannes Weiss. Regarding Weiss' work, Schweitzer wrote:

> "His 'Preaching of Jesus concerning the Kingdom of God,' . . . has, on its own lines, an importance equal to that of Strauss' first Life of Jesus. He lays down the third great alternative which the study of the life of Jesus had to meet. The first was laid down by Strauss: *either* purely historical *or* purely supernatural. The second had been worked out by the Tubingen school and Holtzman: either Synoptic or Johannine. Now came the third: either eschatological or non-eschatalogical! Progress always consists in taking one or other of two alternatives, in abandoning the attempt to combine them."[17]

I believe that the choice Schweitzer offered is not sound. Human beings are capable of changing their minds, of having different sides to their personalities, of holding opinions which are not easily reconciled and even of holding logically contradictory views.

As a human being, Jesus *could* have advocated ideas unconcerned with the immanence of "judgment day" and also at other times he could have "predicted" that day. Furthermore, as long as we are alive in this world we need ways to cope with this existence; at the same time we may have beliefs about the future and an "after-life." For example, Plato discussed both his beliefs about the best way to live the good life and his beliefs about the after-life. It is not necessary to categorize Plato as *either* a philosopher of the here and now *or* a philosopher of the after-life; he was both. In that respect, choosing sides is not necessarily the only way to arrive at an accurate idea of the historical Jesus, even though most modern scholars seem to have taken one side or the other.

Ironically, if Schweitzer were correct then the most certain things we would know about Jesus is that he was crucified and that he predicted the day of resurrection and judgment would occur within the life span of some of his followers. In other words, the most certain things we would know about Jesus would be that he was executed and that he was mistaken in his beliefs. The irony is that many of the "eschatological Jesus" scholars teach in Christian seminaries.

Attempting to resolve the eschatological controversy is beyond the intended scope of this work. Jesus had a philosophy for living in the here and now and it is that philosophy with which I am concerned. His parables and sayings about life here and now can be distinguished from sayings about an after-life, resurrection and judgment day (if he had such beliefs).

It bears mentioning that at least one prominent scholar of the "eschatological school" recognized the similarities between Jesus and philosophers of his era. John P. Meier is one of the most accomplished scholars to tackle the quest for the historical Jesus and one who sides with Schweitzer and others on the eschatological question. Yet Meier also wrote:

> "As a religious figure within the Greco-Roman period, Jesus not surprisingly bore some resemblances to other philosophical or religious teachers of his time . . . while Jesus' resemblance to wandering Cynic philosophers has been greatly overemphasized, one should not deny all similarities to philosophers in the broad Cynic-Stoic stream, mixed as it sometimes was with Pythagorean traits."[18]

A whole new phase of the "quest for the historical Jesus" opened up in the 1940s when ancient manuscripts were discovered near the Dead Sea and in Nag Hammadi Egypt. One of the rediscovered ancient manuscripts was the *Gospel of Thomas*. The *Gospel of Thomas*, which contains many of the "*Q*" sayings, verified the existence of "Sayings Gospels" such as the hypothetical *Q*. "Sayings Gospels" almost certainly circulated among early Christians before the narrative *Gospel of Mark* was written. The earliest layers of "*Q*" and *Thomas* contained the earliest records of remembered sayings of Jesus.

The history of Gospel scholarship indicates that no single Gospel can be considered a complete and entirely accurate portrayal of Jesus. Ancient manuscripts of the Gospels indicate that they were changed, revised, added to, and deleted from. The Gospels must be compared, analyzed, critiqued, and related to historical knowledge in order to discern what the historical Jesus actually said.

I have relied to a great extent on the work of the "Jesus Seminar" in choosing sayings to use for discussing the philosophy of Jesus. I have done so because that work is the closest thing to a scholarly consensus available on the question of "did Jesus really say that?" Some individual authors have done fine work on analyzing the Gospels, but in my view the agreement of many experts is more reliable and less agenda bound than the opinion of any one expert.

## *The Jesus Seminar*

In 1985 the "Jesus Seminar" was initially established by 30 scholars under the auspices of the Westar Institute; eventually more than 200 scholars participated. The participants were reputable and well qualified scholars connected with a wide range of educational institutions. The Jesus Seminar consisted of academics with doctorates in areas relevant to the project of identifying the sayings of the historical Jesus. In addition, many participants had done special studies in Institutes in Jerusalem and Europe. The Jesus Seminar was open to all qualified scholars who chose to participate. No one was excluded on the basis of religious affiliation or opinion.

The Fellows of the Jesus Seminar consisted of professors from Catholic, Protestant and state colleges and universities, including: Notre Dame, Wesleyan University, Texas Christian University, the School of Theology at Claremont, Eden Theological Seminary, Oregon State, Southern Illinois University, University of Minnesota, University of California-Berkeley, Vassar, Vanderbilt, Rutgers, University of Toronto, and University of South Africa. Many of the participants were graduates of Cambridge, Harvard, Oxford, Yale, Cornell, and Princeton.[19] The diversity of backgrounds and affiliations of Jesus Seminar Fellows practically eliminated the possibility of a hidden agenda or conspiracy contaminating the results.

The Jesus Seminar produced the book *The Five Gospels* from

their deliberations. *The Five Gospels* consists of the four canonical Gospels plus the *Gospel of Thomas*, which the scholars determined to be a valuable source of early memories of Jesus' sayings. *The Five Gospels* explains, for each saying, why the Seminar concluded that the saying did or did not originate with Jesus. What follows here is a summary of the main criteria used by the Seminar.

Over the past two centuries, scholars have made a number of observations about how the authors of the Gospels constructed their books based upon careful comparison and analysis of the Gospels. The Jesus Seminar called these observations "rules of evidence" and used the rules to sort through sayings attributed to Jesus. These rules of evidence consist of observations made by scholars over that past century about the structure of the Gospels. The rules of evidence are recorded in *The Five Gospels*[20] as:

(1) *"The evangelists frequently group sayings and parables in clusters and complexes that did not originate with Jesus"* (p. 19). In other words, the same sayings of Jesus were put in different contexts and groupings by "the evangelists" (Gospel authors). Since the clusters and contexts for sayings vary, they cannot have originated with Jesus; they must have been created by the evangelists. From analysis of the complexes of sayings the following three rules emerge:

(2) *"The evangelists frequently relocate sayings and parables or invent new narrative contexts for them"* (p. 19).

(3) *"The evangelists frequently expand sayings or parables, or provide them with an interpretive overlay or comment"* (p. 21).

(4) *"The evangelists often revise or edit sayings to make them conform to their own individual language, style, or viewpoint"* (p. 21).

Careful scholarly analysis of the Gospels also revealed:

(5) *"Words borrowed from the fund of common lore or the Greek scriptures are often put on the lips of Jesus"* (p. 22). For example, when Gospels portray Jesus as quoting scripture, it cannot be determined whether or not he quoted that particular scripture. The words quoted did not *originate* with Jesus and so tell us nothing about him, except possibly that he had some familiarity with "common lore" and Hebrew Scriptures.

(6) *"The evangelists frequently attribute their own statements to Jesus"* (p. 23).

(7) *"Hard sayings are frequently softened in the process of transmission to adapt them to the conditions of daily living"* (p. 23). This means that sayings which were difficult to accept were sometimes modified to make them easier to apply.

(8) *"Variations in difficult sayings often betray the struggle of the early Christian community to interpret or adapt sayings to its own situation"* (p. 23).

(9) *"Sayings and parables expressed in 'Christian' language are the creation of the evangelists or their Christian predecessors"* (p. 24). "Christian language" just means terminology and doctrines that were formulated by Christians *after* the crucifixion.

(10) *"Sayings or parables that contrast with the language or viewpoint of the gospel in which they are embedded reflect older tradition (but not necessarily tradition that originated with Jesus)"* (p. 24).

(11) *"The Christian community develops apologetic statements to defend its claims and sometimes attributes such statements to Jesus"* (p. 24).

(12) *"Sayings and narratives that reflect knowledge of events that took place after Jesus' death are the creation of the evangelists or the oral tradition before them"* (p. 25). The assumption in rule 12 is that it is more likely that gospel authors attributed predictions to Jesus *after* the fact than that he made such predictions himself. It is of course possible that Jesus made accurate predictions about the future, but the predictive sayings are composed from Hebrew Scriptures and common lore. The predictive sayings are unlike the style and content of other sayings that most probably originated with Jesus.

Since Jesus himself did not write anything, what he actually said would have to have been *remembered* by his disciples. The sayings would have to have had a *memorable* form. Based upon the nature of oral traditions, the Jesus Seminar also used what they called "rules of oral evidence" in their deliberations:

1. *"Only sayings and parables that can be traced back to the oral period, 30-50 C.E., can possibly have originated with Jesus"* (p. 25).

2. *"Sayings or parables that are attested in two or more independent sources are older than the sources in which they are embedded"* (p. 26).

So if, for example, a saying is found in both *Mark* and *Q* in different forms, the saying is older than either Gospel and consequently probably originated with Jesus.

3. *"Sayings or parables that are attested in two different contexts probably circulated independently at an earlier time"* (p. 27).

If, for example, *Matthew* and *Luke* use the same saying but put it in a different context, the saying is earlier than either Gospel.

4. *"The same or similar content attested in two or more different forms has had a life of its own and therefore may stem from old tradition"* (p. 26).

5. *"Unwritten tradition that is captured by the written gospels relatively late may preserve very old memories"* (p. 26).

Rules 2-4 help objectively identify the material older than gospels. Rule 5 recognizes that some traditions may go back to the "oral" period even when strong written attestation is lacking.

From study of transmission of sayings in oral cultures, the Seminar added the following rules:

6. *"The oral memory best retains sayings and anecdotes that are short, provocative and memorable – and oft-repeated."*

7. *"The most frequently recorded words of Jesus in the surviving gospels take the form of aphorisms and parables."*

8. *"The earliest layer of the gospel tradition is made up of single aphorisms and parables that circulated by word of mouth prior to the written gospels"* (28).

The Seminar's "rules of evidence" provide sound objective criteria for identifying the sayings that most probably originated with Jesus and the sayings that most probably were invented or drawn from other sources. Similar criteria could be applied to discern sayings of other historical figures known only through an oral tradition, such as the historical Socrates or the historical Siddhartha Gautama (the Buddha).

The Fellows of the Jesus Seminar deliberated regarding each saying found in the four canonical Gospels and the *Gospel of Thomas*. After the reading of papers and discussion, the Fellows voted (and sometimes re-voted) on each verse. The voting process used different colored beads: **red** for *"Jesus said this,"* **pink** for *"Jesus probably said this or something like it,"* **grey** for *"Jesus probably did not say this"* and **black** for *"Jesus did not say this."* The votes in favor of pink and red sayings ranged from 51% to over 90% of the scholars.

An example of a saying considered authentic (part of the core list) is "the mustard seed parable" which is found in *Mark*, *Q* and *Thomas* (in slightly different versions); of the "Five" gospels, only John does not include it. Some parables and sayings found in only one gospel were still overwhelmingly considered authentic, due to style and content consistent with the "core" list of sayings that did have multiple attestations.

From the resulting database of sayings, the Jesus Seminar

concluded that Jesus' sayings: *"cut against the social and religious grain"*; *"surprise and shock"*; "call for a *reversal of roles* or *frustrate ordinary expectations"*; "are often characterized by *exaggeration, humor, and paradox"*; use images that are *"concrete and vivid"*; and are "customarily *metaphorical* and *without explicit application"* (pp. 31-32).

The methodology and conclusions of the Jesus Seminar are sound enough that the resulting list of "red" and "pink" sayings can be considered the sayings most likely to have originated with Jesus. That is the reason I have chosen to use all of those sayings as the basis for exploring Jesus' philosophy.

It is important to note here what *is* being claimed and what is *not* being claimed. What *is* being claimed is that a significant number of scholars would agree that the sayings discussed here originated with the historical Jesus. What is *not* being claimed is that these sayings are the *only* known statements that originated with the historical Jesus. The sayings chosen for discussion provide sufficient data for identifying Jesus' main ideas and style of expression. When I've made reference to a "grey" or "black" saying, I have indicated as much in the text and explained the reasons for doing so.

## Methodology for Identifying the Historical Jesus

The method I have used in my quest for the historical Jesus is holistic and pragmatic. A holistic and pragmatic epistemology draws upon different disciplines to seek conclusions that are coherent with what is already known. A holistic approach is similar to what scientists do when they seek theories that are coherent with the available evidence. A pragmatic approach seeks theories that can be tested in experience; again this is similar to what science strives for. The most significant pragmatic aspect of my approach is found in discussions of how Jesus' ideas are related to health research.

The best biblical scholarship is to some extent holistic, in that scholars employ knowledge from the disciplines of archaeology, anthropology, geography, historical documents and methods such as "source criticism" drawn from historians and literature scholars. New Testament scholar Marcus Borg noted this holistic approach:

"Lately, largely in the last ten years, Jesus

scholars (and biblical scholars generally) have begun systematically to use insights and models gleaned from the history of religions, cultural anthropology, and the social sciences. These not only provide comparative material and theoretical understandings, but also models constructed from either empirical or historical data which can then be used to illuminate historical periods for which we have only fairly scanty data."[21]

In this work, I expand the holistic and pragmatic scope of biblical scholarship to include insights and methods from psychology, health research, comparative religion, and philosophy. I do that in an attempt to infer the nature of Jesus' consciousness, the possible influence of his consciousness on his followers, and how his ideas may be relevant to health and healing.

Identifying Jesus' basic ideas begins with a thematic and systematic consideration of his sayings. I have extracted the sayings from the narrative contexts and grouped them according to the central topics, ideas and concerns of the sayings. I have attempted to order the sayings so that the first sayings present general ideas providing context for understanding those discussed later.

To *interpret* the sayings for meaning and intention requires more information. The role Jesus played in the context of his culture and comparison of his views to those of his culture must be taken into account. In addition Jesus' *style* of expression is important for identifying his meaning and intention. Religious figures, philosophers, literary figures, historians and other types use styles of expression appropriate to their intentions. By identifying which styles Jesus' teachings most closely resemble it is possible to gain insight into his intentions. For example if a saying resembles a comic saying, we can deduce that his intention was to be humorous. If a saying resembles the rabbinical style of the era, we can deduce his intention was to teach and interpret Judaic law. If his style resembles philosophical styles of his era, we can deduce that his intention was to philosophize.Some understanding of Jesus' early life provides a helpful background for understanding what he said. Therefore, the next chapter examines Jesus' life up to the time he set out to teach.

# Chapter Two:    About 30 Years

The following account of Jesus' early life takes into consideration the work of biblical scholars, historians, philosophers, archaeology, and my own experimental research.  Since there is disagreement among scholars on what conclusions can be drawn from the Gospels, this account is based upon my own analysis of information about and from the era, along with the scholarly arguments I find most compelling.  I have not provided footnotes for every detail when the information is available in many sources.  My bibliography includes all the sources I have drawn upon for biographical information.

Jesus was born in Nazareth of Galilee sometime during the reign of Herod the Great (37-4 BCE).  Jesus was crucified during the prefecture of Pontius Pilate (26-36 CE).  New Testament scholars generally date Jesus from 4 BCE to 28 CE, since this range corresponds with the information that Jesus was about 30 when he began his ministry and lived 1 to 3 years after he began.

If Jesus lived from late in Herod's reign (4 BCE) to early in Pontius Pilate's prefecture (26 CE), then he would have been 30 years old when he was crucified.  If Jesus lived from early in Herod's reign (37 BCE) to late in Pilate's prefecture (36), then Jesus would have been about 73 years old when he was crucified.  In one Gospel incident some people say to Jesus, "You are not yet 50," (John 8: 57), indicating that he *could* have been in his late 40s when they talked with him.  However, the common estimate of Jesus being in his early 30s when he was crucified is probably correct.

The authors of the Gospels of *Matthew* and *Luke* wrote different stories about Jesus being miraculously conceived, possibly in part as a response to his hometown nickname "son of Mary."  The author of *Mark*, the Gospel which was the primary source of *Matthew* and *Luke*, was the first to mention the hometown appellation "son of Mary"; and *Mark* did *not* include a "virgin birth" story.  The letters of Paul, written earlier than the Gospels, and the *Gospel of John*, the last gospel written, also make no mention of a "virgin birth."

Paul did, however, mention that Jesus was descended from David (Romans 1: 3).  The belief that Jesus was the Messiah and so had to be a descendent of David was undoubtedly circulating among Jesus' followers before Paul's conversion.  *Matthew* and *Luke* (written after Paul's letters) both have genealogies of Jesus' father Joseph in which he is descended from David, but the two genealogies are traced through entirely different ancestors after David.  Only one of the genealogies could be accurate and both could be inaccurate. If the virgin birth had actually occurred and God was literally Jesus' father, the genealogies of Joseph would be irrelevant to the issue of Jesus being descended from David.

It is very possible, from a scientific and mathematical perspective, that Joseph was descended from David. Since David by all accounts had many children and lived some 1,000 years before Jesus, there would have been many descendents of David during the time of Joseph. Joseph and Jesus could easily have been of David's lineage.

An article posted on *abroadintheyard.com* (August 23, 2012) notes that "some geneticists estimate that everybody on Earth is at least a 50th cousin to everybody else." The article mentions that Andrew Millard of the University of Durham calculated the probability that anyone with Anglo-Saxon ancestry descends from King Edward III to be as high as 99.997%.

The article further explains the mathematics of why you are almost certainly related to royalty. The article notes that a Yale team of statisticians produced a computer model that estimated that at a point 2,000 to 3,000 years ago there would be an ancestor who appears at least once on *everybody's* family tree. In other words, not only are you almost certainly related to royalty somewhere on your family tree, but there is a mathematical possibility that you too are descended from King David and possibly even from Mary, mother of Jesus, through one of Jesus' brothers James, Joses, Judas, or Simon; or one of Jesus' sisters.

But enough about *your* ancestry – let's get back to the story of Jesus.

Stories of ancient heroes being conceived as sons of gods were common in the Mediterranean world into which the Jesus movement later spread. The non-Jewish audience for Christianity would have expected a "savior" figure to have been fathered by a divinity. That expectation would be reason enough for early Christians to create a virgin birth story.

*Matthew* and *Luke* would also have searched the Hebrew Scriptures for passages that could be interpreted as a prophecy of the Messiah being born of a virgin. The only passage they found that could be used as a prophecy of a virgin birth was Isaiah 7: 14: "Behold, a young woman shall conceive and bear a son, and shall call his name Immanuel." The word translated as "virgin" in the Gospels also means "young woman." The context of the passage in Isaiah clearly refers to a child to be born soon (hundreds of year before Mary), for the rest of the prophecy is not about the birth of a Messiah but is about reassuring the king that within a few years the foreign kings he feared would no longer be a threat.

*Matthew* and *Luke* tell completely different stories about how Jesus came to be born in Bethlehem but ended up in Nazareth. Both authors were familiar with the prophetic tradition that the Messiah would be born in Bethlehem and so needed to create a narrative to place his birth there, since it was well known that Jesus was from Nazareth.

Jesus' father Joseph may have been a generous and forgiving man, a model for Jesus' idea of God as Father. Whatever his character and influence on Jesus, as far as we can tell from the Gospels, Joseph was out of the scene once Jesus began to proclaim his message. Either Joseph had died by then or had divorced Mary. Jesus expressed a dislike of divorce practices of his time, so if Joseph divorced Mary that could partly account for Jesus' attitude on divorce.

Mary needed to be strong to endure the difficulties of her situation. She gave birth to at least seven children, possibly more; five brothers are named and "sisters" are mentioned but not named or numbered (Mark 6: 3). Mary may have had to raise the youngest children by herself. Due to very limited employment opportunities for women, Mary probably relied upon her sons to provide for her once Joseph was no longer in their lives.

Jesus was known in his home town as "the son of Mary" (Mark 6: 3). Since sons were traditionally referred to by their fathers' names, being known as "the son of Mary" in his hometown indicates that he was conceived out of wedlock and was considered illegitimate by the residents in his hometown. As a child, Jesus might have been taunted about being the "son of Mary," even though Mary probably eventually married Joseph. Such taunting could have contributed to Jesus' sensitivity to and identification with outsiders later in life.

Jesus apparently was not close to Mary and his brothers. By one account, she once came with his brothers to see him out of concern for what people were saying about Jesus (Mark 3: 21, 31-35). According to the story, he refused to see her or even acknowledge her as his mother.

After the crucifixion, Mary and Jesus' brothers reportedly joined with his disciples. His brothers, especially James, quickly became prominent in the new movement, probably because of the claim that Jesus was the Davidic heir. James would have been next in the Davidic line.

Nazareth was a village with a population of about 400. The

people of Nazareth were mostly poor tenant farmers or artisans. Nazareth was an agricultural community, so most of the population would have worked for landlords, though a few may have had their own property. Those who did not work at farming would have been artisans, producing pottery or working in construction. The population did not have enough consumers to support all of its artisans and farmers, so most residents would have traveled to nearby towns to work, sell goods, and make purchases.

Galileans were descended from many nationalities and spoke Aramaic among themselves. Many Galileans would have been bilingual, speaking Aramaic amongst themselves and Greek in interactions with Romans and others from the Mediterranean world. At least one Galilean of the era, historian Flavius Josephus, wrote extensively in Greek, which indicates that attaining Greek literacy was possible in that place and time.

Most Galileans were Jewish, but their Judaism was less rigid and ritualistic than that of the inhabitants of Judea to the south. The Galilean form of Judaism was considered inferior by Judeans. There may have been a synagogue in or near Nazareth, but whether or not there was, Jesus gained some acquaintance with Jewish law, rabbinical lore and folklore.

Five miles from the tiny village of Nazareth was the city of Sepphoris, which had all the usual cosmopolitan elements of a Greek or Roman city: a theater, a gymnasium, a marketplace and so forth. Inhabitants of Nazareth would have traveled frequently to Sepphoris looking for work, business and merchandise. There was considerable construction going on in Sepphoris during Jesus' youth, so Sepphoris would have been a natural destination for artisans in Nazareth, including carpenters.

Jesus may have been a carpenter as affirmed by Christian tradition. The only reference to his occupation (Mark 6: 3) is the Greek word "tekton." The word "tekton" could refer to any number of occupations; it means "artificer" or "producer." He could have been a carpenter, stone mason, fabric maker, potter or even a peasant farmer. In any case, he is likely to have gone to Sepphoris regularly to work or to sell goods. His father Joseph and his brothers would also have been "artificers," regularly going to Sepphoris.

"Artificers" were paid subsistence wages in those days. Jesus' family would not have been wealthy. Jesus' sayings indicate a strong identification with the poor and also a fascination with the wealthy. "Rich men" figured prominently in his parables and sayings. Some of the rich men were portrayed as admirable and others as not so much.

If Jesus was an "artificer," it is probable that he would have traveled to Sepphoris many times during his working years, from about age 12 (or even earlier) until about the age of 30.

In Sepphoris, Jesus could have heard conversations about Greek philosophical ideas. He could have met Cynic philosophers, who traveled all over the Mediterranean world. Jesus could also have heard discussions of philosophy including Stoic and Pythagorean ideas, for in that era philosophers tended to be somewhat eclectic. As will be seen, Jesus' philosophy certainly has elements akin to Greek philosophies, along with elements indicating some familiarity with Jewish law and rabbinical teachings. While we cannot be certain that Jesus traveled to Sepphoris and heard philosophical ideas, it is more probable that he did than that he did not.

Some have hypothesized that Jesus traveled to India in his youth and learned Eastern philosophies and religions. Such hypotheses are explanatorily unnecessary and historically unlikely; Jesus did not need acquaintance with Hindu or Buddhist ideas to formulate the philosophy he developed. Jesus' philosophy did not require any more foundation and influence beyond what he could have heard within 5 miles of Nazareth. What he could have heard in Galilee was sufficient basis for the ideas he expressed and his style of expression.

Jesus' philosophy was certainly impacted by what he witnessed happening in the lives around him. His mind gravitated to concrete events and experiences rather than the abstract thinking commonly associated with philosophy. However, like Jesus, Cynic philosophers made use of parables and Pythagorean philosophers made use of concrete images in enigmatic aphorisms. In those times, not all philosophy was about abstract thought; the most popular philosophies were about how to live a good life.

In Sepphoris, Jesus also could easily have heard about plays presented in the city's theater; he may even have attended some of them. Some of his parables have the basic plot structure of comedies and tragedies.

Was Jesus married? Jesus' disciples had wives according to Paul's letters. The Gospels mention Peter's mother-in-law, so according to the Gospels at the very least Peter had a wife. Nevertheless, it is doubtful that Jesus was married. Even though early traditions support the idea that he was especially close to Mary Magdalene, none of those accounts explicitly say that she was his wife. In addition, there is the tradition that Jesus did not believe in making vows and a Jewish wedding involved making vows. It is possible that Jesus and Mary Magdalene were married, but there is not enough evidence to assert that they were and some reasons to believe that they were not. The most that can be said, based upon current evidence, is that Jesus had women disciples and was especially close to Mary Magdalene.

At about the age of 30, Jesus heard about John the Baptist and went to see him.

Gospels record that John preached repentance for sins and expectation that God's kingdom would soon be ushered in by a Messianic figure. His baptismal rite and eschatological expectations, as reported in the Gospels, were similar to those of the nearby Qumran ("Dead Sea Scrolls") community, which suggests that John had some connection with that community. However, the Jewish historian Flavius Josephus provided a different view on John the Baptist.

Josephus wrote around the same time the Gospels were being written, not long after the destruction of Jerusalem in 70 C.E. Josephus composed the only extensive history of Judaism written in that era. As with most historians, Josephus had his own agendas, but his books are the most important and detailed primary sources of information about the personalities and events in the Middle East region up through the first century.

Josephus made no mention of eschatological proclamations of John. Josephus wrote of John that he:

> ". . . was a good man, and commanded Jews to exercise virtue, both as to righteousness towards one another, and piety towards God, and so come to baptism; for that washing would be acceptable to him, if they made use of it, not in order to the putting away of some sins, but for the purification of the body; supposing still that the soul was thoroughly purified beforehand by righteousness."[22]

It is possible that the Gospel authors, having adopted the view that Jesus would return, invented the Messianic prophecies they attribute to John.

The ancient Mandaean religion claims John the Baptist as one of their prophets, but rejects Jesus as a "false Messiah." The name "Mandaean" is probably derived from an Aramaic word meaning "knowledge." The Mandaean religion is a form of Jewish Gnosticism and ascribes Gnostic type teachings to John. While intriguing, it is historically uncertain if the Mandaean Gnosticism derives from or accurately represents John's message. If John was really a Gnostic it would be plausible to assert that Jesus, as a student of John, also had Gnostic elements in his teaching. Many early books about Jesus, including the *Gospel of Thomas* and to some extent the *Gospel of John*, have Gnostic-like sayings.

Whether or not John publicly proclaimed Jesus as his successor, Jesus had a spiritual experience not long after being baptized by John. Jesus formulated his philosophy and work after seeing and hearing John. A saying that may have originated with Jesus indicates that Jesus saw his own message as different and superior to John's, while at the same time indicating the highest regard for the Baptist: *"I tell you, among those born of women none is greater than John; yet, the least in God's Realm is greater than he."* (Luke 7: 28)

How influential John was on Jesus' thought is unclear, but John seemed to be a catalyst for Jesus to change from being an artificer to being a spiritual teacher. It is likely that some of John's disciples eventually followed Jesus, especially after John's execution by Herod the Tetrarch. Jesus clearly had an experience that was different from others who came to John. Jesus' message was different from any of those ascribed to John. No other disciples of John became well known.

The Synoptic Gospels (*Matthew*, *Mark* and *Luke*) tell us that after his baptism by John, Jesus went alone into the wilderness for 40 days. It is likely that Jesus went off by himself after having his spiritual experience with John. The number 40 is symbolic for a time of renewal in the Hebrew Scriptures, so may not be an exact number of days Jesus spent in the wilderness. However long he was there and whatever happened there, Jesus came out and began teaching.

*"Jesus was about thirty years old when he began his work."* (Luke 3: 23)

## Jesus' Healing Work

The Gospels report that Jesus performed many healings and that he cast out demons. However, the "exorcism" and healing stories in the Gospels cannot be accepted at face value as accurate historical accounts. The stories were first recorded in *Mark* some 40 years after they were supposed to have occurred. At best the stories are based on events remembered, told, and retold over a 40 year period; over such a long oral history, mistakes and exaggerations could enter into the accounts. At worst, the stories are all fabrications based on folk tales about Jewish prophets or other Mediterranean folklore. We do not know who the sources of the accounts were or how reliable those sources were.

On the other hand, there are reasons to believe that at least some of the stories originated in actual events. There are multiple independent sources for some of the stories, indicating the stories are older than any of the Gospels that report them. At least one healing story has very little in common with the usual form of miracle stories found in that era.

Finally, as will be shown over the course of this work, Jesus' philosophy had therapeutic elements consistent with modern scientific health research. If Jesus' philosophy contained therapeutic elements, then the healing stories could well have had a basis in actual events, even if the reports of those events are not entirely accurate.

The healing stories indicate that Jesus spoke to and touched people with the intention of conveying healing to them. There is no evidence that Jesus used formulas or long prayers when healings were requested. Rather, according to Gospel reports, he spoke directly and affirmatively in the imperative mood. The following examples sum up the type of healing stories that were told and show that Jesus was remembered as simply affirming the cure of those who came to him.

### Was Jesus an "Exorcist"?

Several Gospel stories report that Jesus "drove out demons."

In the Capernaum synagogue, Jesus drives out a demon: *"Shut up and get out of him!"* (Mark 1: 23-27)

In Gerasenes, Jesus drives a "Legion" of spirits out of a mad man: *"Come out of that fellow, you filthy spirit."* He sends the Legion into some pigs. (Mark 5: 1-20)

In Tyre, Jesus is approached by a woman whose daughter has an unclean spirit: *"The demon has come out of your daughter."* (Mark 7: 24-30)

Near Caesarea Philippi Jesus drives a demon out of a boy who is deaf, mute and who has seizures: *"Deaf and mute spirit, I command you, get out of him and don't ever go back inside him!"* (Mark 9: 14-29)

A thorough discussion of Jesus as healer must include some discussion of the concept of exorcism. There are a few sayings suggesting that Jesus was accused of driving out demons by the power of Satan or Beelzebul. There is also a parable about "unclean spirits" which probably originated with Jesus. A close examination of Jesus' sayings related to "demons" leaves one in doubt as to whether or not he believed in demons and performed exorcisms.

Most of the people in the Middle East in the first century believed in demonic possession. In the first century erratic behaviors which are today associated with a variety of psychological illnesses were believed to be caused by demons. Many people today also believe in demons and exorcisms, but probably most people do not. There are psychological explanations for behavior interpreted as "demonic possession" which do not require belief in demons or in effectiveness of exorcisms. Consequently today the world is divided between the scientific non-belief in exorcism and religious belief in exorcism. The world is divided on an ontological question: do demons *exist*? Some who are religiously conservative would answer "yes"; the scientifically minded would answer "no."

Many cultures, going back to the earliest ones, have had "specialists" to deal with "demonic possession." Such specialists have been variously named "shamans," "priests," and "exorcists." The specialists used a variety of methods to "cast out demons" including prayers and offerings to deities, incantations and other rituals. If Jesus did use particular prayers, incantations, offerings or rituals to cast out demons, it is surprising that his methods were not recorded. The exorcism stories about Jesus (originating with Mark) have no special formulas. Generally speaking, without formula or ritual, Jesus just tells the demon to be quiet or to get out.

The synoptic gospels report that Jesus performed exorcisms; the Gospels of *John* and *Thomas* make no mention of anything related to exorcisms. Also Paul's letters, which are earlier than the canonical Gospels, make no mention of driving out demons or of Jesus casting out demons. Nor do any of the other New Testament epistles mention such things. The evidence that Jesus performed exorcisms is from only one book (*Mark*); *Matthew* and *Luke* copied *Mark's* account. The report of one source out of many does not make a very strong case.

The case that Jesus was a healer is much stronger since all Gospels, including *Thomas*, are agreed on that point. If Jesus was a healer by some means other than "exorcism," his contemporaries might still have thought of him as casting out demons since *they* believed that illnesses were caused by demons.

However, the Jesus Seminar concluded that the synoptic Gospels' reports of exorcisms were based upon actual events and that a few sayings related to exorcism were authentic.

The case for the authenticity of the "exorcism" *sayings* is solid. The main problem with the "exorcism sayings" of Jesus is that a person who did *not* perform exorcisms could have truthfully made the same statements. Two of the three sayings are responses to *accusations* that Jesus cast out demons by Satan or Beelzebul. The sayings record responses to accusations. In those two sayings Jesus makes conditional statements that neither affirm nor deny that he cast out demons. Instead, the statements propose logical dilemmas to his accusers. The third saying is like a parable and implies that it is better *not* to cast out demons. The nature of the sayings and the lack of support for *Mark's* tradition cast some doubt on the notion that Jesus performed exorcisms.

Jesus apparently was accused of driving out demons by the power of "Beelzebul." "Beelzebul" means either "Lord of heaven" or "Lord of the house" but the name is derived from a god worshipped by the Philistines: Baal-zebub "Lord of the flies." "Baal-zebub" and the Greek form "Beelzebul" were used by rabbis as derogatory names for "Satan," Baal worship and idolatry in general. Based on the preserved sayings of Jesus it would seem that some people accused Jesus of casting out demons by the power of a foreign deity or of Satan rather than by the power of the God of Israel. Jesus' responses to the charge were logical:

*"Every government divided against itself is devastated, and a house divided against a house falls. If Satan is divided against himself - since you claim I drive out demons in Beelzebul's name - how will his domain endure?" (Lk. 11: 17, 18)*

This saying is found in both *Q* (*Matthew* and *Luke*) and *Mark*. *Mark* 3 follows the saying with the saying about tying up a strong man. *Q* followed the saying with an additional response:

*"Even if I drive out demons in Beelzebul's name, in whose name do your own people drive them out? In that case, they will be your judges. But if by God's spirit I drive out demons, then for you God's imperial rule has arrived." (Mt. 12: 29)*

The responses are subtle; they are not admissions or denials. The first statement implies that *if* Satan is casting out his own demons, there would be nothing to worry about since he would only be destroying his own domain. The second part of the saying is conditional too: "*if* in Beelzebul's name . . . . *if* by God's spirit."

When the two responses from *Q* are put together, we see that Jesus' response to his accusers was to put them on the horns of a dilemma. The dilemma may be stated this way: "If I drive out demons, either I do it by the power of Beelzebul or by the power of God. If I do it by the power of Beelzebul, Satan is divided against himself and his house will fall; in which case there is no problem. If I drive out demons by the power of God, then God's realm is here. Either way, there is no reason to object to my work." Jesus adds to the dilemma an additional point: if he was doing the same thing as his accusers' own people, then they were also doing the same thing as he. "In that case they will be your judges" implies that if demons are cast out by Satan, then any other exorcists of the era must also have been working for Satan.

Jesus' response logically refuted any objections his accusers could make regarding his driving out demons. Yet his response leaves open the question of whether or not he was actually performing exorcisms. The "if" in his responses is not an admission; it is a hypothetical response. It is a little like a person accused of slander saying, "If I did say something that offended someone, I would apologize; but if what I said was true, why should I apologize?" That would be a non-apology, neither admitting nor denying the charge. In effect, the speaker just changes the subject.

The following saying of Jesus, from *Q*, suggests a good reason *not* to drive out "unclean spirits":

*"When an unclean spirit leaves a person, it wanders through waterless places in search of a resting place. When it doesn't find one, it says, "I will go back to the home I left." It then returns, and finds it swept and refurbished. Next, it goes out and brings back seven other spirits more vile than itself, who enter and settle in there. So that person ends up worse off than when he or she started." (Lk. 11: 24-26)*

If a person is *worse* off for having an "unclean spirit" leave, it would seem to be better for a person if the unclean spirit had just stayed. The story makes a case for *not* practicing exorcism. It is a strange thing for a supposed exorcist to say. It indicates that Jesus might have been *opposed* to "driving out demons." The story could have been intended as a satirical criticism of the exorcism practices of the era.

The saying may not have been originally descriptive. If the word "when" at the beginning of the passage is dropped, the rest of the passage sounds like a story rather than a description of supernatural phenomena. It is like Jesus' other parables and could be seen as just a story to make a point. That *story* form is more like other sayings of Jesus.

What would the point of the story be? Perhaps the point could be something like "it's sometimes better to let people be as they are, rather than trying to fix them." That message fits with Jesus' saying about getting the log out of your own eye before trying to remove a speck from your neighbor's eye (Matthew 7: 3-5). If the saying was intended as satirical criticism, the point would be something like "your exorcisms leave people worse off than when they had a so-called 'unclean spirit.'"

Examining what evidence there is regarding Jesus and exorcism, there is some reason to doubt that Jesus performed exorcisms in the conventional sense.

Of course, if there are no such things as demons, then Jesus clearly could not have driven out demons. If he had some positive effect upon people who were thought to have demons, then that effect requires an explanation other than that "he cast out demons."

No one has ever observed a demon; all that has ever been observed was aberrant and disturbing human behavior. What were called "demons" in those times today would be diagnosed as physical illness or psychological disorders rooted in traumas or maladaptive habits.

There are a number of possibilities for how Jesus might have cured psychological disorders or gotten a reputation as an exorcist. It is possible that Jesus responded to aberrant behavior by using the power of suggestion, speaking directly to the person's subconscious or "alternate persona." It is possible that through prayer or "psychic ability" Jesus cured people who were thought to have demons. It is also possible that such behavior happened to stop when Jesus came upon it and his disciples interpreted the temporary cessation of aberrant behavior as Jesus casting out a demon. It could be that Jesus' extraordinary empathy, peaceful presence and faith had a therapeutic effect on psychologically disturbed people.

In the end, we cannot be certain about how Jesus might have affected people with psychological disorders. It is uncertain that Jesus thought of himself as an exorcist. What we can do is relate the ideas in his philosophy to modern understanding of healing and determine if his philosophy had and still has therapeutic value.

The only source of "exorcism" stories is Mark, so it is possible that Mark simply invented the stories. It is likely that Jesus was accused of exorcising demons, but it is uncertain whether or not he believed in demons or spoke commands to them. It is likely that people who came to him were believed to have demons, and so, when such people were cured, it was believed that he cast out demons. He may have spoken as if speaking to the "demons" but he may also have simply affirmed healing as in the following stories. Whatever he said, it is clear that *he held a conscious intention of healing* for those who came to him, and his words and actions expressed that intention.

## *H e a l i n g s*

There are other "non-exorcism" healing stories in the Gospels. The consensus of the Jesus Seminar scholars was that some of those healing stories were based upon actual cures by Jesus. Below when I mention agreement of "scholars," I am referring primarily to the work of the Jesus Seminar, although other scholars also agree with those conclusions. The following are a few of the healing stories that are most probably based on actual events.

*Peter's mother-in-law is sick. Jesus takes her by the hand and her fever breaks.* (Mark 1: 29-31)

This story is unlike other miracle stories, since fevers often break naturally they are not as seemingly impossible to cure as blindness and other more serious illnesses. Scholars affirm that this story is based on an actual event. If so it indicates Jesus' conscious intention of healing conveyed by touch.

*A leper wants to be made clean. Jesus touches him and says, "Okay – you're clean." The leper is healed.* (Mark 1: 40-45)

This story is also believed by scholars to have a basis in an actual event. A slightly different version of the same story has also been found in the "Egerton Gospel," a fragment of a gospel different than those known. According to the Jesus Seminar, "In biblical times the word leprosy embraced a wide range of disorders, including rashes, acne, eczema, psoriasis, and other forms of dermatitis."[23] It is probable that people who came to Jesus with skin conditions were healed, since many skin conditions are known to respond to hypnosis and the "placebo effect." Jesus likely touched "lepers" in defiance of the laws of Moses and the authority of the temple priests. Being touched and pronounced clean could have relieved the "leper" of anxiety and guilt and produced a placebo effect with a quick cure.

*In Capernaum, some people lowered a paralytic through the roof of the house where Jesus is staying. Jesus says: "Child, your sins are forgiven" and "You there, get up, pick up your mat and go home." The paralytic is healed.* (Mark 2: 1-12)

Scholars believe that this story has a basis in an actual event; that Jesus healed a paralytic (there are cases of psychosomatic paralysis, so this cure need not be considered a miracle of supernatural intervention). This case indicates that Jesus sometimes pronounced forgiveness as well as "commands" to be healed. As will be discussed here later, forgiveness, forgiving and feeling forgiven, can have a powerful therapeutic effect on a person's psyche.

*In Capernaum a Roman officer requests a cure for his sick slave. The officer sends the message that Jesus doesn't need to come to the slave, he only needs to speak the word. Jesus praises the officer's faith, but no words of command are reported. The slave is healed.* (Luke 7: 1-10)

John 4: 45-54 contains basically same story as in Luke, but John's version takes place in Cana of Galilee and it is the officer's *son* who is sick. Jesus says: *"Go, your son is alive."*

Scholars affirm that the story originated as an early oral tradition and probably had an authentic basis in an actual event. However, the exact details can't be determined. The story indicates that Jesus had a healing intention and that distance was no obstacle to his consciousness or that the officer's faith effected the healing.

*Synagogue official Jairus requests healing for daughter on the verge of death. When they arrive at official's home, people tell the official that his daughter is dead. Jesus says, "Don't be afraid, just have trust." "The child hasn't died; she's sleeping." He takes the girl by the hand and speaks in Aramaic: "Talitha kuom" (translated as "Little girl get up.") To the astonishment of all, the little girl gets up.* (Mark 5: 21-24, 35-43)

According to scholars, there may have been a historical basis for this story. It may have involved a case in which a girl appeared to be dead but had only been sleeping or in a coma. In any case, the story again indicates the tradition that Jesus used touch and command in some cases.

*On the way to Jairus' house, a woman with vaginal hemorrhage touches Jesus' cloak. The hemorrhage stops and she believes she is cured. Jesus says, "Daughter, your trust has cured you. Go in peace, and farewell to your illness."* (Mark 5: 25-34)

Scholars believe this story is based upon an actual case of a psychosomatic healing of hemorrhaging. In this case the woman touched Jesus and he affirmed that her faith was the curative factor and verbally reaffirms that she is cured.

*Traveling through the Decapolis region, Jesus heals a deaf-mute. Jesus sticks his fingers in the man's ears, spits, touches the man's tongue, and says, "Ephphatha" (which means "Be opened").* (Mark 7: 32-35)

This healing is thought to be historical, but not details of the story. Healing intention, touch and command are again the elements of Jesus' treatment.

*In Bethsaida, a blind man is healed. Jesus spits in the man's eyes and touches him. "Do you see anything?" The man has some vision, but it is blurred. Jesus puts hands on the man's eyes a second time and the man sees clearly.* (Mark 8: 22-26)

Scholars believe that Jesus healed at least one blind person, mainly because there are four different stories: here, Mark 10: 46-52, Matt 9: 27-30, and John 9: 1-7. The Mark 10 story has Jesus simply say, *"Be on your way, your trust has cured you."* Matt 9 has two blind men - Jesus touches them and says, *"Your trust will be the measure of your cure."* John 9 has Jesus use spittle and dirt to make mud for man's eyes and has him go wash in pool of Siloam.

The healing of a psychosomatically blind person is possible. The stories collectively involve healing intention, the faith of the one cured, touch and spit. Evidently it was a common belief that a holy person's spittle could produce cures and Jesus may have accessed that belief, but we do not know the precise details or how many, if any, blind persons were cured by Jesus.

*In Nain, a widow's only son had died. Jesus said: "Don't cry. Young man, I tell you, get up." The young man revives.* (Luke 7: 11-15)

This is another version of reports that Jesus raised someone from the dead. We cannot be certain about the historical accuracy of the story. Here again Jesus heals with a command.

These stories are the only clues we have as to how Jesus interacted with those who sought healing. Collectively the stories indicate that Jesus expressed a healing intention by means of spoken command and, on occasion, touch and/or spittle; and in at least some cases he attributed the healing to the faith of the one seeking healing. On the basis of Jesus' philosophy we can also affirm that his consciousness of love, faith, and forgiveness was the foundation of his intentions, words and actions.

### Entering the Healing "Christ-consciousness"

To truly become a disciple of a philosophy, one must contemplate the ideas contained in that philosophy. To truly become a disciple of Jesus, one must contemplate what he said. Through such contemplation, one may become imbued with a consciousness similar to the healing consciousness of Jesus.

You can only establish in yourself a "Jesus-like" or "Christ" consciousness by following him – seeking to adopt his ways of thinking and feeling, his attitudes and intentions. The discussion of Jesus' philosophy which follows provides context and ruminations to help you understand and relate to what Jesus said. However, no amount of reading about Jesus can establish you in "Christ-consciousness." To enter into that consciousness or "realm," it would seem necessary to follow Jesus by contemplating his actual sayings and attempting to live in accordance with your understanding of the sayings.

For those who would adopt the philosophy of Jesus, it is not simply a matter of affirming certain beliefs. Jesus' sayings almost invariably are suggestive of ways of thinking rather than rules to follow or ideas to believe. The reason many gospels were written is that each author thought about what Jesus said and formulated interpretations from their own perspective. Once you recognize that the sayings are open to interpretation, those sayings can become instruments for meditation.

One simple and effective means for meditating on the sayings of Jesus is to record them in your own voice. You could use the translations found in this text or choose your own favorite New Testament translations. Since no one today knows what Jesus' voice sounded like, you may as well listen to a recording of your own voice reading the sayings as listen to the voice of another. Your subconscious tends to accept your voice as authoritative. What you say out loud your subconscious hears and tends to accept as truth.

Jesus' disciples heard his words, remembered them, and undoubtedly thought about what the words meant during moments of quiet reflection. You can do the same thing Jesus' original disciples did. After each saying, leave space on the recording to allow time for contemplation. During the silence you can reason about the saying or better yet simply sit in silent receptivity to allow insights to form.

The amount of silence after each saying may be as long or short as you choose. I would suggest just recording one passage and see how long you feel you want to contemplate it. Then leave that amount of silence after each saying you add to the recording. There is no hard and fast rule for how long to contemplate a saying to get the most out of it. However a total time of at least 15 minutes for meditation per day is recommended in many teachings as a healthful practice to reduce stress and derive other benefits. Some people prefer even longer meditation periods.

Spending time in meditation on the sayings of Jesus can lead you into a fuller and more powerful realization of his consciousness of God. In that realization you may find healing for yourself and even become an instrument of healing for others.

# Chapter Three: God, Faith, and Healing

In the first century God was understood to be the Supreme Being who created and governs the universe. Judaism affirmed worship of only one God, but many Jewish sects also believed in angels which were, in effect, intermediary supernatural divine beings. The polytheistic religions of the era generally believed in one Supreme God and various lesser deities. An important exception to polytheistic beliefs among non-Jews was the Stoic philosophy, which was pantheistic. Pantheism affirms that the universe is God. Panentheism is a similar position which affirms that the universe is in God, but God is more than the universe. The Apostle Paul expressed a panentheist position when he wrote: *"One God and Father of us all, who is above all and through all and in all"* (Ephesians 4: 6). Paul's affirmation of God as "above, through, and in all" suggests that a panentheistic idea of God was common in earliest Christianity and that idea may well have derived from Jesus.

Another important exception to the general polytheism of the time was the philosopher Parmenides (c. 515 – 450 BCE). Parmenides was the most radically monistic thinker before that age. He argued that there can only be one being and that multiplicity, sensory appearances and "voids" are illusions. His views had a strong influence on Plato and subsequent philosophy as well as upon the development of science and mysticism.[24]

Jesus was a Jew who believed in only one God. He did not explicitly express a radically monistic philosophy like that of Parmenides or a pantheistic philosophy like the Stoics. Using selected sayings attributed to Jesus in the Gospels, arguments can be made for a variety of theological positions. Using only the sayings considered in this work to originate with the historical Jesus, reasonable cases can be made that Jesus was a theist or pantheist or panentheist, depending upon how the sayings are interpreted.

Jews and philosophers such as Socrates, Plato, and the Stoics all believed that the Supreme God was truly good and wise. Jesus undoubtedly also believed the same. There is some reference to God as "Our Father" in the Jewish tradition and also in the beliefs of the Stoic[25] philosophers before Jesus. Jesus' frequent references to God as "Father" do not necessarily imply that he thought of himself as the *only* son of God.

In the first century C.E. nearly everyone believed in God, but the concepts of God were so varied that we ought to say everyone believed in a *concept* of "God." And that is still true today.

The God concept of Judaism was generally theistic and affirmed that God is just and merciful, concerned with the affairs of the nations (Gentiles), but primarily concerned with the people of Israel. The Jewish God had specific commandments and intervened in human affairs to motivate his people to keep those commandments.

The God concept of other nations of the time revolved around God's status as head of a hierarchy of deities. It was generally thought that human affairs were only of secondary interest to the deities. The gods of Homer and Virgil manipulated human events to resolve divine disputes, rather than to benefit humanity.

The God concept of the philosophers could be quite abstract. The Stoics conceptualized God as: Law, Right Reason, Mind, and Destiny. Aristotle thought of God in these terms: "the divine thought thinks . . . and its thinking is a thinking on thinking."[26] Only a philosopher would come up with such a concept of God. That is the type of concept that discourages young people from taking up philosophy.

Jesus' concept of God was partly Jewish and partly philosophical, as will be seen.

Jesus also spoke frequently of the "kingdom of God" or the "kingdom of Heaven." The Greek word "βασιλεια" ("basileia"), has usually been translated into English as "kingdom." "Basileia" does not specifically signify a geographical territory ruled by a king,[27] so it is better translated as "domain," "realm" or "rule." Jesus thought of God as ruling all of nature, so the words "rule" and "realm" are appropriate translations of "basileia" in his sayings.

Most of the quotations from Jesus used here are taken from the Jesus Seminar translation (SV or "Scholars Version") of the Gospels. In that translation, "basileia" is translated either as "Imperial Realm" or "Imperial Rule." I've chosen to use either *"realm"* or *"rule"* in the quotations, but have dropped the SV modifier "Imperial" because there is no Greek word for "Imperial" used in the passages. Also, in my view, the word "Imperial" at best adds nothing to understanding Jesus and at worst is misleading.

*Jesus on God*

## God First

As a Jew, Jesus undoubtedly believed in the "two greatest commandments": *"Hear, O Israel: The LORD our God, the LORD is one. Love the LORD your God with all your heart and with all your soul and with all your strength."* (Deuteronomy 6: 4-5 and Mark 12: 29-30) and *"love your neighbor as yourself"* (Leviticus 19: 18 and Mark 12: 31).

The idea of loving God above all else and loving humankind was also a central idea in the Stoic philosophy. For example, the Stoic philosopher Epictetus (c. 50-138 C.E.) agreed with what he described as the path of the Cynic philosopher:

*"Consider carefully, know yourself; consult the Divinity; attempt nothing without God; for if he counsels you, be assured that it is his will, whether you become eminent or suffer many a blow. For there is this fine circumstance connected with the character of the Cynic, that he must be beaten like an ass, and yet, when beaten, must love those who beat him as though he were the father, the brother of all."[28]*

From Epictetus' admiring description of the Cynic philosophers we get a picture of a group of individuals living by ideals of obedience to God and love of humanity – even of one's enemies. His description of the Cynic could have easily been a description of early Christians.

There is no inherent contradiction between loving God and humanity and being a philosopher. There is no inherent contradiction between being Jewish and being a philosopher. There is no reason to dismiss out of hand the possibility that Jesus was a Jewish philosopher.

Jesus expressed the idea of loving God in terms of serving God and humanity. He pointed out that one cannot be a servant to two masters:

*"No one can be a slave to two masters. No doubt that slave will either hate one and love the other, or be devoted to one and disdain the other. You can't be enslaved to both God and possessions." (Matt 6: 24)*

The word "possessions" in this passage is a translation of the word "mammon," an Aramaic word meaning wealth or possessions. To enter God's realm, one must serve God. If one slavishly pursues wealth, one is serving greed. From Jesus' perspective, one cannot serve both God and greed. He was not opposed to accumulation of wealth *per se*; "rich men" are sometimes "heroes" in his parables. Jesus was opposed to *serving* the "god" of wealth and possessions at the expense of the higher duty of serving the God of love. This attitude toward wealth is practically identical with the Stoic view.

It is clear from Jesus' frequent use of the expression "God's realm" that the idea of entering "God's realm" and understanding "God's rule" was central to his philosophy. The passage about being a "slave" to God clearly indicates that devotion to God was his highest priority. He put serving God first, above all things. In that sense, Jesus was in agreement with Judaism, Cynicism and Stoicism.

A common challenge for religion is that sometimes loyalty to nation or national laws seems to conflict with one's moral or spiritual principles or religious practices. In Jesus' time the Jewish people felt a conflict between their loyalty to their national aspirations and the requirement to pay taxes to Rome. Jesus famously responded to that question by saying "Render unto Caesar the things that are Caesar's and to God what belongs to God," or as the "Scholar's Version" (SV) translates it:

*"Pay the emperor what belongs to the emperor, and God what belongs to God!" (Luke 20: 25)*

Jesus' answer can actually be interpreted in two conflicting ways: pay your taxes (they belong to the Emperor) or *don't* pay your taxes (everything belongs to God). In the *Gospel of Mark* the saying was set in the context of a conversation, which may reflect the original context. In *Mark's* story, before giving his answer Jesus asks for a coin and asks whose image is on it. When someone responds "Caesar's," Jesus says "Render to Caesar, etc." The story context seems to imply that Jesus was saying "pay your taxes, for Caesar made the coins and they are his." The author of *Mark* seems to have interpreted the saying as implying that taxes "belonged" to the Emperor. That interpretation may have been influenced by the facts that *Mark* was written in Rome and the early Christians sought to convert Romans to their faith.

However, if that context was invented by Mark, we are left with the ambiguity of the saying. The *Gospel of Thomas* includes Jesus' saying about "paying the Emperor" without Jesus asking "whose image is on this coin?" In fact, since Jesus' sayings and stories are often ambiguous, it is entirely possible that the saying originally stood alone, without the clarifying action of pointing to Caesar's image. If that is the case, Jesus' intention was not to answer the question but to provoke his listeners to find their own answer for the questions, "what belongs to the government and what belongs to God?"

The questions raised by the saying remain even today. If the government is using taxes in ways that oppose our spiritual values, is it still right to pay taxes? Since the government prints the money, isn't it appropriate to give back whatever the government requires? Do tithes (10% of income) belong to God as is taught in the Bible?

In nations with freedom of religion, each individual must decide the appropriate spiritual use of personal wealth. If you believe that since money is printed by the government, money belongs to the government, then you should have no objection to paying taxes. And of course in democracies and all forms of government, if you do not pay your taxes you won't have any use of personal wealth - because you'll wind up in jail. If you believe all things, including money, belong to God, the simplest practical solution is to join a religious commune to which you can give all your wealth.

Because Jesus seems to have been indifferent to wealth, in alignment with the Stoic ideal, it is reasonable to conclude that he was not opposed to paying taxes.

Jesus undoubtedly believed in a Supreme Being which was, at least metaphorically, a "father" to humanity. He undoubtedly was able to convey that conviction to others by his words and demeanor. I suspect Jesus also conveyed his conviction by a kind of direct influence of consciousness. Communication and persuasiveness are not merely matters of spoken word; what the speaker conveys non-verbally may have an even greater impact than the words spoken. What the speaker conveys non-verbally includes "body language" and possibly "consciousness."

We will now examine the philosophical case that Jesus made for having faith in God.

## A Case for Faith in God

"Don't worry about your life - what you're going to eat and drink - or about your body - what you're going to wear. There is more to living than food and clothing, isn't there? Take a look at the birds of the sky: they don't plant or harvest, or gather into barns. Yet your heavenly Father feeds them. You're worth more than they, aren't you? Can any of you add one hour to life by worrying about it? Why worry about clothes? Notice how the wild lilies grow: they don't slave and they *never spin. Yet let me tell you, even Solomon at the height of his glory was never decked out like one of them. If God dresses up the grass of the field, which is here today and tomorrow is thrown into an oven, won't God care for you even more, you who don't take anything for granted?"* (Mt. 6: 25-30)

In this saying Jesus expressed clearly his primary concept of God: God is our Father who cares and provides for animals, fields and humans. In thinking of God as Father, Jesus may have thought of God as a "Person," but that is not the only possibility. After all, the Stoics called God "Father" but did not generally speak of God as a person; rather, they thought of "our Father" as Divine Reason, the Universe and Laws of the Universe.

Thinking metaphysically, beyond the literal sense, the concept of God as "Father" is congruent with the philosophical idea of God as "Universal Potential." From the "big bang" beginning until now, actual objects and events are preceded by real potential for those objects and events. If there were no real potential for a thing, then the actual thing could not happen. The "point of zero size" at the beginning of the universe[29] contained the potential for all that has happened from the beginning and all that will ever happen. Plant seeds contain real potential for actual food and clothing. Even before you were conceived, the Universe had the potential to produce you. "Universal Potential" can be considered the invisible source of all beings and the supportive sustainer of all beings, and so is a suitable understanding of Jesus' concept of "our Father."

The concept of God presented in the saying is also congruent with the idea of the benevolence of God found in both the philosophies and religions of the era.

Jesus indicated that divine benevolence extends to all people without regard to human "goodness." Another saying makes the point in a straightforward way: *"God causes the sun to rise on both the bad and the good, and sends rain on both the just and the unjust."* (Matt. 5: 45) The God concept here is not one of a Supreme Judge or King who rewards and punishes, but rather of a benevolent Being intimately concerned for and supportively involved in our lives. The concept is of a Real Power that wills to bless and prosper us.

The passage about the "birds of the sky" and the "wild lilies" is characterized by reasoning, imagery, and humor. In form the saying begins with an imperative ("don't worry") which flows into *suggestive* unusual imagery and questions. In addition, the saying includes a rational argument for *letting go of worrying*. To the extent that worrying is counter-productive to health, the saying also contains a *therapeutic suggestion*. If any of his listeners were persuaded by the argument or receptive to the suggestion, the saying might have relieved them of some degree of stress. The saying is *optimistic* about life and the universe.

The saying introduces us to the therapeutic elements Jesus imparted to his audience: cultivation of faith through reason, letting go of worry, therapeutic suggestion, humor and optimism. The therapeutic value of those and other elements will be examined in the context of other sayings.

The passage about the Father providing for the birds indicates that Jesus believed that God was concerned with the well-being of *all* creatures and especially humans. Another saying emphasizes the relatively higher value of humans in God's sight:

*"What do sparrows cost? A penny apiece? Yet not one of them will fall to the earth without the consent of your Father. As for you, even the hairs on your head have all been counted. So, don't be timid: you're worth more than a flock of sparrows." (Mt. 10: 29-31)*

The passages about birds and wild lilies indicate that Jesus looked to nature rather than history as reason to trust "the Father" to care for humanity. In the Bible writers almost always urge people to have faith based upon references to biblical events rather than with references to nature. For example, in chapter 11 of the New Testament book "Hebrews" the author urges his readers to have faith by citing scriptural stories of God's works.

Jesus may have arrived at his view of God and nature through a process of reasoning from observation. He used an *a fortiori* argument to persuade his listeners to trust rather than worry. His use of the argument illustrates a philosophical turn of mind. The argument may be stated simply in the following form:

*Your Father provides for the birds and fields.*

*You are worth more than birds and grass.*

*Therefore there is an even stronger reason to believe that your Father will provide for you.*

"Your Father" in the argument clearly refers to "that which governs the world." Any name or word that stands for "that which governs the world" could be used in the argument, e.g. "Yahweh provides for the birds and fields," "the Laws of Nature provide for the birds and fields," or "the Universe provides for the birds and fields." In other words, if you substitute the name or word which to you means "that which governs the world," the argument would be equally valid for trusting a Higher Power.

The saying has logic within it yet at the same time it is humorous. Jesus is taken so seriously that it may seem irreverent to suggest that he had a sense of humor. Nevertheless, *forms* of humor are found in his sayings. In the passage in question the form of satire is present: the saying gently mocks a human tendency to worry. The human tendency to worry about life, food and clothing is compared to the apparently relatively less worrisome existence of other creatures. Birds do not have to farm to survive – why should we? The second illustration borders on absurdist humor: fields of grass are "decked out" with lilies but of course humans cannot *grow* clothing on their bodies. On the other hand, there is a sense in which we do grow clothing, for we make clothing from plants such as cotton and flax. Jesus' point is serious but also humorous when seen in terms of the *form* of the passage.

Jesus' idea of God as "our Father" was foundational to his ethical ideals and his ontological concepts of humankind. For Jesus, "Father" is God's name and defines our fundamental relationship with God. Jesus saw humans as valued *offspring* of God rather than as disobedient *creations* of God. Because Jesus generally expressed his ideas in metaphorical terms his idea of humans as God's offspring was no doubt a spiritual idea rather than a physical one. Even so, Jesus may have thought of the physical world as part of God. Jesus may have seen God as *permeating* nature rather than as supernaturally *intervening* in nature.

Having faith, trusting in God, was a core idea in Jesus' philosophy. Faith can have a powerful healing influence, whether it is faith in God, relics, a human authority, or a medical treatment.

Assuming Jesus' words and consciousness persuaded some listeners to let go of worries and trust God to heal them, Jesus could have had, at the very least, what medical researchers call a "placebo effect" on those who came to him to learn and to be healed. Therefore at this point it is appropriate to consider the nature and power of the "placebo effect."

## *Faith: Placebo Effects and Exceptional Patients*

*"The placebo effect yields beneficial clinical results in 60-90% of diseases that include angina pectoris, bronchial asthma, herpes simplex, and duodenal ulcer."* - Doctors Herbert Benson and Richard Friedman[30]

If belief in a capsule devoid of medicinal properties can produce healing for some people, as happens consistently with placeboes, then it is no stretch of credulity to suppose that faith in an individual's healing abilities or faith in God can also produce healings in at least some cases.

I do not mean to suggest that there was nothing more to Jesus' healing influence than a placebo effect. While it cannot be proven that Jesus' consciousness and energy healed people, it is highly probable that in at least some cases a person's faith in Jesus or God could heal by a kind of "placebo effect." In addition, there are other elements of Jesus' philosophy which could also have facilitated healing.

The "placebo effect" is commonly assumed to involve a change in belief. The phenomena in medical research commonly known as "the placebo effect" are probably too complex to be understood by laypeople; and probably too complex to be completely understood by medical professionals. The complexity of the effect results from the complexity of the nature of belief. That complexity is three-fold: (1) beliefs are formed in a variety of ways and involve a variety of factors, including but not limited to genetics, education, environment, emotional responses, imagination and internal reasoning processes; (2) the word "belief" is not precisely defined in common usage, since it is used to mean "expectation," "opinion," "trust," or "conviction"; (3) it may be that for some just having hope of recovery associated with a treatment may be sufficient to trigger a cure; and (4) the neurophysiology of belief (or hope) involves interactions of brain structure, the nervous system, and physiological chemistry; there is probably no single identifiable neurological pattern of belief or hope formation.

There are many factors that may be part of what causes "the placebo effect," but study after study has shown that a "fake" treatment can be followed by cures of all kinds of illnesses. In a report to the National Institutes of Health, the authors noted that "The placebo response is almost ubiquitous. Studies show that in virtually any disease, roughly one-third of all symptoms improve when patients are given a placebo treatment without drugs (Goleman and Gurin, 1993)."[31]

In the same report the authors note that "The placebo response relies heavily on the interrelationship between doctor and patient. . . . Doctors who believe in the efficacy of their treatment communicate that enthusiasm to their patients; those who have strong expectations of specific effects and are self-confident and attentive are the most successful at eliciting a positive placebo response."[32] That point is significant because it indicates that not only does a patient's beliefs affect outcome, but also that the therapists' beliefs and behaviors can impact results.

The effect of the doctor's belief on the patient is an especially significant point when it comes to the healing work of Jesus. His faith in God's willingness and power to heal and provide would have had, at minimum, a "placebo" effect on some of those who came to him. Faith healers, Christian Science Practitioners, New Thought practitioners and other unconventional therapists can have similar effects on their clients. The healer's belief in God or the healer's belief in a personal special healing "gift" can affect the patient's response to the healer's words or treatments.

Elmer Green, one of the pioneers of biofeedback studies, described the placebo effect in these terms:

> "Humans, through visualization, are able to self-trigger physiological behaviors . . . . The placebo, by definition, is something false by means of which a patient is tricked into using his or her own visualization powers for physiological manipulation."[33]

Green's definition of the placebo as "something false" applies to most medical research placeboes. Yet if a patient is instructed how to "use his or her own visualization powers" and that practice produces the desired "physiological manipulation," the "placebo effect" cannot rightly be called the result of "something false." Likewise, if encouragement to trust or have faith results in desired effects, the words used cannot rightly be called "something false."

Doctors Herbert Benson and Richard Friedman, experts in the field of mind-body research, described the placebo effect in the following terms:

> "The placebo effect yields beneficial clinical results in 60-90% of diseases that include angina pectoris, bronchial asthma, herpes simplex, and duodenal ulcer. Three components bring

forth the placebo effect: (a) positive beliefs and expectations on the part of the patient; (b) positive beliefs and expectations on the part of the physician or health care professional; and (c) a good relationship between the two parties. Because of the heavily negative connotations of the very words 'placebo effect,' the term should be replaced by 'remembered wellness.' Remembered wellness has been one of medicine's most potent assets and it should not be belittled or ridiculed. Unlike most other treatments, it is safe and inexpensive and has withstood the test of time."[34]

The Benson-Friedman explanation of the placebo effect is illuminating. "Remembered wellness" may be a more accurate label for the placebo phenomena. Patients generally experienced health before their illness. The mere suggestion that a treatment will work can trigger a memory or sense of a previous state of health. The patients' bodies and emotions can recall that state and work to reproduce it in the physiology. However it works, the "placebo effect" is a misnomer. The inert substance called a placebo is not what causes healing response; rather the cause is psychological, either belief or hope. The phenomenon would be better named "the remembered wellness effect," "the belief effect" or "the positive expectation effect."

Benson and Friedman further explain the "remembered wellness" effect in terms of beliefs, expectations, and relationships. In addition to the role of positive beliefs, they acknowledge the role of optimism in their phrase "positive expectations." Finally, the Benson-Friedman explanation acknowledges the role of the good relationship between professional and patient, which indicates the social dimension of belief. However, the social dimension of belief is probably much broader than supposed by the authors. Our beliefs regarding health and healing are influenced by family, social affiliations, religious affiliations, educational associations, and vocational associates. The strength of social support systems plays a role in supporting optimism and belief.

Since a social group with shared beliefs formed around Jesus, it is appropriate to consider the role relationship systems play in belief, optimism and general well-being. An exploratory study of speed of recovery from athletic injuries indicated that a number of factors were associated with relative speed of recovery. Researchers found that quicker recovery from injuries was associated with positive attitude, stress control, goal setting, positive self-talk, mental imagery, and *social support.* Athletes with strong support from their social network recovered more quickly than those who lacked such support.

While the studies about recovery from injuries do not directly address the "belief effect," we do see elements associated with that effect. Positive self-talk and use of mental imagery are commonly advocated by teachers of "positive thinking" to establish positive *belief.* Positive attitude (optimism) is also part of the "positive thinking" approach to well-being and success.[35]

The phrase "positive thinking" was popularized by the minister Norman Vincent Peale with his book "*The Power of Positive Thinking*" published in 1952. Peale's work was a simplification of the metaphysically based therapeutic religious philosophies variously known as "Mind Cure," "New Thought," "Christian Science," "Religious Science," and "Unity." In all such spiritual philosophies, establishing belief in health is the primary mechanism for healing and sustaining health. Each system has its own idealist metaphysical theory and way of interpreting scriptures, but the theories are similar enough to be considered together under one category. For simplicity I will refer to all such groups and methods as "metaphysical."

Metaphysical systems are not "faith healing" in the traditional sense. Traditional faith healing involves belief in leaders with special gifts (faith healers) who have a supernatural connection to God, or belief in sacred objects or places with special sacred connections to God. The metaphysical systems focus on the omnipresence of God-Mind, the power of human consciousness to connect with God-Mind, and the power of consciousness to transform physical experience. These systems claim that anyone can change their consciousness in ways that will establish physical and emotional health.

The metaphysical systems focus on divine *laws* rather than divine gifts and divine intervention. While sometimes using the word "miracle" in reference to their work, metaphysical healers explain "miracles" as the effects of working with divine law. Faith healing emphasizes that God is a Person (or three persons, according to traditional Christian doctrine) who hears and responds to our prayers and faith in the mysterious ways or whims of a Divine Super Person. Metaphysical healing emphasizes God as Infinite Mind and Impersonal Principle which responds to our thoughts in accord with divine law. Faith healing emphasizes belief in supernatural intervention usually connected with a sacred object or special person; metaphysical healing emphasizes changing our thoughts with faith in divine law and in God as Unchanging Principle rather than as mysterious Person.

In the final analysis, the faith healers and metaphysicians are working with belief for healing; they are just doing the work using different language and explanations.

There is an abundance of anecdotal evidence for healing through faith in religious publications, as one would expect. Even respected physicians have given credence to faith healing, in books extending back at least to the great American philosopher and psychologist William James and continuing up to recent books such as those by physician Bernie S. Siegel, M.D.

Bernie Siegel, a respected physician and professor at Yale, provided a number of cases of healing through belief in *Love, Medicine and Miracles*. One case he described was that of a woman diagnosed with terminal cancer who had "gone home to die." She returned several months later, all sign of cancer gone. Her explanation: *"I decided to live to be a hundred and leave my troubles to God."* Siegel commented, *"I could really end the book here, because this peace of mind can heal anything. I believe faith is the essence, a simple solution, yet too hard for most people to practice."*[36]

William James was one of the first academics to have a serious interest in metaphysical healing. William James' lecture on "The Religion of Healthy-Mindedness"[37] cites testimonies to metaphysical healing by individuals known to him. James stated in the lecture that the metaphysical healing philosophy (a.k.a. "mind-cure" and "New Thought") produced significant results: "The blind have been made to see, the halt to walk; life-long invalids have had their health restored. The moral fruits have been no less remarkable."[38] James was not engaging in hyperbolic flourish; he was taking at face value various testimonies by people known to him. One of his fellow faculty members in the Harvard philosophy department was Horatio Dresser, a metaphysical healer and author of some renown in his time.[39] This is not to claim that James himself was a "New Thoughter"; in fact James had significant philosophical differences with the metaphysical movements. However, as a pragmatist William James saw in the metaphysical movements results that commanded his respect and curiosity.

## *H o w   t o   T r u s t   G o d   t o   P r o s p e r   a n d   H e a l   Y o u*

From Jesus' example we see one way to turn our attention away from anxieties and shift into a trusting state of mind and feeling. Jesus gently mocked human anxieties by pointing to the conditions of other animals in nature. He directed his listeners' thoughts from worries about food and clothing to how "your Father" provides plenty of food for the birds; they do not even have to farm for food! He pointed out that fields are decoratively "clothed" with lilies; the fields do not even have to make clothing! Our worries are funny from the perspective that, despite our sense of superiority over other animals, we worry about provision while animals simply take their food from the abundance of nature. No doubt our own earliest ancestors, like other animals, simply foraged or hunted for food until they discovered agriculture. So why worry?

By taking time to reflect on nature and the circumstances of other animals it is possible to let go of worries and enter into a state of faith. For example, consider the lowly tortoise. It moves slowly and never exercises beyond slowly ambling through the grass. It does not worry about its diet; it just eats grass and whatever else is available. It has no health care, no tortoise physicians; yet the tortoise lives longer than humans - some have lived over 200 years! If your Father cares for the tortoise enough to let it live 200 years, won't your Father care for you just as much?

When one observes nature, it becomes clear that most human experiences and worries are built upon unnecessary human constructs. Most of what we have we do not actually need. We do not need any human inventions to survive. We do not need electrical power to thrive. We do not need fame to enjoy life. We do not need to be millionaires to live happily. We do not even *need* houses for shelter; caves worked nicely for our ancestors.

I, for one, do not wish to go back to the cave dwelling days of humanity. I enjoy modern conveniences as much as anyone. My point is that much of what we desire and worry about isn't necessary for life or happiness. We can trust that nature provides all we need and work for what we desire - without worrying.

In addition to this kind of "naturalistic reflection" there are other ways to develop the kind of faith that results in provision and healing. The first step in developing healing and prospering faith is discovering what moves *you* to have faith. What kinds of words do you find compelling and convincing with regard to trusting God (or "the Universe")? Are you moved by preachers of faith-healing or metaphysical teachers? Then you need only follow their directions on how to pray or meditate. If you are not moved by Christian or New Thought preaching and teaching, then look for another path that teaches a healing God or at least a "friendly Universe."

There is no "God-pill" and so can be no "God-placebo" that one could ingest to receive healing. It could be argued that when medical researchers provide placeboes, they are deceiving the patients. I don't think that is the case because researchers do not know if the experimental treatment will work any better than the placebo treatment. In any case, preachers and philosophers who would help others have faith in God must be themselves convinced, if they would remain in ethical integrity. An important role that teachers of religion can play for healing is to produce believable cases for God's existence and goodness and thereby facilitate the power of faith in those who need healing.

For those who would adopt the healing philosophy of Jesus, one important principle is: *There is no cause for worry, for God is our Father and has made provision for all living creatures, including humans.*

We are, in some sense, offspring of the Universe and/or Source of the Universe. As offspring of the Divine Source we have a divine potential for creativity and other divine attributes. Our resources are not limited to what can be found in the world outside of our minds, for our inner knowledge, understanding, imagination and other inner resources give us a capacity to establish health and create wealth. For all we know, the "outer world" is also within our minds, for we know that world only as it is inside our minds. What we think about the world and the attitudes we have toward it form our experience of the world.

If you worry about scarcity your experience is scarcity. If you think of the world as having plenty of good, your experience is plentiful good. If you look for good you experience good. One indirect effect of releasing anxiety by focusing on thoughts of plenty is a reduction of stress - and that is good for your health.

As we continue the exploration of Jesus' philosophy we will see that one general effect of what he said and how he said it would have been reduction of stress for those who believed him. We will discuss the negative effects of stress on health and the positive effects of stress reduction on health in the context of other aspects of Jesus' philosophy.

## *The   Unconditional   Love   of   God*

One example of Jesus' teaching that God is our loving Father is one of his best known parables, "The Parable of the Prodigal Son." We cannot assume that any character in any parable is intended to allegorically represent God. However, the father in the prodigal son story is consistent with the character ascribed to the Father God portrayed in other Jesus sayings. The father in the parable expresses unconditional love toward both sons. It is probable that Jesus intended this parable to illustrate the nature of the "heavenly Father." The "Scholar's Version" of the parable is as follows:

*"Once there was this man who had two sons. The younger of them said to his father, 'Father, give me the share of property that's coming to me.' So he divided his resources between them. Not too many days later, the younger son got all his things together and left home for a faraway country, where he squandered his property by living extravagantly. Just when he had spent it all, a serious famine swept through that country, and he began to do without. So he went and hired himself out to one of the citizens of that country, who sent him out to his farm to feed the pigs. He longed to satisfy his hunger with the carob pods, which the pigs usually ate; but no one offered him anything. Coming to his senses he said, 'Lots of my father's hired hands have more than enough to eat, while here I am dying of starvation! I'll get up and go to my father and I'll say to him, "Father, I have sinned against heaven and affronted you; I don't deserve to be called a son of yours any longer; treat me like one of your hired hands."' And he got up and returned to his father.*

*But while he was still a long way off, his father caught sight of him and was moved to compassion. He went running out to him, threw his arms around his neck, and kissed him. And the son said to him, 'Father, I have sinned against heaven and affronted you; I don't deserve to be called a son of yours any longer.'*

*But the father said to his slaves, 'Quick! Bring out the finest robe and put it on him; put a ring on his finger and sandals on his feet. Fetch the fat calf and slaughter it; let's have a feast and celebrate, because this son of mine was dead and has come back to life; he was lost and now is found.' And they started celebrating.*

*Now his elder son was out in the field; and as he got closer to the house, he heard music and dancing. He called one of the servant boys over and asked what was going on. He said to him, 'Your brother has come home and your father has slaughtered the fat calf, because he has him back safe and sound.'*

*But he was angry and refused to go in. So his father came out and began to plead with him. But he answered his father, 'See here, all these years I have slaved for you. I never once disobeyed any of your orders; yet you never once provided me with a kid goat so I could celebrate with my friends. But when this son of yours shows up, the one who has squandered your estate with prostitutes - for him you slaughter the fat calf.'*

*But the father said to him, 'My child, you are always at my side. Everything that's mine is yours. But we just had to celebrate and rejoice, because this brother of yours was dead, and has come back to life; he was lost, and now is found.'"*
*(Luke 15: 11-32)*

The parable found in Luke has a general theme and structure similar to a riddle attributed to Jesus in Matthew's gospel. While the Jesus Seminar concluded that the riddle in question could not be attributed to Jesus, the vote was close to even. Matthew's parable again has a father and two sons:

*"A man had two children. He went to the first, and said, 'Son, go and work in the vineyard today.' He responded, 'I'm your man, sir,' but he didn't move.*

*Then he went to the second and said the same thing.*

*He responded, 'I don't want to,' but later on he thought better of it and went to work.*

*Which of the two did what the father wanted?" (Matt. 21: 28-31)*

Understood in the context of the culture of the time, in both stories each son *both* honors and dishonors the father. The commandment to honor one's parents was understood to mean in both word and deed. In the prodigal son story, the younger son dishonors his father by leaving home and wasting his inheritance, but then upon return honors the father by acknowledging his sin and offering to do the father's will as a hired hand. The elder son first honors the father by doing his will, but at the end of the story dishonors the father by refusing his father's request to join the celebration. In the parable the father reaches out in compassion to both his sons despite their temporary disobedience.

In Luke's story the honor/dishonor dichotomy is expressed in terms of actions. In Matthew's riddle, the honor/dishonor dichotomy is drawn sharply in terms of saying and doing. The son who at first says he will go to work honors the father with his words, but dishonors the father with his actions. The son who at first refuses to do his father's will, dishonors the father with his words, but honors the father with his actions.

It is possible that both Luke's parable and Matthew's riddle go back to the same orally transmitted original parable by Jesus. If that is the case, then both Luke and Matthew may have edited the original parable. One of Luke's concerns in the book of *Acts* (*Luke* and *Acts* were by the same author) was the conflict between Jewish and Gentile Christians. Luke may have added the younger/elder son distinction to encourage an *allegorical* interpretation of the prodigal story as being about the Gentile Christians (younger sons) and the Jewish Christians (elder sons). Luke may also have added a few details to expand the story for effect.

Matthew was concerned to show that Jesus was the *Jewish* Messiah, i.e. that Jesus supported the laws of Moses and fulfilled the prophecies. Consequently, Matthew may have been uncomfortable with a parable suggesting that God loves and "embraces" even those who break the commandment to honor one's parents. Matthew might have turned the parable into a riddle to make it about how to honor one's parents with action, thereby dropping the theme of the Father's all-embracing love.

There is no way of knowing if Matthew and Luke edited the same parable in different ways; we can only say that both included a story with two sons who both honored and dishonored their father in different ways. Luke's "prodigal son" parable is probably closest to the original, according to the scholars of the Jesus Seminar. Jesus frequently had surprising twists in his parables, such as the surprise of the "prodigal son" being embraced and rewarded by his father. It also reflects Jesus' idea of God as unconditionally supportive, as seen in the passage about the birds and lilies discussed previously and the passage about God's sun and rain being given to both the good and the bad.

The second principle of Jesus' healing philosophy is:

*God loves us unconditionally.*

We may make mistakes. We may waste our resources. We may experience anger about the blessings of others and envy others. We may behave in ways that are not "holy" according to conventional ideas of "holiness." According to Jesus, even if we behave in ways that are not honorable and do not deserve to be called "a child of God," we can always turn back to ways that honor and serve the good. No matter what our behavior, we are always embraced in the love of God.

We have a role to play in our own experience of God and God's love, according to the parable. The father never stopped loving his sons, but the sons each in turn did not realize it. The younger son was so occupied with the world of the senses that he forgot who he was and forgot about his father. Even once he remembered who he was as a son of a wealthy father, the younger son did not realize how much his father loved him. Once he turned back to his father, the younger son came into a higher realization of his father's love. When the elder son became consumed with envy about the party for his brother, the elder son forgot that all that his father had was also his. As long as he stayed stuck in envy, the elder son could not experience the celebration of abundance – the party for his brother.

The father came to the elder son to remind him of the truth; the story ends without telling us how the elder son responded to his father's plea. The ending of the story in effect proposes this question to the audience: while remembering your own blessings, can you also rejoice in the blessings of others?

So, according to the teaching of Jesus, God always loves us like beloved children, but it is up to us to receive and accept that blessing. It is up to us to choose to honor and serve the good. When we make that choice, we will experience the blessings of God that are already ours for the asking. Just as we experience the world filtered through our attitudes, we also experience God filtered through our attitudes.

While the idea of God as Father was not uncommon, the teaching about the *unconditionally loving* Father God was a departure from the prevailing religious and philosophical ideas of God in Jesus' time. In Jesus' time God was seen by most people as a punishing judgmental King. The Jewish prophets sometimes spoke of God's everlasting love, but usually also preached the idea that people had to be punished and had to return to obedience before God would forgive and bless. In that belief system, mercy was offered only after the demands of justice and repentance had been fulfilled. In the prodigal son parable, the father embraces his prodigal son before the boy has a chance to give his speech of repentance. The father attempts to persuade the older son to join the party even though the boy refuses to heed his father's request. In neither case does the father seek or threaten punishment for disobedience.

In Jesus' philosophy, mercy and blessings are *always* available in relation to God. We may suffer the natural consequences of foolish mistakes, as the prodigal did; we may be deprived of enjoying life by our own envy, as the elder brother was. But the suffering and deprivation the brothers experienced were natural consequences of *their* choices; the father did not impose the consequences as punishment – there were no conditions imposed by the father to receive the father's embrace. The only repentance required is recognizing the error of our ways so we can remember that God loves us.

If you find yourself worrying about your life, you may find it helpful to contemplate the words of Jesus and remember:

*There is no cause for worry, for God is my Father and has made provision for all living creatures, including humans and including me.*

*God loves me unconditionally.*

# Chapter Four: Optimistic Thinking, Health and Healing

Research, published in the *Journal of Personality and Social Psychology,* examined self-perceptions of aging and discovered a correlation between "positive self-perceptions" and longevity. The self-perceptions labeled as "positive" were derived from responses to statements such as "things keep getting worse as I get older," "I have as much pep as I did last year," "as you get older, you are less useful," "I am as happy now as I was when I was younger," and "as I get older, things are (better, worse, or the same) as I thought they would be." Those who did not feel less useful, who affirmed "pep" and happiness, and who felt things in general got better had "positive self-perceptions" and could certainly be considered optimistic.

Optimism is often thought to be an attitude of positive expectations about the future. However, a truly optimistic attitude is as much about the present moment as about future expectations. Someone who hopes for a better future could also think of the world in the present as essentially bad – an attitude indistinguishable from pessimism. The true optimist is one who sees the world as basically good; optimism is as much an ability to appreciate good in the present moment as the ability to expect good in the future. A positive self-perception and a positive appreciation of the present truly indicate optimistic thinking. Seeing the world as basically good, the optimist expects things to continue to be good or better in the future.

The study that showed a correlation between positive self-perception and longevity can be understood as measuring a correlation between optimism and health.

"This research found that older individuals with more positive self-perceptions of aging, measured up to 23 years earlier, lived *7.5 years longer* than those with less positive self-perceptions of aging."[40] The authors of the article noted that

> "The effect of more positive self-perceptions of aging on survival is greater than the physiological measures of low systolic blood pressure and cholesterol, each of which is associated with a longer life span of 4 years or less. . . . also greater than the independent contribution of lower body mass index, no history of smoking, and a tendency to exercise; each of these factors has been found to contribute between 1 and 3 years of added life."

If optimistic positive self-perception on aging has a greater impact on longevity than blood pressure, cholesterol, non-smoking and exercise, it must have *some* benefit for health and/or recovery from illness.

The philosophy of Jesus was radically optimistic and that optimism undoubtedly had positive effects upon those who followed him. In some cases that radical optimism could have been a catalyst for healing. The optimism of Jesus' philosophy can be seen in his words about: the already present realm and rule (kingdom) of God, the principle of expansion, and the law of asking and receiving. In this chapter we will explore those ideas and some health research on how optimism is related to wellbeing.

## The Presence of God's Realm and Rule

Jesus' ideas regarding the realm and rule of God were different from those held later by his followers. The prevailing Jewish belief about the Kingdom of God of his time was political, territorial, and related to future events and hope for divine intervention. Jesus' disciples never let go of the idea of a future territorial kingdom, even though Jesus spoke about God's realm as being already present.

Jesus' idea of the realm of God had deep roots in Jewish tradition. In Hebrew scriptures God is sometimes portrayed as already ruling all of nature; that is the concept Jesus connected with. That theme is prominent in the book of Job and in many Psalms, e.g. *"The heavens are telling the glory of God; and the firmament proclaims his handiwork."* (Ps 19: 1, RSV) Jesus adopted that "God rules nature (including humanity) now" theme as his primary idea of the realm of God, and used illustrations from nature and everyday human behavior. He rarely directly referred to the politics of the time.

*There is nothing hidden that will not be revealed. (Thom. 5: 2; see Mt. 10: 26)*

Jesus implied in this statement that he was concerned with knowledge: revealing that which is hidden. Viewed in that light, he was optimistic about discovery of truth and what he called "God's realm."

The historical Jesus spoke of the realm of God as already present, although not "observed" by people. He stated forthrightly, according to the *Gospel of Luke*, that *"You won't be able to observe the coming of God's realm. People are not going to be able to say, 'Look, here it is!' or 'Over there!' On the contrary, God 's realm is within you"* (Luke 17: 21). This is very clear: God's realm is not located in any external place or future time; the realm is already present within the individual. Presumably, Jesus was affirming that God's realm must be sought in the mind and heart, not in the sky or political conditions.

The idea of God's realm "within you" is logically consistent with characterizing God as "Father." Our human parents are "in us" in a biological and psychological sense; God can be said to be "in us" in a psychological and spiritual sense. Those who think at all about God, even those who deny that God exists, have a psychological relationship with the idea of God's existence; in that sense "God" is psychologically within us. If we take "God" to signify the ultimate good and Creative Energy of the universe, God can be said to be "spiritually" within us as our moral ideals and creative aspirations. If we think of our lives as emanating from God (or a Benevolent Universe), then our very life and consciousness is the presence of God within us. If we think of God as the Potential of the Universe, then the potential within us is God within us.

According to the *Gospel of Thomas*, Jesus said:

*"It will not come by watching for it. It will not be said, 'Look, here! Or 'Look there!' Rather the Father's realm is spread out upon the earth, but people don't see it."* (Thomas 113: 4) This passage reflects Jesus' idea of God's realm as "hidden" and affirms that God's realm is present "spread out on the earth." The idea that God's realm is spread out on the earth is consistent with Jesus' idea that the Father-God supports all life here and now.

Also according to *Thomas*, Jesus said:

*"If your leaders say to you, 'Look, the Father's realm is in the sky,' then the birds of the sky will precede you. If they say to you, 'It is in the sea,' then the fish will precede you. Rather, the Father's realm is within you and it is outside you."* (Thom. 3: 1-3)

Here Jesus chides people for their ideas that the realm of God is up in the sky or in the sea. The idea of a divine realm in the sea was a "Gentile" idea rather than a Jewish one, but there is no reason to suppose Jesus was *only* familiar with Jewish ideas. This saying was not selected by the Jesus Seminar as probably originating with Jesus, but there are good reasons for thinking it did originate with him. The saying clearly has the same message as the passages from Luke 17: 21 and Thomas 113: 4. Furthermore, the passage reflects Jesus' style of satirizing conventional ideas using references to nature, as well as affirming the idea of Divine Presence everywhere.

I would like to note here that the above sayings found in the *Gospel of Thomas* do not reflect "Gnostic" ideas as generally portrayed. The Gnostics supposedly thought of the material world as a defective creation of a demi-god rather than having God's realm spread out (though unseen) upon it. The Gnostics supposedly focused on realms (aeons) beyond this world (aeon), rather than on God's realm here and now. In other words, the above passages in *Thomas* are more like a Jesus saying in *Luke* than sayings in so-called "Gnostic" gospels.

Jesus' naturalistic, non-supernatural and non-political sayings suggest a description of the way the universe works. The phrase "God's realm/rule" as Jesus used it is equivalent in meaning to what we would call the "universe." The *way* the universe works is properly a *metaphysical* and *cosmological* topic, not a prophetic one. The *way* of the universe is primarily a *philosophical* concern even though cosmological assumptions are often found in religious beliefs.

His idea that God's realm and rule is "hidden yet present" indicates Jesus was a mystic. The effect of "mystical consciousness" for healing is not known and difficult to test; nevertheless I suspect it is the most important and powerful aspect of Jesus' role as healer. Studies of the effects of prayer are the closest thing we have to substantiation of spiritual consciousness as being efficacious for healing. Some of those studies will be discussed in Chapter 8.

## Principle of Expansion

Scientific knowledge indicates that expansion is at work in the universe, everywhere from the very beginning. Scientific theory posits that the universe expanded from a single point of energy and recent evidence indicates the universe continues to expand at an accelerating rate. Organisms likewise expand from tiny seeds into their full grown forms; in fact organisms expand from the invisible "seeds" of DNA molecules.

The principle of expansion is one of the primary ideas in Jesus' philosophy of how the universe works. This principle of expansion can be interpreted with relation to ideas of health. Such an interpretation supports an optimistic perspective regarding healing: as you focus on the presence of God, health expands within you. The principle can also be interpreted with relation to ideas of goals, supporting an optimistic outlook on attaining those goals.

Jesus compared God's realm and rule to examples of expansion in nature. He may not have known about the "big bang" or DNA, but he observed expansion as ubiquitous in nature and identified expansion as the way God's rule works in the world. In that way he identified what can be called a "cosmological principle of expansion."

*What does God's rule remind me of? It is like leaven which a woman took and concealed in fifty pounds of flour until it was all leavened.* (Luke 13: 20-21)

Leavening is an example of the principle of expansion that is a part of everyday life. The leaven here could symbolize any kind of expansion, so any number of interpretations could be given. The leaven, being hidden, works best as a symbol for an invisible agent of expansion. Expansion of ideas, wisdom, faith, love, spiritual awareness, or "hidden" physical agents such as DNA, can all be represented by the analogy. Jesus probably mainly intended to represent expansion of God-awareness and spiritual qualities in the individual and in humanity collectively.

In the analogy of the leaven we see Jesus' sense of humor again in the form of a surprising image that reverses a conventional metaphor. "Leaven" was conventionally used as a metaphor for *false* doctrines or being *unclean*. Unleavened bread was usually associated with the "clean" and sacred. Unleavened bread was associated with the Passover meal commemorating escape from Egypt.

*"Seven days you shall eat unleavened bread, but on the first day you shall remove leaven from your houses; for whoever eats anything leavened from the first day until the seventh day, that person shall be cut off from Israel." (Exodus 12: 15, New American Standard Version)*

Leavened bread was forbidden for some of the offerings in the temple:

*"No grain offering, which you bring to the LORD, shall be made with leaven, for you shall not offer up in smoke any leaven or any honey as an offering by fire to the LORD." (Leviticus 2:11)*

In the New Testament the association of leaven with false doctrine or uncleanness continued. One saying in which leaven has its conventional negative implication is attributed to Jesus:

*"And Jesus said to them, 'Watch out and beware of the leaven of the Pharisees and Sadducees.'" (Matthew 16:6)*

According to the Jesus Seminar the saying probably did not

originate with Jesus but was added later when the early Christians found themselves competing with the Pharisees for converts.

Even after Jesus told the leaven parable, some Christians continued to associate leaven with uncleanness. Paul uses the metaphor of leaven in his letters, with the common negative implication:

*"Your boasting is not good. Do you not know that a little leaven leavens the whole lump of dough?" (1 Corinthians 5:6)*

*Clean out the old leaven so that you may be a new lump, just as you are in fact unleavened." (1 Corinthians 5:7)*

It is clear that Jesus' use of leaven as a simile for God's realm and rule is a reversal of common associations. Likewise, his comparison of God's rule to a woman's work is unusual but not entirely unconventional, since e.g. God's Wisdom is referred to as feminine in Proverbs and other wisdom literature. Jesus may very well have had the expansion of spiritual wisdom in mind as the meaning of this parable.

Another unusual use of imagery in the same simile is the amount of flour that the woman is leavening. Fifty pounds of leavened flour is enough to make about 100 pounds of leavened bread. Since there were no preservatives in that time, people generally made only enough bread for one or two days. Clearly the woman in the simile is expecting to feed a lot of people that day!

Mention of large quantities is typical in Jesus' parables; the exaggerated quantity was probably a device to help people remember the saying. In addition, by implication the parable fits another common theme in Jesus' sayings: the theme of celebration. The large quantity of bread being prepared by the woman was suitable only for a great feast, some kind of celebration. Jesus' parables referring to celebration include the man who finds a lost sheep, the woman who finds a lost coin, the return of the prodigal son, the man who finds a treasure in a field, and the man who prepares a great feast.

Finally, by saying the woman "concealed" the leaven rather than "mixed" it, the saying suggests that God's realm is hidden from ordinary perception. The idea of God's hidden-yet-present realm is found in many of Jesus' sayings.

The fundamental meaning of the parable is that God's rule involves a principle of expansion. The parable does not explicitly say *what* expands in God's realm and rule. That ambiguity allows the listener or reader to reflect upon the idea of expansion and formulate applications. Reflection on unusual and ambiguous sayings can be a way to induce meditative states (this concept will be discussed in *Chapter 7: Meditation Induction and Prayer*).

The parable of the mustard seed is similar to the leaven parable in style, theme and meaning:

> *"It's like a mustard seed. It's the smallest of all seeds, but when it falls on prepared soil, it produces a large plant and becomes a shelter for the birds of the sky." (Thomas 20: 2-3; see also Mt 13: 31-32, Lk 13: 18-19, Mk 4: 30-32)*

Again the main idea in this analogy is that God's rule involves a principle of expansion, this time drawing on the natural metaphor of a mustard seed and plant.

In this simile, Jesus parodies a conventional metaphor of the time: a tall tree as signifying power and/or goodness of nations or individuals. Nations were metaphorically referred to as trees; the larger the nation or empire, the larger the tree in the metaphor. Righteousness and wisdom were sometimes compared to trees. Here are a few examples:

> *"The righteous will flourish like a palm tree, they will grow like a cedar of Lebanon."(Psalm 92:12)*

> *"She is a tree of life to those who take hold of her; those who hold her fast will be blessed." (Proverbs 3:18)*

Chapter 31 of *Ezekiel* compares nations to trees. The size of the tree indicates the power of the nation; the greater the nation the taller the tree. It makes reference to the tall tree having birds in its boughs.

Chapter 4 of *Daniel* compares King Nebuchadnezzar to a mighty tree:

> *"which grew large and strong, with its top touching the sky, visible to the whole earth, with beautiful leaves and abundant fruit, providing food for all, giving shelter to the wild animals, and having nesting places in its branches for the birds - Your Majesty, you are that tree! You have become great and strong; your greatness has grown until it reaches the sky, and your dominion extends to distant parts of the earth." (4: 20-22)*

The mustard shrub of Jesus' parable stands in stark contrast to Daniel's metaphor of a tree "touching the sky." The contrast could be compared to the common modern expression of a person's "family tree" being humorously referred to as a "family shrub." Nebuchadnezzar was compared to a tree so tall that it was visible to the whole earth; Jesus compares God's kingdom to a common shrub that spread rapidly but didn't grow to conspicuous heights. The theme of the parable is again the idea that God's realm and rule expands from something that is practically invisible.

Is it a trivial coincidence that Jesus' description of the universe (God's realm) is a nearly perfect simile for the origin of the universe in the scientific "big bang theory"? Jesus' philosophy expressed elements of reason and observation. His insights are similar to the intuitions of mystics. On the basis of reason, observation and mystical insight Jesus may have intuited that the universe grew from a "God seed." That his seed metaphors express something fundamental about the universe is no more coincidental than that Heraclitus' notion of the universe as an ever evolving process expresses something fundamental about the universe. Like Heraclitus, Jesus discerned the general nature of the universe in observation of natural phenomena.

The philosophers of the era tended to favor primary metaphors for describing the nature of the universe. Heraclitus used fire and water as primary metaphors for his central idea of change or process as fundamental to the nature of the universe. Plato used shadows as his primary metaphor for describing the visible universe as a copy of the real realm of true and ideal forms. Jesus' fondness of seed parables suggests that seed growth was his primary metaphor for the nature of the universe.

Just what the mustard seed represents, beyond its general "likeness" to God's realm, is not specifically stated; hence many interpretations are possible. The expansion of God's realm could refer to Jesus' message or "spirit" spreading to others. It could refer to ideas or spirit growing within individuals. It could refer to both outer and inner expansion. The expansion could refer to how any "idea-seed" can grow into expression. Because there are many applications of the metaphor, it is best understood as a general principle rather than as having one and only one referent. The parable "begs" to be used as a general statement about the nature of the universe or the "way" of God in the universe.

In other seed parables Jesus notes other aspects of the "expansion principle." He notes that expansion is a process with phases. He notes that prevailing conditions influence how much seeds, consciousness, or ideas can expand. He notes that processes have cycles of beginnings and endings.

> *God's rule is like this: Suppose someone sows seed on the ground, and sleeps and rises night and day, and the seed sprouts and matures, although the sower is unaware of it. The earth produces fruit on its own, first a shoot, then a head, then mature grain in the head. But when the grain ripens, that farmer sends for the sickle, because it's harvest time.* (Mark 4: 26-29)

In general terms this parable identifies a process which goes through distinct phases, in which later phases "look" very different from earlier ones. It doesn't take genius to notice that the growth of wheat goes through distinct phases. The genius was in using this as a metaphor for the universe (God's realm). Natural processes have beginnings and endings; they involve expansion and have distinct phases. While clearly applicable to development of vegetation, distinct phases of process are also seen at every level of the cosmos: in animal growth from conception to maturity, in human society growth from tribe to nation to empire, in the cosmic expansion from the "big bang" to energy clusters to galaxies and solar systems.

> *Listen to this! This sower went out to sow. While he was sowing, some seed fell along the path, and the birds came and ate it up. Other seed fell on rocky ground where there wasn't much soil, and it came up right away because the soil had no depth. But when the sun came up it was scorched, and because it had no root it withered. Still other seed fell among thorns, and the thorns came up and choked it, so that it produced no fruit. Finally, some seed fell on good earth and started producing fruit. The seed sprouted and grew: one part had a yield of thirty, another part sixty, and a third part one hundred.* (Mk. 4: 3-8)

The traditional interpretation as found in *Mark* is that Jesus is the sower, the seed is his word and the different types of soil represent different responses to the message. In that interpretation the seed's relative fruitfulness depends entirely upon individual consciousness and response. This is a reasonable interpretation of the parable; it indicates that whether or not Jesus' words bear fruit is dependent upon the faith or consciousness of those who hear. However, if the interpretation does not originally come from Jesus but from Mark, as is argued by many scholars, then the parable could have many applications and interpretations.

Plants require certain soil and climate conditions in order to grow well and "bear fruit." The same could be said of animals, societies, businesses and ideas. The sower in the parable could be God, a teacher, a farmer or any individual who has a product or idea to develop. By another interpretation, the seed could represent people born in different environments. The parable could also be taken as an illustration of the nature of cause and effect. For any effect there must be both necessary and sufficient conditions. The necessary conditions for seed growth as illustrated in the parable are a sower and soil; but those are not sufficient conditions. The seed needs the right *kind* of soil to grow to maturity. Causation can be thought of as a conjunction of conditions which interact to produce something new.

In the leaven and seed parables Jesus was indicating a *general principle of expansion*; he left it to his listeners to interpret how that principle operated and in what cases beyond seeds and leaven it might apply. Besides the general principle, the parables indicate that expansion evolves in distinct phases and the fruitfulness of expansion is partly dependent upon conditions. The parables reflect a principle in the physical world and at the same time are suggestive that the same principle applies in the individual mind and experience. Hence one could interpret the expansion similes in terms of words, ideas and actions being seeds which, when sown in receptive consciousness, expand into the world and bear fruit according to their kind.

Though Jesus did not go into this specifically, the principle of expansion has application to growing businesses, organizations and personal prosperity. Anything one might want to grow begins with an idea. The idea must be sown as words or actions to get the idea started. The idea must be sown in "receptive soil" in order to flourish. A desert would be a great place to start a business of *collecting* sand, but it would *not* be a great place to find a market for *selling* sand. Ideas go through phases as they grow; a business begun in a store front shop can grow into an international corporation, but that doesn't happen overnight. Personal prosperity usually begins with a plan which is implemented step by step.

The expansion principle also can be applied to healing. As seen in the discussion of the placebo effect, a healing can begin with the mind-seed of envisioning health or remembered wellness. The idea can expand into the body. A vision of health can act like a mind-seed sown in a mind-field which eventually expands through the information system of the body until it bears fruit as a physiological effect.

Christianity, as an organization intent on evangelizing the world, would naturally interpret the expansion principle as being about expanding the church. My point is not that the traditional interpretation is wrong; I believe the principle applies to religious organizations as well as to plant life. My point is, rather, that the expansion principle is a marvelous cosmological principle that can be seen operative in every dimension and many aspects of the universe.

## A Friendly Universe: Ask and Receive

Based upon Jesus' concept of God as all-loving Father it is reasonable to say that Jesus held the position that the universe is fundamentally "friendly." His idea of the friendliness of the universe is reflected in his teaching that we get what we seek:

*Ask - it'll be given to you; seek - you'll find; knock - it'll be opened for you. Rest assured: everyone who asks receives; everyone who seeks finds; and for the one who knocks it is opened. Who among you would hand a son a stone when it's bread he's asking for? Again, who would hand him a snake when it's fish he's asking for? Of course no one would! So if you, neglectful as you are, know how to give your children good gifts, isn't it much more likely that your Father in the heavens will give good things to those who ask him? (Mt. 7: 7-11; see Lk 11: 9-10)*

Jesus' statement is in the form of a cause and effect law: if you ask, then you will receive. Is this really a law of the universe? Do we always get what we ask for and find what we seek? Does every door we knock upon open up to us? One is tempted to modify the statement: *sometimes* we receive, find, and have doors open to us; sometimes *not*. That would seem to be a more "reasonable" expectation, given that "prayers" do not always seem to be answered. Why does Jesus make an *unqualified* statement about ask-receiving, seeking-finding, and knocking-opening? Again his position is rooted in his idea of God as loving father: of course a good father would give his children good gifts when they ask.

The word "ask" can mean "order" as in the sentence, "At the restaurant she asked for the salad bar." To ask at a restaurant is not to "pray" or "beg" but to order with the fully justified expectation that you will receive what you asked for. When we order something in a restaurant or store, we are asking for something with the reasonable expectation that we will get what we ordered. This is another way of understanding the "law": "order and you will receive."

Yet another way to think of asking and seeking is to recognize that what we habitually think and speak is a kind of "asking" for something. That interpretation goes beyond the literal meaning, but makes sense psychologically and behaviorally. For example, a person who directs thoughts and actions toward the pursuit of a particular career is, in a psychological and behavioral sense, asking and seeking to have that career.

What we habitually think, say and do is a kind of "asking, seeking, and knocking" to experience the world in a certain way; and we will habitually experience the world that way *even if actual conditions contradict our perceptions.* Suppose a woman habitually says something such as "I can never get a break." As long as she continues in that thought pattern, even if she gets a break she won't "see it" because she filters her experience through the belief that she never gets a break. In everyday language we commonly acknowledge that a person can behave in a way that is "just asking for trouble," even if the person never *says* "give me trouble." In other words, all mental, verbal and physical behavior can be seen as "asking" for or seeking something. In that sense, it is reasonable to hypothesize that we generally get what we "order" from life.

It is important to note that the law, as stated, does not affirm that everything we happen to have is something for which we asked. The law does not say "everything you get, you asked for." Things can happen around us that we did *not* ask for. We may not have consciously asked to be born with our particular genetics or environment, unless it is true that we asked for those conditions before we were born, as is believed by some advocates of reincarnation. Regardless of whether or not such reincarnation theories are true, according to the law of asking and receiving, if we don't like what we've got, the solution is to seek what we *do* want.

It is radically optimistic to believe that you can have whatever you request from God or from the Universe. Is there any way in which Jesus' radically optimistic position on asking-seeking-knocking can be justified, other than from his God-concept? One other way he justifies his concept is by describing a situation involving only humans:

*Suppose you have a friend who comes to you in the middle of the night and says to you, "Friend, lend me three loaves, for a friend of mine on a trip has just shown up and I have nothing to offer him." And suppose you reply, "Stop bothering me. The door is already locked and my children and I are in bed. I can't get up and give you anything." - I tell you, even though you won't get up and give the friend anything out of friendship, yet you will get up and give the other whatever is needed because you'd be ashamed not to. (Lk. 11: 5-8)*

The notion that anyone would give bread to a friend at midnight is based upon the customs of Jesus' culture. There was an expectation of hospitality connected with the honor/shame values of the time. It was considered honorable to do favors for friends and shameful to turn a friend away. Consequently, if a friend asked a favor, the one asked would do his or her best to grant that favor.

The illustration may be more than analogy; it may be that Jesus did not intend the "ask-seek-knock law" to be purely about asking in prayer but intended it to be applied as well in relation to fellow humans and even nature. In other words, the law of asking and receiving does not just apply to prayer but to all possible ways of "asking."

In considering the saying on asking and receiving, it is important to keep in mind that Jesus was not literal minded; that is why he spoke in parables. He sometimes used exaggerated images. His absolute law-like statements may simply have been his way of generalizing from his experience and observations or exaggerating for effect rather than being intended as statements of literal laws.

In the larger context of his teaching, he advocated persistence and perseverance in "asking-seeking-knocking." The following parable illustrates that point.

*Once there was a judge in this town who neither feared God nor cared about people. In that same town was a widow who kept coming to him and demanding, "Give me a ruling against the person I'm suing." For a while he refused; but eventually he said to himself, "I'm not afraid of God and I don't care about people, but this widow keeps pestering me. So I'm going to give her a favorable ruling, or else she'll keep coming back until she wears me down." (Lk. 18: 2-4)*

This parable again shows Jesus' sense of humor. He sets up a confrontation between a powerful judge who cannot be intimidated by God or people and a widow. In prophetic writings "widows and orphans" are proverbially members of society who rely upon others for their well-being:

*"Learn to do right; seek justice. Defend the oppressed. Take up the cause of the fatherless; plead the case of the widow." (Isaiah 1: 17)*

*"Woe to those who make unjust laws, to those who issue oppressive decrees, to deprive the poor of their rights and withhold justice from the oppressed of my people, making widows their prey and robbing the fatherless." (Isaiah 10: 1-2)*

*"I will be quick to testify . . . against those who defraud laborers of their wages, who oppress the widows and the fatherless." (Malachi 3: 5)*

In a confrontation between a powerful judge and "defenseless" widow, the expectation would be that the judge would impose his will on the widow. Jesus reverses the expected outcome by having the widow nag the judge into giving her what she wants. By pure persistent asking, the widow receives.

The story is humorous but not absurd. Any parent knows how persistent children can be in asking and how often the parent gives in. The proverbial "nagging wife" who always eventually gets what she wants is a standard comic character and probably has some basis in actual experiences. In politics, persistent demands can yield positive results, as demonstrated by civil rights movements in the United States, India, and elsewhere. Successful political movements have achieved greater justice by persistently demanding justice. In the parable, justice is what the widow is actually demanding: she demands "dike," which is a Greek word meaning "justice."

I don't believe that the "ask-receive law" is the kind of "law" that can be proven or disproven scientifically; it is a proverb with some practical wisdom in it and an example of Jesus' radical optimism. If the law is true, it suggests a paradox: if the law is true, then when you seek evidence that the law does *not* work, you will find such evidence. You thereby seem to simultaneously "prove" and "disprove" the "law," because you found the disproof you were seeking. Likewise if you seek evidence to prove the "law" *works* you will find it, again "proving" the "law." Perhaps the "law" can be thought of as a practical "rule of thumb," relative rather than absolute. On the other hand, it could simply be an absolute law that happens to be extremely difficult to prove.

What is pretty certain is you cannot get what you ask for if you don't ask in some way; you cannot find what you seek if you don't in some sense seek; doors won't open in any sense if you don't in some sense "knock."

One Jesus parable suggests that at least in some cases it is prudent to place a limit on persistence when seeking:

*A man had a fig tree growing in his vineyard; he came looking for fruit on it but didn't find any. So he said to the vinekeeper, "See here, for three years in a row I have come looking for fruit on this tree, and haven't found any. Cut it down. Why should it suck the nutrients out of the soil?" In response he says to him, "Let it stand, sir, one more year, until I get a chance to dig around it and work in some manure. Maybe it will produce next year; but if it doesn't, we can go ahead and cut it down." (Lk. 13: 6-9)*

There is in this parable once again a humorous element in the form of reversal of conventional expectation. The person of "superior" position is the vineyard owner; the vinekeeper is a mere employee. The conventional expectation would be for the owner to know more or at least as much about farming as the vinekeeper. The owner is impatient with the fig tree because it has not borne fruit after three years. The vinekeeper suggests fertilizer and waiting just one more year. As it happens, fig trees take 3 to 5 years to produce fruit. Hence the vinekeeper takes a more knowledgeable and sensible position: give it another year. Jesus' audience consisted to a great extent of farm laborers who knew about fig trees; they would have understood the humorous tweak of the impatient landowner.

The parable does not suggest being patient and persistent forever; rather if we generalize from growing figs to other projects, the parable suggests that a certain amount of care and time is required for a project to bear fruit. Knowing "how long" depends upon what one is trying to accomplish. I suppose that for some projects, if one has been working on something "fruitlessly" for four or five years it might be wise to reconsider the wisdom of the project. For example, it usually takes four years to complete undergraduate or doctoral courses; U. S. Presidents are given four year terms to prove themselves; businesses and governments often have four or five year plans.

There may be something cosmically or psychologically significant about the numbers four and five as times for completion of a phase of experience. Biblical writers were fond of multiples of 4 as times for completion: e.g. 40 day or 40 year periods (the flood, the years in the wilderness, etc.).

Primarily the fig tree parable is about nurture and patience; secondarily it is about balancing persistence with prudence.

One last note on the fig tree parable: it is probably the basis of the strange story of Jesus cursing a fig tree and causing it to wither. As stories are passed along orally, story-tellers often modify, add detail or even transform the story. One story-teller may well have transformed the fig tree parable into a miracle story, in which Jesus becomes the "impatient master" who destroys the fig tree. The motivation for the change could have been to make a point about bearing fruit: if you don't bear fruit, you will be cursed and destroyed. It is highly unlikely that Jesus advocated *that* idea, even though in another context he did suggest that if you don't use your "talents" you will lose them (Mt. 25: 14-28). The story also may have been invented as a "prophetic" allusion to the destruction of the Jerusalem Temple around 70 C.E.

Another parable of Jesus illustrates the asking-receiving law as well as Jesus' emphasis on the importance of forgiveness:

*Two men went up to the temple to pray, one a Pharisee and the other a toll collector. The Pharisee stood up and prayed silently as follows: "I thank you, God, that I'm not like everybody else, thieving, unjust, adulterous, and especially not like that toll collector over there. I fast twice a week, I give tithes of everything I acquire." But the toll collector stood off by himself and didn't even dare to look up, but struck his chest, and muttered, "God, have mercy on me, sinner that I am." Let me tell you, the second man went back to his house righteous but the first one did not. (Lk. 18: 10-14)*

The issue behind the story is the question: "what makes a man righteous?" The usual assumption of the audience at the beginning of the story would be that the Pharisee was the righteous man and the toll collector was a sinner.

The Greek word rendered here as "righteous" is "δικαιοο" (dikaioo). In this parable it is usually translated as "justified," but that word does not adequately convey the meaning in this story. "Dikaioo" is related to the word for justice and can mean "acquitted, freed, justified, or rendered righteous or just."[41] The story would shock and reverse the expectations of the listeners. The "sinful" toll collector went home righteous but the "holy" Pharisee went home *not* righteous.

In the context of Jesus' teachings the conclusion of the story, however shocking, is perfectly logical. The Pharisee's prayer does not ask for righteousness; therefore, he does not receive it. In addition, the Pharisee condemns others; Jesus taught "condemn not and you will not be condemned." The statement implies that condemning others leaves one susceptible to being condemned. The toll collector's prayer asks for mercy; Jesus taught "ask and you will receive." Consequently, the toll collector would receive what he asked for: mercy or *forgiveness*. Having been forgiven, the toll collector was free of sin; being free of sin, he was righteous.

A common anxiety of humans is a sense of sinfulness and guilt. The story in the context of Jesus' teachings provides a simple solution to be freed (another meaning of dikaioo) of guilt. For those who take the philosophy of Jesus as authoritative, the simple way to be freed from guilt and be rendered "righteous" is to ask for forgiveness – ask and you will receive.

This way of forgiveness is not what Christianity ended up affirming. The parable does not affirm Christian doctrines about forgiveness such as being baptized, accepting Jesus as Savior, repenting, confessing to a priest, doing penance, and participating in sacraments as the ways to forgiveness. Those doctrines may have value to the believer, but they do not reflect the much simpler philosophy of Jesus regarding the two ways to forgiveness: ask and receive *or* forgive and you will be forgiven (the latter point will be more fully discussed later). To the extent that relief from anxiety about guilt is therapeutic, this simple philosophy of forgiveness would have been psychologically liberating for Jesus' audience.

The "law of asking and receiving" can be related to the idea of trusting God to provide, as expressed in the "don't worry" argument (Mt. 6: 25-30) already discussed. The following statement about faith was not identified by the Jesus Seminar as part of the list of "authentic sayings." However, the saying is consistent with the teachings of asking and trusting and therefore consistent with Jesus' philosophy, even if not originating with him. The saying combines asking and trusting in an inspiring way:

*Have faith in God. Truly, I say to you, whoever says to this mountain, 'Be taken up and cast into the sea,' and does not doubt in his heart, but believes that what he says will come to pass, it will be done for him. Therefore I tell you, whatever you ask in prayer, believe that you have received it, and it will be yours." (Mk 11: 22-25)*

The saying affirms that one can "move mountains" through

prayer; figuratively, the mountains represent "big" life obstacles. The idea of believing that you have *already* received is intriguing. How can one believe one has already received before one has actually received? Perhaps a clue can be found in some of the practices of sports psychology.

A number of studies have indicated that vividly imagining attaining certain results works as well or almost as well for improving performance as physical practice.[42] Imagination has also been used with positive effects in therapy for illnesses, including cancer.[43] If imagining affects results, then imagining might also be a way to "believe you have received" *before* you "actually" receive. The effects of imagination on belief and of belief on healing and accomplishment are certainly worthy of further research.

The idea that you get what you seek is an optimally optimistic way of seeing the world. The idea affirms that you can have whatever you want. All you have to do is ask for it, seek it, and "knock on doors of opportunity" until you receive, find or have doors opened for you. A note of caution is sounded in the parable of the fig tree: consider your objective carefully and identify a reasonable amount of time for seeking to attain it. You can be optimally optimistic without having complete disregard for prudence.

Clearly, optimism is another therapeutic factor in Jesus' philosophy.

## O p t i m i s m   a n d   H e a l t h

In 2012 an analysis of 200 studies by Harvard researchers found that "traits like optimism and hope, and higher levels of happiness and satisfaction with one's life were linked with reductions in the risk of heart disease and stroke."[44] The study showed that of various attitudes studied, optimism was "most robustly associated with reduced risk of cardiovascular events."[45] The study found that even when risk behaviors like smoking and poor diet were factored out, optimism still proved to be linked with the reduced risks.

The Harvard study indicates that optimism can, in effect, be a preventative factor for sustaining health. Can optimism also be therapeutic for recovery from illnesses? Research published in the *Journal of Personality and Social Psychology* indicated a connection between optimism and recovery rates from coronary artery bypass surgery. The results of the study indicated that optimism was "associated with a faster rate of physical recovery during the period of hospitalization and with a faster rate of return to normal life activities subsequent to discharge" and "there was a strong positive association between level of optimism and postsurgical quality of life at 6 months."[46] The study does not indicate that people are cured by optimism, but it does indicate that optimism has therapeutic value for recovering from illness.

Recall the study cited at the beginning of this chapter. The study concluded that there is a strong correlation between longevity and positive self-perception with regard to aging. Positive self-perception appears to have a significant impact on overall wellbeing. Self-perception may have a more significant impact on health and healing than we currently know. For example, the Benson-Friedman concept of the placebo effect (discussed in the previous chapter) as "remembered wellness" suggests a shift in a person's self-perception from "I am sick" to "I remember being well." That shift, however characterized, is a shift in how one thinks of oneself.

Another indicator of the therapeutic possibilities of shifts in self-perception is the profound effects that changing one's self-image can have. Plastic surgeon Dr. Maxwell Maltz discovered in his practice that changing how a person looked did not always change how the person felt about herself or how she functioned. Wanting to help his patients, Dr. Maltz began to research self-image psychology and share methods for change with his patients. He claimed to have found many methods to help patients adopt a new self-image consistent with their new physical image.[47]

Dr. Maltz's claims regarding his patients were not quantified in his book. However, he did cite anecdotal and research evidence strongly indicating that how we think of ourselves has significant impact on how well we function. For example, Maltz discussed studies of performance of various tasks at different times, comparing effects of physical practice, no practice and visualization on performance.[48]

One of the studies described by Maltz was published in 1943 in *Journal of General Psychology*.[49] Three groups were tested on throwing darts. They were then dismissed for 18 days. During that period, one group was not to practice throwing darts, another physically practiced, and the third group practiced mentally, i.e. visualized themselves throwing darts effectively. The outcome of the experiment was that those who merely visualized throwing darts improved almost as much as those who physically practiced; those who did not practice did not improve.

A study with basically the same design was done 17 years later, using basketball free-throw shooting as the tested skill. The latter study also indicated that those who did not practice did not improve; those who physically practiced improved the most; and those who visualized improved nearly as much as those who physically practiced.[50]

What do the studies on dart-throwing and basketball tell us about "self-perception" and "self-image"? The studies suggest that if we develop images of ourselves doing some tasks well, the subsequent self-image can help us improve at those tasks. The studies suggest that mental imagery, including image of self, has physiological effects. The studies suggest a field of experimentation that could have significant consequences for physical health. Since imagination can affect motor skills as indicated by the above studies, then it must also have effects on brain, nervous system, and muscles. Since imagination can affect brain, nervous system, and muscles, it can affect other parts of the body to a significant degree.

How are the effects of imagination on the body and health relevant to optimism and the philosophy of Jesus? The subjects in the "mental practice and motor skills" studies mentioned above were visualizing optimistically. They were visualizing doing well, visualizing optimal performance.

*Optimistic imagination* may yet prove to be more powerfully therapeutic than is currently known. In Jesus' philosophy, the self-image suggested by his teaching was the image of self as offspring of God and as having the realm of God within them. That is clearly a highly optimistic self-image. I suspect that some of those who followed Jesus shifted their self-perception from "victim" to "offspring of God having God's realm within"; that shift surely contributed to their psychological and physical wellbeing.

## Practical Applications

The difference between a pessimist and an optimist is how each looks at life. People generally seek out evidence for what they already believe. That is why politically conservative people watch Fox News and liberals listen to NPR. The pessimist seeks evidence that the world is going to hell in a handcart; the optimist seeks evidence for heaven on earth.

In the simplest terms, if you want to be more optimistic and reap the benefits of optimism, look for what is good in yourself, in your life, and in the world. That does not mean that you must ignore or deny problems; it means to look for evidence that problems are being solved or can be solved. Seek out articles, books, programs, and internet information about uplifting stories, people overcoming challenges, and progress toward a better world. Even some television news programs today end with uplifting stories, so the news media is moving toward more optimistic programming. Shifting toward a more optimistic viewpoint involves shifting your attention; changing what you seek, what you look for, and what you look at. That shift includes how you look at yourself and your own life.

An enjoyable way to become more optimistic is using your imagination to describe or picture what you want in life. Visualization and affirmation are powerful tools for shifting your consciousness and changing your life. For example, if you want to have stronger motivation to exercise, you can visualize yourself filled with energy and exercising.

I have found that I can make changes in my life by taking five or ten minutes per day to sit quietly and vividly visualize how I want to be and what I want to achieve. Once I wanted to improve my bowling average, which had remained the same for many years, so I began to take time to relax and visualize myself throwing strikes. Without any additional practice, my bowling average increased twenty pins per game after using that visualization.

You may even find that visualization can increase your income. There is a well known story of Jim Carrey who claimed that when he was a struggling actor he wrote himself a check for ten million dollars and used it for visualization. After a time, he received payment for a movie in the amount he had put on his imaginary check.[51] That payment was of course for his talent and the hard work he did in developing as an entertainer. Even so, Carrey believes that there is a "law of attraction" that was involved in manifesting his success.

I decided to try the technique to receive a specific amount for *not* working – or rather as a reward for work already done. I did in fact receive that amount. Perhaps I should have written an imaginary check for millions instead of thousands, but the technique works best when you can believe in a "real" possibility and opportunity for receiving the amount you imagine. I cannot guarantee that the "imaginary check method" always works, but it is fun and does stretch your imagination of possibilities for good. The method can help shift you into a more optimistic frame of mind.

If you have difficulty relaxing and imagining what you want, use of affirmations can be just as effective and enjoyable. Affirmations are declarative statements of what you want to achieve. Use them with the same confidence and expectation you would have in asking for a meal off a restaurant menu.

The most powerful affirmations are those rooted in your spiritual or metaphysical belief system, because you then link your statements to what you already believe about the way the universe works. If you believe you are a child of God, then "I AM" affirmations can be powerful, e.g. *"I AM a child of God and God's perfect life flows through me,"* or *"I AM a child of God and I can do all things through God who strengthens me."*

Often a simple and well devised statement can lift your energy level. Many Unity students love the affirmation: *"I am alive, alert, awake, joyous, and enthusiastic about life!"* Try saying that statement in a loud voice; if nothing else, it might give you a chuckle. I have found that my favorite and perhaps most powerful affirmation is simply: *"Divine Order is established in my mind, body, and affairs."* To me, saying or thinking that affirmation feels like surrendering to God with positive feelings about the present and positive expectations for the future.

Many people like to regularly use daily devotionals, such as *Daily Word,* to start their day in a positive way. Many people put cards with written affirmations all over their houses, especially on their mirrors and refrigerators.

There are so many books and articles that provide examples of affirmations and instruction in the use of affirmations that no more examples are necessary here. My personal favorite book on affirmative prayer is *Prayer: the Master Key* (Unity House, 1975) by James Dillet Freeman, former longtime Director of Silent Unity. Silent Unity is a 24/7 telephone prayer ministry which has been in operation since 1890. The book is not a "best-seller," but is poetic, deeply spiritual, and written by a man who was deeply engaged in prayer work.

Incidentally, astronauts literally put two of Mr. Freeman's poem-prayers on the moon! One of those poems came to Mr. Freeman in a time of personal despair. The poem is titled *"I Am There,"* the "I Am" of the poem representing God or the Higher Self speaking to the human consciousness and condition. It reflects the idea of God's realm already present and available to provide help in time of need:

*Do you need Me?*
*I am there.*
*You cannot see Me, yet I am the light you see by.*
*You cannot hear Me, yet I speak through your voice.*
*You cannot feel Me, yet I am the power at work in your hands.*
*I am at work, though you do not understand My ways.*
*I am at work, though you do not recognize My works.*
*I am not strange visions. I am not mysteries.*
*Only in absolute stillness, beyond self, can you know Me as I am, and then but as a feeling and a faith.*
*Yet I am there. Yet I hear. Yet I answer.*
*When you need Me, I am there.*
*Even if you deny Me, I am there.*
*Even when you feel most alone, I am there.*
*Even in your fears, I am there.*
*Even in your pain, I am there.*
*I am there when you pray and when you do not pray.*
*I am in you, and you are in Me.*
*Only in your mind can you feel separate from Me, for only in your mind are the mists of "yours" and "mine."*
*Yet only with your mind can you know Me and experience Me.*
*Empty your heart of empty fears.*
*When you get yourself out of the way, I am there.*
*You can of yourself do nothing, but I can do all.*
*And I am in all.*
*Though you may not see the good, good is there, for I am there.*
*I am there because I have to be, because I am.*
*Only in Me does the world have meaning; only out of Me does the world take form; only because of Me does the world go forward.*
*I am the law on which the movement of the stars and the growth of living cells are founded.*
*I am the love that is the law's fulfilling. I am assurance. I am peace. I am oneness. I am the law that you can live by. I am the love that you can cling to. I am your*

*assurance. I am your peace. I am one with you. I am.*
*Though you fail to find Me, I do not fail you.*
*Though your faith in Me is unsure, My faith in you never*
*wavers, because I know you, because I love you.*
*Beloved, I am there.*

Persistence in achieving a more optimistic state of mind is an important factor, as it is in any significant endeavor. Just remember the parable of the widow who nagged the powerful judge into giving her what she wanted. You may receive what you want by asking only once or seeking for only a few minutes or for many years. If your objective is worthwhile, then so is the persistent asking, seeking, and knocking.

# Chapter Five: Ethics, Love, and Healing

In the 1990s a research team performed an ingenious experiment. A key chemical in the human immune system was measured in the participants in the experiment. Higher levels of that key chemical were known to be associated with decreased incidence of disease and infection. The participants then viewed a video of Mother Teresa tending to the ill and poor in Calcutta. The randomly chosen participants had a variety of opinions about Mother Teresa, not all favorable, and a variety of religious beliefs. After viewing the video, the immune system chemical was measured again. The participants had higher levels of the immune system chemical after watching the video.

What did the experiment prove? It demonstrated that just watching another person's compassionate action can result in a strengthened immune system. The relationship between watching compassionate action and strengthened immune system is probably not one of strict causation for all people. Human health is such a complex thing that practically all therapies have only probable benefits for most people. There is practically no treatment that works for everyone. Nevertheless, it would appear that focusing on compassion is, in general, good for your health.

Another research team did follow up research on the "Mother Teresa Effect" experiment. The research involved testing the induction of "positive emotions" (care and compassion) using and comparing both an external method (watching videos, such as the one with Mother Teresa already mentioned) and an internal method. The internal method is referred to as a "self-induction" method. The self-induction method involved having subjects direct their attention to the area around the heart and focus on feelings of care or compassion toward someone or something.[52] This research found that: "Positive emotions . . . produced significant increase" in the immune system chemical levels and "that self-induction of positive emotional states is more effective at stimulating (those) levels than previously used external methods."

In other words: *the universe is structured in such a way that love is good for your health.* I consider this conclusion evidence for the presence of God as love in our bodies and in our world.

If cultivation of compassion strengthens the immune system, it is also probable that the strengthened immune system could *cure* illness as well as prevent it. In any case, cultivation of compassion, as advocated and demonstrated by Jesus, evidently has value for health. The healing energy of his compassion flowed through others and that healing Spirit of love flowed also through the disciples who knew him. Jesus' teaching of love also had a healing effect on those who heard it. Compassion was a therapeutic element of Jesus' philosophy.

## On  Love  and  Justice

Jesus advocated the idea of a generous God and friendly universe; he also spoke about the ideas of law and justice in the universe. The two ideas of love and justice are held in a kind of creative tension in Jesus' parables and sayings, much as they are in politics. Conflicting political positions are often rooted in a values disagreement regarding love and justice. For example, those who favor compassion are likely to be opposed to capital punishment, while those favoring justice are likely to favor capital punishment. That tension between the values of love and justice has already been illustrated in the discussion of the parable of the Prodigal Son: the father's unconditional *love* of his sons is contrasted with the elder son's feeling that his father was not being fair or *just*.

Another parable illustrating the creative tension between justice and love in Jesus' philosophy is the tale of a landowner who acts with fairness to some employees and with generosity to others:

*"Heaven's rule is like a proprietor who went out the first thing in the morning to hire workers for his vineyard. After agreeing with the workers for a silver coin a day he sent them into his vineyard. And coming around 9 a.m. he saw others loitering in the marketplace and he said to them, "You go into the vineyard too, and I'll pay you whatever is fair." So they went. Around noon he went out again, and at 3 p.m., and repeated the process. About 5 p.m. he went out and found others loitering about and says to them, "Why did you stand around here idle the whole day?" They reply, "Because no one hired us." He tells them, "You go into the vineyard as well."*

*When evening came, the owner of the vineyard tells the foreman: "Call the workers and pay them their wages starting with those hired last and ending with those hired first."*

*Those hired at 5 p.m. came up and received a silver coin each. Those hired first approached thinking they would receive more. But they also got a silver coin apiece. They took it and began to grumble against the proprietor: "These guys hired last worked only an hour but you have made them equal to us who did most of the work during the heat of the day." In response he said to one of them, "Look pal, did I wrong you? You did agree with me for a silver coin, didn't you? Take your wages and get out! I intend to treat the one hired last the same way I treat you. Is there some law forbidding me to do with my money as I please? Or is your eye filled with envy because I am generous?" (Mt. 20: 1-15)*

As is typical of most of Jesus' sayings, the parable does not present a didactic moral but instead suggests questions: was the proprietor fair in his dealings with those he hired first? Is fairness better than generosity or vice versa? Jesus' sayings tend to be suggestive rather than directive. That style of suggestiveness indicates an intention to provoke contemplation rather than give rules for behavior. Suggestive stories and sayings provide a natural provocation for meditative states. Meditative states are much like non-directive hypnotic states in that they provide a condition in which the individual can see things in a new way and change old ways of thinking. It is therefore highly probable that generally Jesus' intention was to help people change their minds and thereby change their lives.

It is important to remember that Jesus' original audience would not have interpreted his sayings as being about Christian doctrine; when he spoke there was no Christianity and so no Christian doctrine. That point would seem obvious, yet most of Jesus' sayings and parables are commonly interpreted as being about Christianity and dogmas which were voted upon after the 4th century. For example, the story of the proprietor and laborers is customarily understood as meaning: those who convert to the Church late in life receive the same reward in heaven as those who have long been Christians. However, a silver coin does not provide a particularly powerful representation of the everlasting bliss of heaven. It is therefore reasonable to hypothesize that the silver coin/heavenly reward was not the central point of the parable.

It is understandable that once a professional clergy was established, the clergy would interpret Jesus' sayings as supporting Church policies and doctrines. Nevertheless, if we want to understand Jesus, we cannot assume he was establishing doctrine let alone supporting doctrines established hundreds of years later. The proprietor and laborers parable is not specifically about afterlife reward; it is specifically about one day's pay. At issue is the relative fairness and generosity of the proprietor and how the laborers felt about their treatment. The parable juxtaposes fair treatment (those who were paid what they previously agreed to) and generous treatment (those who were paid a full day's wage for a partial day's work).

This is not to say that the standard interpretation is "wrong," only that the standard interpretation is not the only or even most obvious meaning of the story. The ending shocks and provokes; it does not assert a moral. It raises questions about the relative "goodness" of fair treatment compared to generous treatment. It raises the question: would *I* rather be treated fairly or generously? It has implications for application of the "Golden Rule": if I prefer to be treated fairly, then I should treat others fairly; if I prefer to be treated generously, then I should treat others generously.

Perhaps deep down we want mercy and generosity for ourselves - and justice for others?

Jesus' idea of justice was simple and elegant: what you do comes back to you. That position is exemplified in this passage: *"Do not judge, and you will not be judged; do not condemn, and you will not be condemned. Forgive and you will be forgiven; give, and it will be given to you. . . . for the measure you give will be the measure you get back."* (Lu 6: 37-38)

This statement is the moral equivalent of the Newtonian third law of motion: the mutual forces of action and reaction between two bodies are equal, opposite and collinear. The law is more commonly stated: for every action there is an equal and opposite reaction. Jesus' idea of justice is also roughly equivalent to the Hindu concept of karma.

The idea of justice was central in both Judaism and Greek philosophy. Jesus' statement, *"the measure you give will be the measure you get back,"* is about as simple and elegant a way of defining justice as can be given. This idea of justice suggests a guideline for behavior in terms of expected outcome: give the measure you want to get back. The versions of "the Golden Rule" found in most religions and many philosophies provide guidance consistent with the law that you get back according to the measure you give. While "Golden Rules" are stated in the imperative mood, Jesus' statement of justice is in the declarative mood. He does not say "you *should* do thus and such" but rather affirms in effect that what you do will come back to you. This is similar to the popular expressions: "you reap what you sow" and "what goes around comes around."

Religions generally promise that justice is ultimately fulfilled as one's "final reward," meaning in effect "after you die." That common teaching implies that justice is not fulfilled in this life; that an afterlife is necessary for justice to be fulfilled. This teaching is often mixed in with the teaching of a merciful God. Christianity generally teaches that we are only saved by the grace of God and that there are some who receive God's justice rather than God's grace.

The philosopher Kant made "afterlife justice" a key axiom in his argument for belief in immortality. Bertrand Russell nicely summarized Kant's argument:

> "The argument is that the moral law demands justice, i.e. happiness proportional to virtue. Only Providence can insure this, and has evidently not insured it in *this* life. Therefore there is a God and a future life; and there must be freedom, since otherwise there would be no such thing as virtue."[53]

On the other hand, Emerson affirmed that justice is not deferred to an afterlife but is fulfilled in the here and now: "Justice is not postponed. A perfect equity adjusts its balance in all parts of life."[54] "Cause and effect, means and ends, seed and fruit cannot be severed; for the effect already blooms in the cause, the end preexists in the means, the fruit in the seed."[55] Emerson could affirm present justice because he did not look only at outer conditions as "compensation" for actions; he saw that every act has an immediate and lasting impact in the "soul" of the actor. "In the nature of the soul is the compensation for the inequalities of condition."[56] As examples of "unpostponed soul justice," Emerson wrote:

> *"We feel defrauded of the retribution due to evil acts, because the criminal adheres to his vice and contumacy and does not come to a crisis or judgment anywhere in visible nature. . . . Has he therefore outwitted the law? Inasmuch as he carries the malignity and the lie within him he so far decreases from nature."*[57]

In other words, the "evil act" diminishes the one who commits it and that diminishment is known and felt by the one who committed the act. Likewise, a virtuous deed expands the soul, the very act being felt as reward and pleasure in the actor, regardless of external results. It is through wise and virtuous acts that we express what we truly are: *"There is no penalty to virtue; no penalty to wisdom . . . . In a virtuous action I properly am; in a virtuous act I add to the world."*[58] Our actions make us what we are to ourselves; our sense of self-worth is the "reward" or "punishment."

Jesus' statement of justice neither affirms nor denies "afterlife" fulfillment of justice. There are no "authentic" sayings of Jesus that tell us what, if anything, he believed about the afterlife. From his silence regarding an afterlife, it is entirely possible that Jesus thought more in Emersonian than in Kantian terms, i.e. justice occurs internally/psychologically as well as externally/circumstantially. Justice is fulfilled in *this* life, in our souls if not in our outer circumstances.

Love and justice are cosmological principles in Jesus' philosophy. God the Father is portrayed as unconditionally loving; God's rule is portrayed as having both perfect justice and at the same time unconditional "grace." By "unconditional" I mean "offered without regard to personal merit or demerit." By "grace" I mean God's realm includes freely available beauty, truth, love, and bounty. Jesus' parables often combine justice and grace in creative tension, leaving his audience to ponder that tension and decide which value is better.

## The Love Ethic

In the 1960s Joseph Fletcher, an Episcopalian Priest and philosopher, proposed a moral theory called "situation ethics."[59] Fletcher argued for the idea that the only ultimate good was unconditional love for all people. All other rules and principles are only useful guidelines for determining the most loving thing to do in a given situation. Fletcher's position was rooted in the teachings of Jesus and expanded upon with considerable philosophical sophistication. His theory comes very close to Jesus' ethical ideas, but Fletcher's concept of justice as "equal distribution of love" is compatible with but not identical to Jesus' idea of justice. Furthermore, for Jesus, doing the loving thing was not the *absolute* good but a *practical* good related to the ultimate and absolute good of finding the realm and rule of God.

Jesus' idea of justice was not "equal distribution of love," as per Fletcher, but rather (as noted in the previous section) a principle of "what you do comes back to you." By that concept, justice assures that whatever action one takes for good or ill is balanced by *consequences* equivalent to one's actions. Fletcher's idea of justice is about what we *ought* to do; Jesus' concept is more directly concerned with the *consequences* of our actions. In that sense, Jesus'ethic has some common ground with modern utilitarian and pragmatic ethics.

It should be noted that Jesus' concept of justice does not affirm that judging or condemning others *necessarily* results in being judged or condemned. He only affirms that eschewal of judging and condemning assures one will not be judged or condemned. That those who condemn are themselves condemned is *not* a logical inference from "do not condemn and you won't be condemned"; that statement leaves open the *possibility* of reciprocal condemnation but does not affirm it. It leaves room for grace.

Ethics is primarily concerned with "ought" rather than "is": arguing how we *ought* to behave rather than describing how we *do* behave. Jesus' imperative statements regarding how we ought to behave are consistent with his understanding of God and how God's universe works.

### Generosity and Inclusivity

*God causes the sun to rise on both the bad and the good, and sends rain on both the just and the unjust. Tell me, if you love those who love you, why should you be commended for that? Even the tax collectors do as much, don't they? Be perfect as your Father in heaven is perfect. (see Mt. 5: 45, 46, 48 & Lk. 6: 32)*

"Perfect" morality in Jesus' mind would be to love and bless the bad and the good, the just and the unjust. While Matthew records Jesus as saying "be *perfect* as your Father," Luke records the same saying as "be *compassionate* (in other translations, "*merciful*") as your Father." This discrepancy could be explained by the fact that the Hebrew words "shalam" and "shalem" (related to "shalom") can be translated as meaning either "perfect" *or* "friendly." If the remembered saying of Jesus was in Greek but contained the word "shalam" or "shalem" (or their Aramaic equivalents), Matthew and Luke might simply have chosen different *Greek* words as the translation.

The different translations of Matthew and Luke suggest the possibility that Jesus was bilingual, speaking Aramaic to some, Greek to others, and occasionally a mixture of the two languages. That would not have been unusual in his part of the world where the locals did business with Greek speaking merchants and officials. The situation was not much different from the modern situation in America where immigrants and migrant workers speak their native tongue amongst themselves and English in interactions with the English speaking community.

In any case, Jesus affirmed that the way to be like our Father God is to practice universal love, without partiality to ideas of "good" and "bad" people. He drew this conclusion from the universality and impartiality of natural blessings, rather than from a sacred text. The passage is another indication of Jesus' philosophical approach. His advocacy of universal love is based upon observation of the ways of nature. His idea of love, as found in this passage, is to imitate God's action of giving sun and rain to all. How we are to do likewise is not specified; again the saying is suggestive, though it seems to be directive.

In a few sayings Jesus is a bit more specifically directive about what it means to love. He directs his disciples to give freely:

*If you have money, don't lend it at interest. Rather, give it to someone from whom you won't get it back. (Thom. 95: 1, 2) (See Mt. 5: 42)*

*Give to the one who begs from you. (Mt. 5: 39-42)*

The directive to give freely, besides being a high moral ideal, for Jesus would be practical wisdom, since he believed in a just universe: "give and it will be given to you."

A saying in the *Gospel of Thomas*, while not in the imperative mood, pushes the idea of giving to the point of self-sacrifice for the sake of others. The saying specifically connects giving with happiness:

*Happy are those who go hungry, so the stomach of the one in want may be filled. (Thom. 69: 2)*

Jesus illustrated love as giving with a provocative parable. The parable was provocative for his original audience, but we are so accustomed to the expression "Good Samaritan" that the parable no longer shocks. In his time there was historically rooted animosity between Samaritans and Jews. Along with Pharisees, the Priests and Levites were supposed to be models of religious piety. A Christian could imaginatively recapture the emotional impact of the story in a modern context by substituting a Christian for the man going to Jerusalem, a Catholic priest and a minister for the priest and Levite, and a Muslim for the Samaritan.

The parable suggests both generosity and inclusivity as high moral ideals. The parable shocks by being a realistic portrayal of behavior expected from Priests and Levites in contrast to what is held up as the model generosity of the Samaritan:

*There was a man going from Jerusalem down to Jericho when he fell into the hands of robbers. They stripped him, beat him up, and went off, leaving him half dead. Now by coincidence a priest was going down that road; when he caught sight of him, he went out of his way to avoid him. In the same way, when a Levite came to the place, he took one look at him and crossed the road to avoid him. But this Samaritan who was traveling that way came to where he was and was moved to pity at the sight of him. He went up to him and bandaged his wounds, pouring olive oil and wine on them. He hoisted him onto his own animal, brought him to an inn, and looked after him. The next day he took out two silver coins, which he gave to the innkeeper, and said, "Look after him, and on my way back I'll reimburse you for any extra expense you have had."* (Luke 10: 30-35)

By saying the man who was robbed and beaten was going from Jerusalem, the parable strongly suggests that he was *from* Jerusalem, i.e. he was presumably a Jew. Jesus' audience would immediately identify with the Jewish man on his way to Jericho. What happens to him *empathetically* happens to the listeners in their imagination. They might imagine a friend or even themselves being beaten and robbed. The response of those passing by in effect becomes a response to a loved one or to themselves.

In order to maintain ritual purity required for performing their functions in the Temple, priests and Levites were expected to avoid touching corpses. Seeing a man "half dead," the priest and Levite could not take the chance that the man was "all the way dead." It was to some degree understandable for them to avoid the man from their perspective; but this would not be comforting to the man or the audience. The Samaritan ignored the appearance of uncleanness and demonstrated generous compassion which most people in most places and ages would regard as admirable. The parable suggests that ritual purity is not identical with "holiness" and high morality. In this way the parable was originally more than an illustration of admirable behavior: it was a counter-example to conventional understanding of holiness and a sympathetic reframing of disliked Samaritans.

In his practice, according to the gospels, Jesus associated and ate with Samaritans, Gentiles, "unclean" persons and "sinners." That would have been socially unconventional behavior. In fact even today people associate and eat primarily with others of the same social and economic "status" (with the notable exception of individuals campaigning for public office). Despite Jesus' consistency on the issue of social equality at shared meals, even the early followers of Jesus may have been hesitant to share table with those they perceived as unclean or sinners. According to the book of *Acts* there was even a controversy among early followers of Jesus regarding Jewish Christians eating at the same table with Gentile Christians.

Jesus told a parable about a man who broke the custom of eating only with one's kind:

*"A person was receiving guests. When he had prepared the dinner, he sent his servant to invite the guests. The servant went to the first and said to that one, 'My master invites you.' That one said, 'Some merchants owe me money; they are coming to me tonight. I have to go and give them instructions. Please excuse me from dinner.' The servant went to another and said to that one, 'My master has invited you.' That one said to the servant, 'I have bought a house, and I have been called away for a day. I shall have no time.' The servant went to another and said to that one, 'My master invites you.' That one said to the servant, 'My friend is to be married, and I am to arrange the banquet. I shall not be able to come. Please excuse me from dinner.' The servant went to another and said to that one, 'My master invites you.' That one said to the servant, 'I have bought an estate, and I am going to collect the rent. I shall not be able to come. Please excuse me.' The servant returned and said to his master, 'Those whom you invited to dinner have asked to be excused.' The master said to his servant, 'Go out on the streets and bring back whomever you find to have dinner.'"* (Thomas 64: 1-11)

The shocking twist at the end of the parable is the master inviting *anyone* who could be found. Luke's version of the story is explicit about inviting people considered ritually unclean: the "maimed and blind and lame" along with "the poor." (Luke 14: 16-23) Like the parable of the "Good Samaritan" this parable sets forth moral ideals of generosity and inclusivity.

### How  to  Love  Your  Enemies

The inclusiveness of Jesus' philosophy invited his listeners to change their feelings and behavior toward people toward whom they felt animosity. Jesus proposed an apparently paradoxical moral imperative: *"Love your enemies." (Mt. 5: 44)*

The paradox in the statement is especially evident in the Hebrew word for "enemy" which essentially means "hated one." "Love those you hate" seems self-contradictory. Judging by the history of Christianity this admonition has only rarely been taken seriously except by the earliest Christians. The Church exiled and burned at the stake some whose doctrines were deemed heretical. The Church mounted "holy wars" against "infidels" and "pagans." Even today some Christian groups hurl invectives against homosexuals, Muslims and even people with "liberal" political views. While Christianity is not characterized by hatred, hatred of perceived "enemies" is still a common attitude in many who think of themselves as Christian, as it is with people of other religions and of no religion.

Is it even humanly possible to "love enemies"? Jesus did not provide "technique" for changing one's feelings about persons one hates. He did, however, prescribe *actions* which could be deemed loving towards "enemies."

*Don't react violently against one who is evil: when someone slaps you on the right cheek, turn the other as well. When someone wants to sue you for your shirt, let that person have your coat along with it. Further, when anyone conscripts you for one mile, go an extra mile. (Matt 5: 39-41)*

To modern ears these admonitions may seem merely weak submission. Furthermore, the second and third admonitions do not seem directly relevant in a modern context. Who today sues for a person's shirt? Who can conscript a person for one mile?

Historical context provides rebuttal to the notion that the admonitions advocate merely weak submission. A slap on the right cheek with the right hand would be a back-handed slap, which culturally indicated the one being slapped was considered a "social inferior," such as a slave. While it would be insulting to be slapped on the *left* cheek, the one slapped would be on equal footing and would therefore be socially justified in returning the slap. Hence turning the other cheek would be a challenge to the "slapper" to see the one slapped as on equal footing. To slap the "other cheek" would be an admission that the one slapped was a social equal; not to mention it would set up the slapper to receive a return blow. All this would be immediately understood by Jesus' listeners, but has to be explained today. To turn the other cheek would be to "turn the tables" in the situation.

I suppose an insult might be a modern equivalent of a "back-handed" slap. When someone says something insulting to you, there are at least 7 possible responses: (1) return insult for insult; (2) shout an angry reply; (3) physically assault the person; (4) ignore the insult with suppressed anger; (5) ignore the insult with emotional detachment; (6) ignore the insult with compassion for the person's unenlightened consciousness; (7) reply in a surprising non-violent way, e.g. with a sarcasm such as, "How kind of you to say so."

The first response (return the insult) could cause an escalation of hurt feelings or worse. The next three possible responses (some form of angry response) are probably counter-productive, if only because anger is not generally a healthy emotion. The fifth and sixth responses (detachment or compassion) would probably generally be considered idealistic, enlightened or spiritual responses.

The seventh response may be closest to Jesus' recommendation. Turning the other cheek was a subtle non-violent way of *shaming* the one who struck the blow. Turning the other cheek was not passive submission nor retaliation but an action asserting personal dignity and equality with the one who struck the blow. A sarcastic response would not be *literally* an insult so much as a way of highlighting the insulter's meanness with words that in their literal meaning express praise. On the surface the response would be kind; in effect it could be illuminating, bringing the other person into an awareness of his or her less than admirable behavior.

The "shirt and cloak" advice is another example of a way to respond to an "enemy" with love: be generous. Like the action of "turning the other cheek," giving one's coat would also "shame" the person, because it would highlight that person's meanness. In those times all people wore was a shirt and coat; giving up both would leave a person naked. Obviously it would take some courage to so fully expose oneself in that way. The image is shocking and absurd; another example of Jesus' sense of humor. Perhaps he didn't mean it as literal advice but as comic light on the issue of lawsuits.

There is a case of a medieval youth who responded to a situation in a way very similar to Jesus' admonition to give an adversary all one's clothes. The story is told about St. Francis of Assisi that on his way to becoming a saint he began to give away his wealth to the poor. The problem was that it wasn't exactly *his* wealth; it was his *father's*. His father didn't have the same attitudes about wealth as Francis did. Consequently Francis' father went to the local priest and prevailed upon him to restrain Francis' generosity. When the priest and Francis' father tried to persuade Francis to stop using the father's wealth for charity,

Francis agreed. Then he renounced his inheritance and all of his father's wealth. To make that renunciation complete, Francis literally gave the clothes off his back to his father and walked away in his "birthday suit." We do not know exactly how the father and priest felt about Francis' renunciation, but no doubt it caused them both some discomfort and may have provoked in them some contemplation on wealth and its uses.

It occurs to me that a non-violent "shaming" strategy *could* be employed in modern times by folks whose homes are foreclosed by banks. Suppose your job was "downsized" and you couldn't pay your mortgage. Suppose the bank refused to renegotiate and foreclosed on your home. Not having a house you no longer need furniture. Suppose you decide to give your furniture to the bank and you begin to move your furniture into the bank lobby. Perhaps the bank would have you arrested; at least you would have food and shelter. But the bank would have a public relations disaster; after all, they would have imprisoned you for giving them gifts. Suppose others followed your lead. That might lead banks to consider more flexible lending and repayment policies. This is perhaps an absurd idea, but probably no more absurd than giving all your clothes away to someone who sues for your shirt.

The third bit of advice for "loving your enemies" is proverbial: "go the extra mile." That admonition would have applied only to the power of Roman soldiers, who could legally conscript any subject of the empire to carry their burdens – food, water, etc. – for one mile.

To go an *extra* mile would be to, in effect, do the soldier a favor. In the context of Mediterranean culture, friendships were developed by doing favors. It was considered "shameful" to refuse to return a favor. Social pressure was applied to anyone known to refuse a favor. Consequently any subject who did a favor to a soldier by carrying a burden an extra mile could expect a favor in return. What is more, by doing a favor the person would begin the conventional process of making a new friend. It may be that early Christians took this advice literally and converted their new soldier "friends" to Christianity in the process. We know that many Romans became Christians; it does not stretch credulity to hypothesize that "going the extra mile" had something to do with that.

The three strategies of what is commonly known as "nonresistance" or "passive resistance" are neither truly "nonresistant" or "passive." Each in its way resists oppression with non-violent action rooted in magnanimity. The three strategies address three types of oppression: social oppression ("back-handed slaps"), economic oppression ("suing for a shirt") and military-political oppression ("conscripting to carry a burden for one mile"). These are strategies for loving, non-violent resistance to oppression - gentle strategies for *liberation*. They demonstrate that creative and magnanimous non-violent responses to oppression can effectively subvert oppression. The teachings also suggest the rather subtle point that loving one's enemies can be *self-liberating*.

One other saying of Jesus expresses the idea of defusing adversarial relationships. This bit of advice is sometimes followed today:

*When you are about to appear with your opponent before the magistrate, do your best to settle with him on the way, or else he might drag you up before the judge, and the judge turn you over to the jailer, and the jailer throw you in prison. I tell you, you'll never get out of there until you've paid every last red cent. (Lk. 12: 58-59)*

Most lawyers would probably agree that often it is best to settle out of court. Jesus apparently advised that it is *always* best to settle out of court.

Deeper psychological ways to liberation through love, ways more central to Jesus' ethic, are the practices of forgiveness and non-judgment.

## Forgiveness and Non-Judgment

*Forgive and you'll be forgiven. (Lk. 6: 37)*

This is a deceptively simple idea with cosmological, ethical, and devotional implications. In addition to the elegant and straightforward statement "forgive and you'll be forgiven" and the prayer "forgive us to the extent that we forgive others," Jesus told two parables illustrating how this law might work in the context of practical economic affairs. In plotline, one parable is a tragedy, the other is a comedy.

I have been emphasizing Jesus' sense of humor because it is a little known dimension of his mind and because of the therapeutic value of humor. However, Jesus was, as doctrine holds, "acquainted with grief"; he encountered people who were suffering and saw the negative consequences of certain human behaviors.

Jesus' use of classic dramatic structure in a few parables suggests the possibility that he had some familiarity with Greek theater. If Joseph and Jesus were "carpenters" (the traditional translation of the Greek "tekton" which means "artificer" or "craftsman"),[60] they would have traveled to Sepphoris to do construction work. His hometown of Nazareth was just four miles from the city of Sepphoris, which had a large theater in which Greek and Roman plays were frequently performed. According to the Gospels, Jesus also traveled through other cities and districts (including Jericho, Samaria, the district of Sidon, and the region of Decapolis) which had thriving theaters.[61] Jesus used the word "hypocrites" which was the word used for "actors," and another indication that he may have had some acquaintance with the theater.

While the influence of theater on Jesus is still controversial among scholars, it is clear that he used tragic and comic structures in his parables. In his travels, Jesus could easily have witnessed plays or heard descriptions of them. Common elements of Greek and Roman comedies included the stock character of a slave who outwits his master, women who outwit men, soldiers who brag in an exaggerated fashion about their exploits, the reconciliation of fathers and children (including prodigal sons forgiven by their fathers).[62] Those themes are reflected in Jesus' parables of "The Unjust Steward" (Luke 16: 1-8), "The Widow and the Judge" (Luke 18: 2-4), "The Pharisee and the Tax Collector" (Luke 18: 10-14), and "The Prodigal Son" (Luke 15: 11-32), respectively. This is not to say that Jesus' parables were mere plot summaries of plays, but only that the structure of his parables could have been influenced by some acquaintance with Greek theater.

The "tragic" parable about forgiveness revolves around the central character's "tragic flaw" which results in his downfall, a typical device in Greek tragedies.

*This is why Heaven's imperial rule should be compared to a secular ruler who decided to settle accounts with his slaves. When the process began, the debtor was brought to him who owed ten million dollars. Since he couldn't pay it back, the ruler ordered him sold, along with his wife and children and everything he had, so he could recover his money. At this prospect, the slave fell down and groveled before him: "Be patient with me, and I'll repay every cent." Because he was compassionate, the master of that slave let him go and canceled the debt.*

*As soon as he got out, that same fellow collared one of his fellow slaves who owed him a hundred dollars, grabbed him by the neck and demanded: "Pay back what you owe!" His fellow slave fell down and begged him: "Be patient with me and I'll pay you back." But he wasn't interested; instead, he went out and threw him in prison until he paid the debt.*

*When his fellow slaves realized what had happened, they were terribly distressed and went and reported to their master everything that had taken place. At that point, his master summoned him: "You wicked slave," he says to him, "I canceled your entire debt because you begged me. Wasn't it only fair for you to treat your fellow slave with the same consideration as I treated you?" And the master was so angry he handed him over to those in charge of punishment until he paid back everything he owed. (Mt. 18: 23-34)*

The story revolves around the experience and actions of the first slave; he is the central character. The central character in classic tragedy starts out seeking something. Oedipus starts out seeking to avoid his predicted fate. Hamlet sought to find out if the "ghost" of his father revealed the truth about his uncle and mother. In the parable, the slave starts out seeking forgiveness.

Eventually the "hero" seems to discover what he was seeking. Oedipus leaves his homeland as a way to avoid his predicted "fate." Hamlet discovers that his father's "ghost" told him the truth. The slave receives forgiveness of his debt.

But the "heroes" of tragedy always have a fatal flaw which leads to their downfall. Oedipus is proud and believes that he can avoid a "fate" predicted by an oracle of the gods. This leads him to ignorantly fulfill the predictions *because* of his attempt to evade his fate. Hamlet "over-thinks" things, which results in his being both clever and indecisive. The consequences of his "over-thinking" are the deaths of all the main characters, including Hamlet. In Jesus' parable, the slave cares more about his finances than about his fellow humans; his refusal to forgive a relatively small debt results in his imprisonment. The parable credibly illustrates how refusal to forgive others can lead to tragic consequences for oneself.

The story, though it has the structure of a tragedy, also has a comic touch in the quantities of monies involved. The massive debt which is first forgiven (equivalent to about ten-million dollars in modern terms) immediately gives pause to wonder: how could a slave accumulate such an absurdly large debt? Despite his great fortune in having the debt forgiven, the slave is unwilling to forgive a relatively paltry debt of about one-hundred dollars. How could anyone who had received such great forgiveness be so petty in dealings with others? The slave's behavior seems ridiculously petty and so "laughable." At the same time his fate is tragic in the conventional sense.

Jesus' story of the "unforgiving slave" fits Aristotle's theory of tragedy except that for Aristotle a tragedy was a play rather than a narrative. Aristotle's theory of tragedy was widely accepted by the time of Jesus and even today is influential in aesthetic theory.

Plots, according to Aristotle, should have a change of intention or reversal of fortune; Jesus' parable has both. The plot must include "the incentive moment" which introduces a problem and starts a chain reaction of events. In the parable the "incentive moment" is the ruler collecting debts. The "climax" must be caused by earlier events and must itself cause the incidents that follow. In the parable the "climax" is the slave refusing to forgive after he himself was forgiven. The "resolution" is caused by preceding events but does not lead to events outside the compass of the story. The resolution resolves the problem set up in the incentive moment. The resolution of the parable is the resolution of the problem of debt collection; the slave who was originally forgiven ends up in prison.

Aristotle defined tragedy as having "incidents arousing pity and fear, wherewith to accomplish its catharsis of such emotions."[63] What emotions are aroused by Jesus' parable? Pity is aroused for those in debt, including initially the slave who is at first forgiven, then later for the second slave whose debt is not forgiven by the first slave. Most of Jesus' listeners probably had their own debts which, if not paid, could lead to their imprisonment. The audience's identification with debtors might well have aroused some fear or at least anxiety regarding their own debts. The imprisonment of debtors in the story could have heightened that anxiety. Having aroused the emotions, did hearing the story also produce a catharsis for the listeners? Was that Jesus' intention?

If he intentionally designed the parable to produce a healing catharsis, Jesus was more sophisticated and knowledgeable about Greek philosophy than is usually assumed. I think it is unlikely that Jesus was familiar with Aristotle's *Poetics*. If he intuitively created the parable, his intuition was a remarkably apt fit with Aristotle's theory. Unfortunately these questions about intention and intuition must remain unresolved here.

What can be said is only that some of Jesus' stories may have produced emotional catharsis which may have been psychologically therapeutic. What can be said is that the story was told to illustrate the principle "forgive and you will be forgiven" and suggests a corollary: if you don't forgive, you might not be forgiven. If the first slave had forgiven the second, the first slave would have remained in a state of forgiveness. Because he didn't forgive, his action was reported to the master and the end result was imprisonment.

The second story has a similar dramatic structure and a reversal of fortune, but is comic rather than tragic because the resolution is a happy ending.

*There was this rich man whose manager had been accused of squandering his master's property. He called him in and said, "What's this I hear about you? Let's have an audit of your management, because your job is being terminated."*

*Then the manager said to himself, "What am I going to do? My master is firing me. I'm not strong enough to dig ditches and I'm ashamed to beg. I've got it! I know what I'll do so doors will open for me when I'm removed from management." So he called in each of his master's debtors. He said to the first, "How much do you owe my master?"*

*He said, "Five hundred gallons of olive oil." And he said to him, "Here is your invoice; sit down right now and make it two hundred and fifty."*

*Then he said to another, "And how much do you owe?" He said, "A thousand bushels of wheat." He says to him, "Here is your invoice; make it eight hundred."*

*The master praised the dishonest manager because he had acted shrewdly. (Lk. 16: 1-8)*

The parable is classic comedy: the underdog is "kicked to the curb" yet manages to cleverly reverse his situation and surprisingly comes out on top. The comedy movies "Fun with Dick and Jane" (original in 1977, remade in 2005) are examples similar to the "dishonest steward" parable. In those films, Dick loses his job and, with his wife Jane, he turns to robbery to survive. Eventually the couple turns the tables on Dick's employer, thus their livelihood is restored. Their restoration to good fortune involves dishonesty, but the story is told in such a way that the audience sympathizes with the couple's plight.

As in other parables of Jesus, this one contains a shocking surprise. The manager is portrayed as "dishonest" yet is also praised for his shrewdness. The story does not promote the conventional morality of "honesty is the best policy." What it does indicate is the idea that forgiving debts can have a very practical worldly economic benefit: you will make friends who owe you favors. That was the "shrewdness" of the manager's actions, the assurance of employment after job termination. By forgiving part of his clients' debts, the manager assured himself of favors after he was released from his master's employ. Giving discounts to clients and customers is no doubt good business and is a lesson that can be drawn from the parable.

It is not entirely clear why the manager is labeled "dishonest" at the end of the parable. It may have been the case that business managers, then as now, were empowered to offer discounts to customers, in which case the manager in the story did nothing wrong in discounting his customers' payments. In that case, his "dishonesty" was not in his actions toward customers but in being guilty of the original accusation of "squandering his master's property." The parable says he was "*accused*" but does not say he was *actually* guilty of squandering resources. In any case, it is interesting that Jesus chose to commend the behavior of a dishonest man.

Was Jesus advocating dishonesty as a means to improving one's situation? That shallow interpretation of the story is troubling and may explain why this particular parable was included only in Luke and is not as familiar to Christians as some of the others. The shocking element of the manager getting away with dishonesty makes the story memorable and making the story memorable may have been Jesus' primary motivation for framing the story as he did. However, I believe there is more to the story.

Jesus famously associated with disreputable characters: tax collectors, harlots and other "sinners." He sympathized with the oppressed, the poor, and the sick. It makes sense that if his sympathies were with people oppressed by the political and religious establishment, he would also be sympathetic to those who subverted the oppressive system, including outlaws and outcasts. His parables and sayings feature persons who are dishonest, dishonorable ("the prodigal son"), thieves (someone who wanted to rob a "strong man"), murderers (someone who wanted to kill a "powerful man"), religiously unorthodox (the "good Samaritan"), and those generally considered sinners (the tax collector).

Jesus did not condemn or judge people for their conditions or behaviors. It is probable that Jesus did not think a person's conditions or momentary behavior defined the person. He believed in second chances; he may have believed in "seventy times seven" chances as indicated by the saying attributed to him "forgive seventy times seven." (Matthew 18:

22) He believed "we are all God's children" and thought our worth was defined by that relationship rather than earthly conditions, status and even behavior. His forgiving and non-judgmental consciousness made it possible for him to imagine a "disreputable" character to illustrate the practical business value of debt forgiveness.

Perhaps a lesson to be drawn from the "dishonest manager" is that it is good to give people a second chance; perhaps even to give 490 second chances. If we set aside the difficulty of the literal sense of the story and look to the consciousness behind the story, we get a glimpse of a forgiving and non-judgmental mind transcending conventions and perceiving the divine in all things.

Another way Jesus attempted to promote a more forgiving society was by directing listeners' attention to their own attitudes and behaviors and away from the human tendency to criticize the perceived faults of others. This provocation to self-exploration and self-knowledge is implicit in the ambiguity, humor and counter-cultural tone and content of practically all Jesus' sayings. He uses stories and aphorisms which invite the listener to re-think (the original literal meaning of "repent") opinions and see the world through different eyes. This provocation is not merely implicit in his sayings but actually explicit in a particular saying:

*"Why do you notice the sliver in your friend's eye, but overlook the timber in your own? How can you say to your friend, "Let me get the sliver out of your eye," when there is a timber in your own? You phony, first take the timber out of your eye and then you'll see well enough to remove the sliver from your friend's eye." (Mt. 7: 3-5)*

The saying is a classic example of Jesus' use of humorous exaggeration. It suggests the ridiculous image of a person with a log in their eye attempting to remove a perceived sliver in another's eye. The word here translated as "phony" is the Greek "hypocrite" which literally meant "stage actor," a person who pretends to be something other than what they really are.

The term "hypocrite" did not inherently carry a negative connotation; in fact theater was popular with the Greeks and Romans. Greeks generally held actors in high regard. Although in Roman culture actors generally had low status, some actors were celebrated as great artists. The fact that Emperor Augustus, King Herod the Great, and Herod Antipas all built lavish theaters and sponsored performances indicates that royals and aristocrats of the period held theater arts in high regard. Herod the Great held competitions in performing arts, awarding high honors and generous prizes to the winners.[64] Just as today people are fascinated with actors and awards ceremonies for film, television, and live theater, many in Jesus' era admired and were somewhat fascinated with acting skill. The context indicates that Jesus used the word for "actor" to provoke self-examination rather than to condemn the listener.

Based upon his emphasis on imitating God, serving God, and finding the realm and rule of God, Jesus clearly believed that finding God was the ultimate good and that practicing unconditional love and forgiveness is a crucial part of that quest.

## *Love, Forgiveness, Health & Healing*

It is indisputable that Jesus' philosophy and behavior promoted the value of compassion and that Christianity adopted that value. Christianity has generally believed in faith healing, but has not generally thought in terms of compassion healing. As noted at the beginning of this chapter, medical research now indicates that the cultivation of compassion strengthens the immune system. Since cultivation of compassion strengthens the immune system, it is possible that the strengthened immune system could also cure illness as well as prevent it. In any case, cultivation of compassion, as advocated and demonstrated by Jesus, evidently has value for health.

Jesus' emphasis on forgiving also appears to be sound psychological therapy, as illustrated by a recently developed and researched "forgiveness therapy." "Forgiveness therapy" is a process developed by psychologists to help clients work through issues of anger and resentment. The process has 17 steps which can be summarized as follows: awareness of psychological defenses, feelings and habitual ways of thinking (steps1-5); insights attained regarding counter-productive ways of thinking (steps 6-8); rethinking and changing feelings and strategies in relation to offender (steps 7-13); and various realizations building up to "awareness of internal, emotional release" (steps 14-17).[65] Forgiveness therapy defines forgiveness as "an unjustly hurt person's act of deliberately giving up resentment toward an offender while fostering the undeserved qualities of beneficence and compassion toward that offender."[66]

The forgiveness therapy process has been used with clients who have serious emotional issues, including people with substance abuse issues and incest survivors. A study of forgiveness therapy used in drug abuse treatment indicated that participants who went through forgiveness therapy "had significantly more improvement in total and trait anger, depression, total and trait anxiety, self-esteem, forgiveness, and vulnerability to drug use than did the alternative treatment group."[67] In a study of incest survivors, forgiveness therapy also proved effective. Those who were treated with a process model of forgiveness gained more than the control group in forgiveness and hope and decreased significantly more in anxiety and depression. "In forgiving, the injured party may give up the qualities of resentment or even hatred but not necessarily enter into relation with an untrusted offender."[68]

Jesus did not offer a 17 step psychological process for forgiveness. However, what he did offer was a logical and elegant solution to a primary religious concern for the people of his time and motivation to apply that solution. In Jesus' era, people believed that God might forgive their sins if they made sacrificial offerings and if the priests were ritually pure and performed the sacrifices correctly. There were several uncertainties involved in that view: was the offering sufficient? Were the priests pure? Were the sacrifices offered correctly? Would God accept the offerings? In addition, temple sacrifices placed increased economic stress upon the poor and the stress of travel on those Jews who lived at great distances from Jerusalem.

Jesus offered an alternative based upon the common view that God was just: forgive and you will be forgiven. To illustrate how it was just to receive forgiveness as compensation for forgiving others, Jesus also told parables to show how forgiveness worked practically in human affairs. Jesus' followers were probably motivated to work on forgiving others by a combination of factors: the strong desire to have sins forgiven; the logical elegance of the principle "forgive and be forgiven"; and the practical illustrations in Jesus' parables. The effect of the motivation may well have been sufficient to produce results similar to modern "forgiveness therapy." What is clear is that Jesus' philosophy emphasized forgiving others and forgiving others has psychological benefits.

Although the studies of forgiveness therapy did not include data on physiological effects of forgiveness, the diminishment or release of emotions such as anxiety, anger and resentment indicates release of stress. Release of stress is known to have a positive impact on physical health; consequently effectively releasing negative emotions by practicing forgiveness likely could be physiologically as well as psychologically therapeutic.

## A Practical Application

One can choose to regularly meditate to cultivate and experience increased feelings of compassion. An article in the *New York Times* (7/7/2003, "Sunday Review" section, p. 12) described research indicating that practicing meditation results in increased compassion, not only in terms of feeling but also in action. The author of the research and *Times* article was David DeSteno, professor of psychology at Northwestern University. DeSteno cited not only his own study but also a research by neuroscientists indicating that even relatively brief training in meditation techniques "can alter neural functioning in brain areas associated with empathic understanding of others' distress."

One form of meditation you could use to cultivate love would be to make a meditation recording of Jesus' sayings on love and forgiveness. For suggestions about making such a recording, see the section titled "*Entering the Healing 'Christ-consciousness'*" at the end of Chapter 3.

You could also try directing your attention to the area around the heart and focusing on feelings of care or compassion toward someone or something. Relax, sit still, and think of someone you love. You can think of yourself as sending the energy of love to them or simply sending the thought "I love you." This technique can be deepened by broadening it, that is: expand your meditation to include many people you love, then acquaintances, then people you dislike.

Another meditation for love is to think of yourself as immersed in and filled with an ocean of love-energy which connects you to all people and all things. Think of the area around your heart as a center through which the love-energy flows. From the space of this embracing compassionate energy it becomes easier to forgive others and set yourself free of grudges and resentment.

To cultivate compassion in meditation, you can also use affirmative prayers, such as *"The Infinite Love of God flows through my heart, establishing harmony in my world."*

# Chapter Six: Jesus on the Laws of Moses

An ethic based upon a few principles or upon an idea of "the highest good" does not need a list of rules. Rules in a principle based system are secondary to the principles and therefore serve only as guidelines. For example, in situation ethics the principle of "do the most loving thing" can conflict with some rules of conventional morality. While most often it is the loving thing to tell the truth, in some situations it could be better to lie. If Nazis were hunting for Jews and the Nazis come to your door and you know where the Jews are hiding, would it be the most loving act to tell the truth? I believe a pretty good case could be made that in that situation the loving and right thing to do would be to prevaricate as convincingly as you could. I believe that pragmatic and utilitarian ethicists could also make a case that lying is, in certain circumstances, the right and best thing to do.

Jesus' ethic is consistent with a Jewish idea of the highest good, i.e. loving God. At the same time, because Jesus' philosophy was situational and pragmatic, he could reasonably challenge the rule based ethic of Judaism.

One saying of Jesus clearly challenges the conventional interpretation of one of the "Ten Commandments." Jesus said, *"The Sabbath day was created for Adam and Eve, not Adam and Eve for the Sabbath day. So the son of Adam is lord even over the Sabbath day."* (Mk. 2: 27, 28) Jesus' statement about the Sabbath *could* be extrapolated to encompass all the laws of Moses, i.e. the laws were made for humans and not humans for the laws so humans are "lord" over the laws. The "logic" is that Adam, Eve, Abraham and other humans existed before the laws; so the laws were made for their sake, they were not made for the law's sake. Jesus saw that Mosaic laws are not absolute but relative to the well-being of humanity.

Beyond his situational attitude toward Sabbath laws, Jesus challenged purity and kosher laws. He was apparently as situational about "fasting" rules as about the Sabbath: *"The groom's friends can't fast while the groom is present, can they? So long as the groom is around, you can't expect them to fast."* (Mk. 12: 19) It is clear from this saying that Jesus was not rigid about fasting rules.

What is not entirely clear is what he means by "the groom is present." One can certainly understand why his disciples interpreted the saying as being an affirmation of Jesus' special status as "Messiah." However, when Jesus made the statement about the groom, he had not yet been recognized as the Messiah. Hence, those who heard him make the statement would not necessarily have interpreted it as being about Jesus as Messiah.

There is another possible interpretation of the "groom and fasting" saying. We have seen that Jesus thought of God's realm and rule as present. Some biblical prophets made use of the metaphor of God as "groom" and "husband" of Israel and Jerusalem:

*"As a young man marries a young woman, so will your Builder marry you; as a bridegroom rejoices over his bride, so will your God rejoice over you."* (Isaiah 62: 4-6)

*"For your Maker is your husband— the LORD Almighty is his name— the Holy One of Israel is your Redeemer; he is called the God of all the earth."* (Isaiah 54: 4-6)

*" 'Return, faithless people,' declares the LORD, 'for I am your husband.' "*(Jeremiah 3:14)

Jesus may simply have been making reference to that prophetic metaphor. If by "the groom" Jesus meant to refer to God, then "the groom is present" simply refers to the Divine Presence: there is no need to "fast" in mourning or supplication when one is celebrating the Presence of God (the groom or husband). The statement can be understood as another affirmation of the presence of God's realm.

*"Why do you wash the outside of the cup? Don't you understand that the one who made the inside is also the one who made the outside?"* (Thom. 89: 1)

The meaning of this saying is unclear. It may refer to purity rules or conventional practices; it may be about keeping up appearances of purity (the outside) while being "unclean" in thoughts (the inside). It *sounds* like a challenge to purity laws or at least conventional ideas about purity. Was Jesus suggesting that it is not necessary to wash the outside of the cup? Or was he implying that it is necessary to wash both the inside and the outside? Today it seems a trivial and irrelevant point; we are accustomed to washing both inside and outside. We can't help but wonder why anyone would comment on cup washing and why anyone would remember the comment. If we reflect on the saying and view the cup as a metaphor for consciousness (inside) and expression (outside), it becomes suggestive of self-examination and psychological cleansing. That interpretation would certainly fit with Jesus' philosophy, insofar as his philosophy promoted the attainment of "self-knowledge."

More overtly challenging to conventional practices are sayings regarding eating:

*"It's not what goes into a person from the outside that can defile; rather it's what comes out of the person that defiles." (Mk. 7: 15)*

*"Stay at one house, eating and drinking whatever they provide. Whenever you enter a town and they welcome you, eat whatever is set before you." (Lk. 10: 7, 8)*

One important thing to notice about Jesus' sayings is that many are in the indicative mood and only a few in the imperative mood. He more frequently makes observations in the indicative mood than commands in the imperative. One of the above sayings is an observation; the other is a command. The reason it is important to make the distinction is that followers of Jesus have tended to turn his indicative observations into imperative commands. That tendency is a misreading of Jesus' philosophy, for it misses the subtlety of his thought and his intention to induce the new way of seeing life that is "entering God's realm" which is "within you" and "seeing God's realm spread out on the earth."

The two sayings about eating, taken together, broke down a fundamental social barrier that existed between Jewish and "Gentile" followers of Jesus. Eating is a primary form of socializing. When people are forbidden to eat together as a matter of food taboos, it sets up a barrier to social interaction and friendship. What Jesus said about food ultimately had far reaching consequences for the movement that emerged in his name. There were in Jesus' time many Gentile sympathizers with Jewish religious ideas; these Gentiles were known as "God Fearers." Undoubtedly those God Fearers and Jewish followers of Jesus were able to become better acquainted and form friendships as a result of eating together.

Other barriers, even circumcision, undoubtedly became non-issues as bonds of friendship and mutual respect formed. There is a saying about circumcision attributed to Jesus, though it probably did not originate with him. Whether or not Jesus said it, the saying provides an example of what could plausibly be attributed to him because of what he said about the Sabbath and about eating. The saying is found in Thomas 53: *"If it were beneficial, their father would beget them already circumcised from their mother. Rather, the true circumcision in spirit has become completely profitable."* The saying "sounds like" Jesus in both its use of surprising logic and its content which undermined traditional Mosaic Law. Since Jesus' original Jewish followers did not insist upon circumcision, they must have believed that Jesus would not have insisted upon it.

The sayings about food not defiling a person and eating "whatever is set before you" indicate that Jesus rejected the concept of "unclean" foods. These sayings are undoubtedly the basis of the early church controversy, referred to in *Acts* and Paul's letters, about eating with Gentiles and eating non-kosher foods. The sayings imply a blanket rejection of the entire Mosaic code regarding "clean" and "unclean" foods.

The first saying, in addition to indicating that Jesus rejected concepts about clean and unclean foods, also contains a rather shocking suggestion that some might have regarded as humorous. By juxtaposing "what goes into a person" with "what comes out of a person" he brings to mind the fact food passes through us. Another saying attributed to Jesus, while it may not have originated with him, makes the point explicitly: *"Do you not see that whatever goes into the mouth enters the stomach, and goes out into the sewer?"* (Matt. 15: 17, NRSV)

The saying about "food not defiling a person" illustrates Jesus' ingenious and elegant use of logic to undermine conventional beliefs and practices. If food just passes through, it does not stay in you. If it does not stay in you, it cannot make you "unclean." Certainly "what comes out" can "defile," but once it is buried in the earth, it cannot defile the one through whom it passed. Early Christians interpreted the "what comes out which can defile" as meaning "unclean" words and actions; probably Matthew added that bit of interpretation to his Gospel and attributed it to Jesus. I am not convinced that the traditional interpretation captures Jesus' intended meaning, but it does not contradict the spirit of his teachings.

The second saying about "staying in one house" appears to be instructions for the road. The instruction would have allowed his disciples to be "good guests." Rather than making an issue about non-kosher dishes offered to them, they would have eaten whatever was set before them. The disciples would have been unhindered by food taboos in their social interactions and so able to form bonds with "Gentiles" in any city. And of course that is exactly what they did.

## *H a t e   Y o u r   F a m i l y   a n d   Y o u r   L i f e ?*

Jesus also appeared to contradict the commandment "honor your father and your mother" by saying: *"If any come to me and do not hate their own father and mother and wife and children and brothers and sisters - yes, even their own life - they cannot be my disciples."* (Lk. 14: 26)

This saying is one of the most disturbing sayings attributed to Jesus. The saying is puzzling in the context of an ethic centered in universal love. "Love your enemies," but "hate" your family and even your own life? It seems *prima facie* preposterous.

The first thing to notice is that the statement is not in the imperative mood; it is not a command but rather an observation (this time in the subjunctive mood). He did not say "hate your family" but *"if* you don't hate your family and even your own life, you can't be my disciples." The implication is that to "go" where Jesus went in consciousness entails, in some sense, "hating family and your own life." The implication is that Jesus himself must have "hated" his own family and his own life in order to "enter God's realm."

The word "hate" in Hebrew can mean "oppose" and so does not necessarily convey the strong sense of *"feeling* animosity." In English, "hate" is also sometimes used to mean "oppose" or "refuse" rather than to mean "animosity." For example, I have said, "I hate beets," by which I mean I don't like the taste and prefer not to eat beets; I do not have any personal animosity towards beets. I hate political advertisements; I hate their misleading words and insinuating tone. However my "hatred" of political advertisements does not include any personal animosity, desire to harm, or intention to destroy. All my "hatred" of political advertisements entails is my intention to avoid seeing and hearing them whenever possible. The meaning and consequences of "hate" depend upon context.

There is in the Jewish rabbinical tradition a position that one's rabbi should be more authoritative than one's own parents; that may provide part of the explanation for Jesus' saying about hating family. If a prospective disciple's family opposed following Jesus as rabbi, the prospective disciple would have to choose between family and following Jesus. To follow Jesus, one would have to prefer his teaching to honoring the wishes of one's family.

One might *have* to choose between opposing one's family and opposing Jesus. Since the Hebrew and Aramaic words for "oppose" are the same as the words for "hate," a reasonable interpretation of Jesus' saying is simply that one may have to be opposed to one's family in order to follow Jesus' teachings. Since Jesus' teachings in a few cases opposed Mosaic traditions, it is likely that conservative Jewish families would have pressured their clan to oppose Jesus. To enter God's realm one must prefer the "way" advocated by Jesus to the "way" advocated by family traditions. Nevertheless, accepting the rabbi's authority as higher than that of one's parents would not seem to entail "hating" one's family in the sense of "having animosity" toward one's family.

As for the call to hate one's own life, surely Jesus was not advocating animosity towards oneself. Overall, his message gives no indication of being a call to self-loathing; he called people to see themselves as children of God, which is the most positive self-image possible. I have heard people say, "I hate my life." What they have clearly meant is that they wanted to *change* their lives, to go in new directions. People whom I've heard say "I hate my life" were not suicidal; they were just discontented with their current situations and wanting to pursue happiness in new directions. New directions were what Jesus offered. People who were content with their lives were not likely to follow him; only those who "hated" their lives would have followed him.

Christians have conventionally interpreted the statement about "hating one's life" as a call to martyrdom for the cause of Christianity. However it is just as plausible to interpret the saying as meaning one must want to change one's life in order to adopt Jesus' philosophy. To truly change your life you must let go of old behaviors, situations and conditions. Following Jesus was clearly a life-changing decision for anyone who followed him. His disciples would have left behind their occupations as fishermen, tax collectors, etc. to become wandering advocates of a new philosophy. They would have let go of conventional family ties and religion to embrace a new way of living. They loved Jesus and what he represented to them more than they loved their old lives.

I believe Jesus spoke of "hating" relatives in order to shock his listeners into letting go of their identification of themselves with blood-ties and open their minds and hearts to a broader identification with the "family of God." Identification with one's genetic family can have detrimental effects on personal and spiritual development, especially in cases of emotional and physical abuse. Selective love, as for tribe or nation, often results in enmity towards "outsiders." To expand consciousness toward universal love is to love all equally, to bless all like the sun and rain. Such love may entail less emotional attachment to tribe or nation; in effect, to oppose or "hate" the boundaries of tribal and national divisions.

We know that conservative elements in his society resisted Jesus' message and mission. Anyone who joined Jesus might well encounter resistance from their own family members. Even today individuals, when adopting a new religion, can encounter considerable resistance from family members. Jesus was challenging his listeners to put new spiritual values ahead of family traditions, beliefs, and emotional ties.

In any case, Jesus also taught his disciples to love their enemies, hence any "hate" toward family ultimately would have to be transformed into love; but love from a different perspective on the relationships.

In *Jesus the Healer*, Steven Davies makes an interesting conjecture regarding a possible therapeutic effect of the "hate your family" idea. First Davies marshaled evidence for the theory that "demon possession" as depicted in the Gospels was probably an effect of family dysfunction. Citing modern psychology and cross-cultural anthropology, Davies showed that modern cases of dissociative identity disorders and "demon possession" in other cultures are frequently connected with childhood abuse of some kind. Davies concludes that:

> "The primary causal factor in cases of demon-possession is intrafamily conflict wherein subordinate family members . . . adopt a demon persona so as to respond and cope with their familial superiors. It can be said rather confidently that a person exorcised of such a demon persona who returns to his or her family situation with the situation unchanged will sooner or later . . . again respond to the unchanged stresses by the same coping mechanism he or she previously used. . . . we do have reports that Jesus offered a method by which the formerly demon-possessed might avoid further instances of demon possession. He advocated that individuals leave their families entirely and offered those who did so and became his associates a surrogate family headed by God the Father."[69]

Today we know more about the frequency and the tragic effects of child abuse. Some cases of dissociative identity disorder are caused by extreme child abuse. We know that often the abuse is perpetrated by family members. It may be that psychological symptoms caused by child abuse can be alleviated by the abused child being given permission to "hate" the parents. It is probably the case that people who were thought to be demonically possessed in Jesus' time actually had severe psychological disorders such as dissociative identity disorder. If these admittedly speculative premises are true, the tentative conclusion we could draw is that Jesus may have helped alleviate symptoms of psychologically disturbed people by giving them permission to hate their parents. While this conclusion may not be scientifically provable, it is plausible and is suggestive of therapeutic experimentation and possibilities.

Therapeutic or not, by loosening obligation to biological family, Jesus redefined the core unit of civilization for himself. *"My mother and my brothers - who are they? Here are my mother and my brothers. For whoever does the will of my Father in heaven, that's my brother and sister and mother." (Matt 12: 48-50)* In Jesus' philosophy, "family" was spiritual rather than biological. Those who act according to the ethic of God's realm were the true family for Jesus. One who would "follow" him in consciousness would have to do likewise, but again the statement is an observation not a commandment.

## Reason, Intuition, and the Ten Commandments

It is not likely that Jesus *rejected* the Ten Commandments as moral and spiritual precepts. However, his statements treat the commandments as subject to human reason. He *reasons* that the Sabbath was made for humanity's sake, not humanity for the Sabbath's sake; therefore exceptions to the rule can be made. He *reasons* that food cannot defile a person, so food taboos in the Laws of Moses can safely be ignored. He *reasons* that to follow him his disciples might have to go against their family's wishes, which might entail "not honoring" parents and opposing the wishes of other family members. This pattern of using reason *against* religious rules is a pattern found in *philosophical* traditions. Religious traditions tend to use reason to *defend* religious rules. Jesus' attitude toward religious rules supports the hypothesis that he was more like a philosopher than like a preacher of conventional religious morality.

A few of Jesus' statements simply observe that, in actual life, people *do* make exceptions to the prohibitions against killing and stealing. Opponents of abortion may cite the commandment "thou shalt not kill" to support their position, but may ignore that commandment when taking a position in favor of war or capital punishment. Likewise, pacifists may cite the commandment to oppose war, but ignore it when advocating "death with dignity" arguments for euthanasia. Whether or not the commandment "Thou shalt not steal" is kept seems often a matter of interpretation. When local governments cite "eminent domain" to take property from those who do not wish to give up their property, such confiscation is akin to stealing. Historically, Christians seemed to have no problem with taking land from indigenous populations in America, Africa, etc. Western governments supported displacing the natives of Palestine to make way for the new nation of Israel. Yet politicians, Christians and Jews look upon such confiscations as "in the public interest" or even "God's will."

I am not taking positions on these issues; my point is only that in practice even people who proclaim their belief in "the Ten Commandments" make rationalizations for killing and stealing. I suspect Jesus was perceptive enough in his day to recognize this fact too.

According to the *Gospel of Thomas*, Jesus shockingly compared the realm or rule of God to a successful murder:

*"The Father's rule is like a person who wanted to kill someone powerful. While still at home he drew his sword and thrust it into the wall to find out whether his hand would go in. Then he killed the powerful one." (Thom. 98: 1-3)*

According to The Gospel of Mark, Jesus made an observation about how to rob a powerful man:

*"No one can enter a powerful man's house to steal his belongings unless he first ties him up. Only then does he loot his house." (Mk. 3: 27)*

These two sayings do not advocate murder and theft, rather they recognize that humans kill and steal, despite the commandments and laws against such actions. Considering the love ethic of Jesus, it is practically certain that he did not intend these sayings to give instruction for successful murder and burglary. We are compelled to do one of two things: ignore the sayings or reflect upon them and try to find interpretations and application in our lives consistent with Jesus' love ethic.

First we should notice that the examples of killing and stealing given by Jesus in the sayings are *observations* of the *difficulty* of committing such acts. In that sense they can be seen as caveats for anyone contemplating such actions. The caveat would have been especially apropos for zealots in his audience.

If the strong and powerful men are seen as symbolic, they could be seen as representing strong and powerful individuals, nations or impulses. Certainly his audience might have thought of the Roman occupiers in connection with the strong and powerful men; in which case, the sayings can be seen as cautions against thinking of successful armed rebellion as easy to accomplish.

Some of his disciples might have thought in terms of the difficulty of "casting out demons." In modern terms we might think of "personal demons" – inner impulses – which are difficult to overcome. With that interpretation, "going into one's house and practicing sword thrusts" could symbolize *mentally* practicing or visualizing the overcoming as a way to build up the inner strength to overcome. "Tying up the strong man" could symbolize use of will and thought to control impulses. "Tying up the strong man" could also be interpreted in terms of non-lethal acts of resistance to the Roman Empire. In light of Jesus' creative non-violent strategies, the "strong man" illustration could be seen as an enigmatic allusion to those practices.

What is certainly true about these sayings is that they provoke reflection. It may be that all Jesus was intending was to provoke people to look inward for answers. Many sayings and parables of Jesus are enigmatic enough to provoke contemplation, which suggests that his intention was to help people get in touch with their own intuitions rather than blindly following conventions. Provoking people to contemplate unconventional ideas is traditionally a primary role of the philosopher.

Sometimes Jesus' *observations* have come to be seen as *commandments*. The human tendency to seek rules to live by, rather than living by their own intuitions and reason, is probably the cause of such misreading. An example of such a misreading is a saying of Jesus regarding divorce. The saying appears to be a reinterpretation of the meaning of adultery.

One challenge regarding the saying on adultery is that alternative versions are found in the different Gospels:

*"Anyone who divorces his wife and marries another woman commits adultery against her. And if she divorces her husband and marries another man, she commits adultery." (Mark 10: 11-12, NIV)*

*"Anyone who divorces his wife, except for sexual immorality, makes her a victim of adultery, and anyone who marries a divorced woman commits adultery." – (Matt 5: 32, NIV )*

*"Anyone who divorces his wife, except for sexual immorality, and marries another woman commits adultery." – (Matt 19: 9, NIV)*

*"Anyone who divorces his wife and marries another woman commits adultery, and the man who marries a divorced woman commits adultery." – (Lu 16: 18, NIV)*

The first thing to notice is that *none of these statements forbid* divorce and remarriage; they are stated as *observations* about what constitutes adultery. It is understandable that people take the observation to be a prohibition, but *technically* an observation is neither a prohibition nor a command.

Based upon the difference between *Mark's* version and the versions found in *Matthew* and *Luke*, it appears that Matthew and Luke preferred a version in "*Q*" to Mark's version. Three versions (one of Matthew's, along with Mark and Luke) say that a man who divorces *and* re-marries commits adultery. This is likely an accurate version of the first part of the saying. Matthew and Luke both have the second part "anyone who marries a divorced woman commits adultery." That is likely the second part of the original aphorism; hence Luke's version is probably the only one that is accurate in its entirety. Only Matthew adds the "exception": "except for sexual immorality," which was already a part of Jewish law. Mark changes the second half to mention a wife who divorces her husband, but women were not then allowed by *Jewish* law to initiate divorce. *Mark's* version probably was written for Romans and other Gentiles, who did allow women to initiate divorce.

The difference between Jesus' saying and Jewish law was that he expanded the meaning of adultery. He added two definitions not found in previous tradition: (1) divorcing one woman and marrying another and (2) marrying a divorced woman. This would seem to be a case of Jesus suggesting that Mosaic Law was not strict enough; the opposite of his perspective on other aspects of Mosaic Law. However, he did not literally forbid divorce, as some churches have supposed; he only said divorce *followed by re-marriage* is adultery.

If we look at the logical implications of the statement and the context of culture and of other New Testament sayings we can see that there is something more interesting than a new marriage rule behind the statement.

In Judaism of the time, marriage was a consecrated contract which involved the family of the bride along with the married couple. According to Mosaic Law a man could divorce his wife for "displeasing him" (Deut. 24: 1-4), but there was always the possibility of reconciliation. A man was *required* to divorce his wife if she committed adultery. Because only men could initiate divorces under Mosaic Law, no doubt Jesus meant his interpretation of divorce and adultery to protect women from being divorced in a cavalier fashion.

Adultery was considered a very serious offense; adulterers were supposed to be stoned according to Mosaic Law (Leviticus 20: 10). The Jewish philosopher Philo of Alexandria was highly regarded within Judaism and a contemporary of Jesus. According to Philo, adultery was "the greatest of all violations of the law."[70] Philo defined adultery as a man having intercourse with another man's wife (but not a married man having an affair with an unmarried woman) and refers to it as a "violation of vows."[71]

Jesus' statement about divorce and remarriage is logical *if* we take it that a *consecrated* marriage contract must be considered *sacred and inviolable*. A divorce followed by remarriage would in effect break the original marriage contract; hence those actions *taken together* would break the marriage covenant and so be adultery. Just divorcing a woman would not by itself constitute a breaking of the contract as long as the man did not make a new marriage contract with another woman. If a man married a divorced woman, he would be having intercourse with another man's wife because the original contract was consecrated and so inviolable. In effect the Mosaic Law, which allows divorce and remarriage, contradicts the Law which makes marriage a contract in the "eyes of God." Jesus must have interpreted the marriage contract as inviolable; that is the only interpretation by which we can make sense out of his expansion of the meaning of adultery. This is not a far-fetched notion; marriage vows even today do not generally include an escape clause.

Was Jesus actually opposed to divorce and remarriage or was there something else behind his observation? The question cannot be answered without looking at the broader context of Jesus' life and the traditions found in the New Testament.

A wedding ceremony is essentially a vow or oath of fidelity. That was the understanding in Jesus' time as well as in ours. Vows and oaths in Judaism were related to the commandment not to take God's name in vain; the rabbinical traditions have over the years discussed what kinds of oaths are acceptable. Philo made this comment on not taking God's name in vain as related to oaths:

*"Next to swearing not at all, the second best thing is to keep one's oath; for by the mere fact of swearing at all, the swearer shows that there is some suspicion of his not being trustworthy."*[72]

Philo took the position that one should avoid taking oaths whenever possible. For him, keeping one's oaths is good, but not taking oaths at all is better.

Jesus probably had a position on vows similar to that of Philo. There is an early tradition, recorded in the Gospels and the *Epistle of James*, that Jesus told his disciples not to make any oaths at all. After the passage on adultery in Matthew 5, Jesus reportedly said: *". . . do not swear an oath at all . . . All you need to say is simply 'Yes' or 'No'; anything beyond this comes from the evil one."* (5: 34, 37) The juxtaposition of the adultery and oath sayings probably indicates that in Matthew's mind the two issues were related in Jesus' philosophy. That Jesus opposed taking *any* oaths is supported by the passage from *James*: *"Above all, my brothers and sisters, do not swear . . . . All you need to say is a simple 'Yes' or 'No.' Otherwise you will be condemned."* (5: 12) The phrase "above all" indicates that this idea was very important to James; it may also have been to Jesus. Since not taking oaths at all is not a traditional rabbinical position, it is likely that the position was original to Jesus (and Philo) rather than to James, who was Jesus' brother, according to the earliest traditions.

If Jesus did think it unwise to make vows, it is entirely plausible that he thought marriage covenants were unwise. That idea puts a different light on his saying about divorce and adultery. The statement about divorce, in light of the statement opposing vows, might have been intended to make his disciples wary of marrying. According to Paul, Jesus' apostles and his brothers were married (1 Corinthians 9: 5). From the fact that apostles married we can conclude that Jesus did not *prohibit* marriage for his followers; he just wanted them to contemplate their options.

Paul advised unmarried Christians not to marry, but he probably did so for reasons different than those of Jesus. Jesus was probably wary of the vow involved in marriage, especially as related to his ideas about divorce and adultery. Paul was wary of marriage because he believed the resurrection and new world was coming soon and that Christians should focus upon preparing for that. Paul wrote:

*"Now to the unmarried . . . I say: It is good for them to stay unmarried, as I do . . . . the time is short. From now on those who have wives should live as if they do not . . . . For this world in its present form is passing away." (1 Cor 7: 8, 29, 31)*

Jesus, like the Cynic philosophers, was skeptical about traditional ideas concerning family obligations. Cynics generally did not marry. A notable exception was Crates who married Hipparchia. However, Hipparchia adopted the Cynic philosophy and traveled with Crates; Hipparchia was not a traditional wife and theirs was not a traditional marriage. Like the Cynics, Pythagoreans, Platonists and Epicureans, Jesus had women disciples. In the Greek and Roman traditions women could be philosophers; in the Jewish tradition women could not be rabbis. Jesus' attitude toward women was closer to that of philosophical schools than that of Jewish rabbis.

In his rejection of conventional moral and religious absolutes, Jesus' approach to morality, like Fletcher's, was situational. I would add here that "situationalism" is not identical with "relativism." A relativist holds that there are no moral absolutes, i.e. that every moral idea is relative to culture or some other limited grouping; a situationalist (at least in the cases of Fletcher and Jesus) can hold to one or more "moral absolutes."

Jesus was not opposed to the Ten Commandments. He said nothing against the Commandments to have only One God, to make no graven images, or to not take God's name in vain. On the other hand, he did seem to think of other Commandments as relative to situation and to reject the value of kosher laws.

# Chapter Seven:  Meditation
# Induction  and  Prayer

*"Whoever discovers the interpretation of these sayings will not taste death" (Thomas 1).*

*The Gospel of Thomas* begins with a statement that interpreting the sayings of Jesus will result in not "tasting" death.  Even though this saying probably did not originate with Jesus, it does tell us at least three interesting things about how followers of Jesus responded to his life and sayings.  First, his early followers felt a need to *interpret* his parables and provocative sayings.   This  point  should  already  be  obvious  from discussion  of  the  different  ways  the  gospel  authors  interpreted  his message  and  the  alternative  interpretations  explored  here.   Second, interpretation  requires  *contemplation*.   Contemplation  can  lead  to meditative  states  in  which  psychological  and  physiological  changes  can occur.  Third, Jesus' disciples believed that understanding Jesus would lead to conquest of death.

Based  upon  personal  experience,  I  have  no  doubt  that contemplating  the  parables  and  sayings  of  Jesus  can  lead  to  deep meditative  states  –  altered  states  of  consciousness  with  physiological effects.  This chapter is an exploration of various sayings of Jesus that could have induced meditation or "hypnotic" states in those who heard and contemplated his sayings.  The next chapter will look more closely at the therapeutic value of such altered states as demonstrated by significant health research.

Since  Christianity  came  to  emphasize  everlasting  life  through Jesus, it is appropriate here to consider what Jesus said about "not tasting death," before moving on to discussion of contemplating and interpreting his sayings.

Each  of  the  canonical  Gospels  contains  one  saying  using  the phrase "will not taste death."  The phrase is not found anywhere else in the Bible.  None of the sayings about "tasting" death were assessed by the Jesus Seminar as originating with Jesus.  However, the appearance of the phrase "will not taste death" in all four canonical Gospels as well as in *Thomas* strongly indicates that some such expression was remembered by disciples as being used by Jesus.

The  sayings  preserved  in  the  synoptic  Gospels  most  probably came from two different sources, *Mark* and *Q* (*Luke* and *Matthew* versions*)*:

> *And he said to them, "Truly I tell you, some who are standing here will not taste death before they see that the kingdom of God has come with power." (Mark 9: 1)*

> *"Truly I tell you, some who are standing here will not taste death before they see the kingdom of God." (Luke 9: 27)*

> *"Truly I tell you, some who are standing here will not taste death before they see the Son of Man coming in his kingdom." (Matthew 16: 28)*

The existence of different versions of the saying in the independent sources of *Mark* and *Q* indicates that the saying preceded those Gospels and may have originated with Jesus. It is also possible that Luke and Matthew simply modified Mark's saying to suit their own perspectives.

The version in *Mark* affirms that people still alive will see that the kingdom *has already* come, which agrees with sayings of Jesus that affirmed the realm of God as already present. *Luke* affirms that some people will see the kingdom of God before they taste death; it is ambiguous whether the God's realm is present or future. Matthew's modification is clearly about Jesus returning at the future imminent apocalyptic event. Assuming Jesus taught that God's realm is already present, then either Mark or Luke's version could be originally from Jesus, but Matthew's version could not.

*John's* reference to "not tasting death" is actually closer in meaning to *Thomas'* version than to the synoptic Gospels. Both versions affirm that Jesus' word is the key to "not tasting death." In John's version Jesus speaks of not *seeing* death; his audience responds by quoting him as saying "*taste death*":

> *"'Very truly, I tell you, whoever keeps my word will never see death.' The Jews said to him, 'Now we know that you have a demon. Abraham died, and so did the prophets; yet you say, 'Whoever keeps my word will never taste death.'" (John 8: 51-52)*

The Greek word translated as "keeps" means "attends to carefully." While "attending to" and "understanding the interpretation" are not identical in meaning, both expressions indicate the importance to early Christian communities of contemplating Jesus' sayings. Both *John's* and *Thomas'* communities believed that Jesus' sayings were the keys to "not tasting death." Only the *Thomas* saying indicates that Jesus' words had to be *interpreted*, yet as we look at what Jesus said it is clear that interpretation is necessary if one is to discover meaning and application for his sayings.

The Greek word "taste" also can mean "to experience" or "to perceive." To "not taste death" is subtly different in meaning from "will not die." To not perceive or experience death could mean to not be *affected* by death. It could mean not being affected by the death of others as well as not being affected by one's own death. Anticipating death and losing loved ones can produce pain, anxiety and fear. To "not taste death" would then be freedom from pain, anxiety and fear related to death.

Freedom from fear of death was an important theme in the Greek philosophies, especially in Cynicism, Stoicism, Pythagoreanism and Epicureanism. It could be that in some way Jesus' sayings freed his original disciples from fear of death and that freedom, for them, was "not tasting death."

The communities that used *Thomas* thought of "not tasting death" as the most important and ultimate outcome of studying and reflecting upon the sayings of Jesus. That attitude may have been more prevalent among the first generation of disciples than is commonly recognized. After all, the early church preserved and treasured words ascribed to Jesus.

The *Gospel of Thomas* also shows that those who esteemed Thomas' Gospel recognized the sayings as having deeper meanings which had to be interpreted to be understood. The process of interpreting sayings would have acted as a *catalyst* for contemplation, insight, feeling and other inner experiences.

## Catalytic Aphorisms

Altered states of consciousness often result from use of language, in the form of meditation instruction and methods of hypnosis.

Language is used most often to convey or seek information. Descriptive sentences are usually intended to convey information and questions are usually intended to seek information. However, language is also sometimes used to provoke thought, feeling, internal experience or insight. Such language acts, in effect, as a *catalyst* for inner experience. Some sentences are not intended to convey or seek information; rather, they are intended to act as *catalysts* for changing consciousness.

Hence, some language can be "catalytic" as well as descriptive or questioning. For example, stories and poetry are primarily descriptive yet can be intellectually or emotionally provocative as well. Philosophical treatises are explanatory and exploratory, yet at the same time they are intended to provoke thinking in their audiences. Likewise, questions can be intended to provoke thought and feeling as well as to evoke information.

When a saying is not intended to describe or inquire but only to *provoke* inner experience, that saying can be called a "catalytic aphorism." Examples of catalytic aphorisms are Zen koans and the "Symbols of Pythagoras," which will be discussed a bit later in this section along with examples from Jesus' sayings.

Catalytic aphorisms are in their literal sense usually obscure or paradoxical. The obscurity or paradoxical nature neither conveys nor seeks information; rather, it *confuses* and may even temporarily block conscious rational thinking. With the conscious mind partly "disabled" an opportunity occurs for deeper subconscious levels of feeling and insight to emerge into awareness. The temporary state of conscious confusion is similar to sleep, in that subconscious mentation "takes over" and can emerge into awareness through words and images. In meditation we may "hear" a voice or receive a vision; in sleep we dream. The experience and remembrance of a dream is awareness of subconscious mentation. Feeling and insight provoked by catalytic aphorisms are likewise awareness of subconscious mentation.

## Jesus: An Early "Hypnotherapist"?

In his discussion of Jesus' parables, New Testament scholar Stevan Davies concluded, in agreement with many scholars before him, that the parables would have produced an altered state of consciousness in some of his audience.[73] Davies found a modern parallel in the work of Milton Erickson, the innovative and influential hypnotherapist. Erickson wrote that hypnotherapists have found that shocking, surprising, and confusing stories and statements can be used to induce trance states which allow patients to activate and access unconscious creative and therapeutic potentials to solve their own problems.[74] He believed that drawing forth guidance and solutions from the subconscious was a more effective use of hypnosis than attempting to implant solutions by direct suggestion.

Erikson developed methods for quickly inducing hypnotic and autohypnotic states. He discovered some of his methods as ways to cope with the pain of his affliction with polio. Through autohypnosis he regained some control over his muscles so that he was able to become physically active. He took canoe trips and eventually was able to walk. He thus dramatically demonstrated in his life the physically therapeutic power latent in the mind.[75]

It is probable that the philosophers, including Jesus, who used catalytic aphorisms were, like Erikson, individuals who did experimental self-exploration and who entered into states similar to those known today as meditative and hypnotic.

Davies summarized Erickson's work in the following terms:

"A therapist should enable the client to gain access to his or her own unconscious functioning so that the client can thereby work to resolve his or her own difficulties. As the conscious ego structure has limited access to the unconscious (practically by definition) the therapist should enable the client to put aside his or her conscious ego structure so that access to the unconscious is made possible. The way to do this is to place the client into trance and to make nondirective suggestions to the client to facilitate him or her in making use of already present unconscious potentials. Thus trance facilitates resolution of the client's problems with the assistance, but not the direct advice of the therapist."[76]

The Ericksonian method for inducing trance "used confusion to break up clients' ordinary reality orientation."[77] The method involved "confusion due to [verbal] shock, stress, uncertainty, etc. [leads to] unstructuring of usual frames of reference [leads to] restructuring needed [leads to] receptivity to therapeutic suggestions."[78]

After briefly describing Erickson's method, Davies notes, "If we take seriously what specialists in the study of Jesus' parables tell us over and over again, we see that they conclude, with lines of reasoning wholly unrelated to considerations of Ericksonian therapy, that Jesus used parables to produce confusion, unstructuring, restructuring, receptivity."[79]

In his work, Davies was contending for a view that Jesus was attempting to induce the state he called "the kingdom of God," which Davies described as a dissociative state in which Jesus was "possessed" by an alternate persona. Davies further surmised that Jesus' sayings caused his listeners to enter a dissociative or "spirit possessed" state.

I do not personally find Davies' arguments for possession by an alternate persona compelling; however, assessing those arguments is beyond the intended scope of this work and is not relevant to my hypotheses. I will only say here that Erickson did not take on an alternate persona and his work did not result in dissociative alternate persona in his clients comparable to "spirit possession"; therefore the analogy to Erickson's work does not support the "spirit possessed Jesus" of Davies' theory. Erickson characterized his work in terms of accessing resources in the unconscious and not in terms of inducing possession by an alternate personality (Davies' theory of "spirit possession").

However, the parallel between Erickson's methods and Jesus' sayings, as noted by Davies, is illuminating. The exploration of Jesus' philosophy in the preceding sections noted time and again the elements of shock and surprise in Jesus' sayings as well as the countercultural content of those sayings (the "unstructuring-restructuring" aspect). There are parallels between Erickson's methods and Jesus' style of expression. For example:

Erickson: "apposition of opposites" – Jesus used such appositions, e.g. "do not let your left hand know what your right hand is doing."

Erickson: "Surprise" – Jesus' parables had elements of surprise within and at the end, e.g. the "justified" tax collector and the "not justified" Pharisee.

Erickson: "Confusion"- Jesus' sayings were often confusing, e.g. "love your enemies" and "whoever does not hate his family cannot be my disciple."

Erickson: "Shifts in frames of reference" – practically all of Jesus' sayings and parables represented shifting one's frame of reference, seeing the world in a different way.[80]

Just as Erickson employed "a rich repertory of analogies drawn from everyday life" to induce trance and help his clients access the potential of their unconscious, Jesus primarily used analogies to direct the attention of his listeners to "God's realm" to access their potential. Many of Erickson's analogies were "about the perceptions and experiences of childhood; the child's way of functioning are closer to unconscious, which Erickson is trying to facilitate in trance work."[81] Jesus told his disciples that they had to become like little children to receive "God's realm."

Based upon the parallels between Erickson's approach to hypnotherapy and Jesus' approach to entering God's realm, I believe Davies is correct in his argument and position that Jesus' sayings induced trancelike states similar to if not identical with hypnotic states. I believe those states helped Jesus' audience access "unconscious resources" and made Jesus' audience "receptive to therapeutic suggestion." Jesus did not use the language of "accessing unconscious resources"; in his terminology a person could "enter God's realm" which was "within them."

What were the "therapeutic suggestions" in Jesus' sayings? Some "suggestions" were contained in the *content* of Jesus' philosophy; his sayings *indirectly* suggested optimism, faith, love, forgiveness and joy. In Jesus' sayings, the "suggestions" were part of the content; the style, how he shaped the content, was what likely "induced" trance states or hypersuggestibility. Jesus' language did not suggest that people become "spirit possessed"; he was instead suggesting a restructuring of outlook and emotions.

The comparison of Jesus' philosophy to Erickson's approach to hypnotherapy is not to say that Jesus was a "hypnotherapist" in the modern sense; that would be anachronistic. Rather, I would say that, like Erickson, Jesus naturally found ways to access his own "unconscious potentialities," what he referred to as "God's realm." Having gained that access, Jesus expressed from that altered state of consciousness (but not necessarily from an "alternate persona") in a way that facilitated altered states in his disciples.

How did he discover those ways? He was probably partly influenced by contact with the language of Pythagorean, Stoic and Cynic philosophers, who used obscure or paradoxical sounding statements and parables, and who had unconventional alternative ways of seeing and being. Jesus was probably also influenced by the preaching of John the Baptist, perhaps mainly by the Baptist's preaching of the "nearness" of God's realm. John the Baptist probably saw that "nearness" in terms of future outward conditions; Jesus saw the nearness in terms of a present inwardness. John may also have influenced Jesus to feel that he was in a state of forgiveness through the baptism ritual. I suspect that mainly Jesus discovered his methods by internal experimentation and external observation of people, as Erickson himself did.

Considering the effectiveness of hypnosis to cure psychosomatic symptoms, it is very possible that the use of catalytic aphorisms resulted in what appeared to be "miraculous" cures in ancient times. Certainly Pythagoras and his followers used "catalytic aphorisms" and had an accepted reputation as healers.

Perhaps the most widely known examples of catalytic aphorisms are Zen koans. The koan is a riddle with no definitive answer. The Zen Master gives the student a koan as a focal point for meditation, which is intended to lead the student to a different state of consciousness called "satori." The koan *"what is the sound of one hand clapping?"* does not seek information or rational analysis; it seeks to provoke a state of mind called "satori." Modern Zen practitioners claim that Zen meditation has therapeutic value.

Zen Buddhism undoubtedly developed the koan technique as a result of interaction with Taoist philosophy in China. The Taoist seminal text, the *Tao-Te-Ching*, is filled with obscure and paradoxical sentences, for example: *"To yield is to be preserved whole. To be bent is to become straight. To be empty is to be full. To be worn out is to be renewed. To have little is to possess. To have plenty is to be perplexed."*[82]

About the same time that Lao-Tzu was confusing Chinese followers with obscure sayings, in the West the philosophers Heraclitus and Pythagoras were also using catalytic aphorisms to sow the seeds of later Platonism and Stoicism.

Heraclitus of Ephesus (535-475 B.C.E.), who was known as "the Obscure One," intentionally used obscure statements to direct his listeners' minds through appearances to a deeper reality. One of his "mottos" was "Nature loves to conceal herself." This is strikingly similar to Jesus' idea of God's realm as "hidden."

Examples of Heraclitus' obscure sayings are:

*"You cannot step twice into the same river."*

*"The dry soul is the wisest and best."*

*"All things come out of the one, and the one out of all things."*

*"Mortals are immortals, and immortals are mortals, the one living the other's death and dying the other's life."*[83] .

The Pythagoreans had a widespread reputation as healers; it seems likely that they utilized to some extent the therapeutic power of induced "hypnotic" states. Pythagoras taught by means of enigmatic commands, which disciples contemplated for deeper meaning (they also contemplated "number" i.e. geometry and music theory). Iamblichus was one of the few ancient writers to record information about the

Pythagoreans. He asserted that "All Pythagoric discipline was symbolic, resembling riddles and puzzles, and consisting of maxims."[84]

Some of the "Golden Verses of Pythagoras" were straightforward commands such as: "Worship the Immortal Gods by making your sacrifice: keeping your faith, honoring great heroes, living in harmony in the world" and "Remember about the law of cause and effect in your life."

Another set of sayings, "The Symbols of Pythagoras," consists primarily of commands and prohibitions. Many of these are obscure in meaning and so fit the category of "catalytic aphorisms." The "Symbols of Pythagoras" included:

*"Eat not the heart."*

*"Do not sit upon a bushel basket."*

*"Do not walk in the public way."*

Pythagoras probably used such sayings to provide memorable images for contemplation, provoking his disciples to turn inward. They would have contemplated the sayings not merely to interpret them but also to explore the depths of their own consciousness.

The greatest challenge to understanding verses of Pythagoras and other ancient sayings of the type is that the context of the sayings is lost. It is unlikely that the list of sayings was simply presented as a speech. The sayings more likely were responses to specific questions or situations. Without the context, we have to guess at the context, meaning, and purpose of such sayings.

Consider as a more modern example an aphorism of Benjamin Franklin: "Gentlemen, we must all hang together or assuredly we will hang separately." Suppose we had practically no context for the saying; that it was just part of a list of Franklin's aphorisms. Without context we can guess the saying is about the importance of humans working together, since we know that "hanging together" can be taken idiomatically as meaning working together. If we happened to know that "hanging" was a form of execution, we could guess the "hanging separately" part to be an allusion to execution. We might suppose Franklin was exaggerating for effect in his reference to being hanged. If we had practically no knowledge of Franklin's era, we might hypothesize that he was part of a gang of criminals who worried about being caught and executed. Knowing he was actually addressing conflict within the Continental Congress during the American Revolution, the wit and wisdom of the saying become more evident.

Ancient wisdom teachings, such as Aesop's Fables, originally were spoken in some unknown context. The fables were remembered and eventually recorded. Those who collected "Aesop's Fables" added "morals" to the end of the stories. We know this because different collections had different morals. We also know that at least some of the fables attributed to Aesop were actually invented by others.[85] Even so, some of the collectors of Jesus' sayings provided different interpretive contexts and interpretations; and undoubtedly some of Jesus' followers invented sayings and attributed those sayings to him.

## Catalytic Aphorisms of Jesus

In the case of the New Testament Gospels, the authors probably had lists of remembered sayings without the contexts. Consequently, the authors in writing their narratives had to imagine the contexts and provide settings for interpreting the sayings.

Like Pythagoras and Heraclitus, Jesus also used "paradoxical" and obscure sayings. It is possible that he had heard sayings of Pythagoras and/or Heraclitus and was influenced by them. It is also possible that catalytic aphorisms found in Jesus,' Pythagorean, Taoist, and Zen Buddhist philosophies were products of similar states of consciousness rather than of direct influence of one tradition on others.

Jesus probably spoke his aphorisms for the same purpose as the other philosophers of his era: to provoke contemplation. As with the parables, the sayings "stuck" in the minds of Jesus' disciples. Undoubtedly at least some disciples would have contemplated the sayings in solitude, trying to understand and apply the meanings. In that way, the aphorisms could act as focal points to lead the disciples into meditative states. Jesus himself probably practiced contemplation using scriptures, ideas about God's nature, and his observations of nature and human behavior. Some of his aphorisms indicate that Jesus contemplated his own body, states of mind, and memories. By contemplating his sayings one can enter into meditative states, just as contemplation of Zen koans can lead to meditative states.

Logical analysis of many of Jesus' aphorisms indicates that they were not intended to convey descriptive information and could only have acted as *catalysts* for thought and inner experiences.

What follows is commentary on the catalytic aphorisms of Jesus. The commentary is intended to provide context for understanding and possible interpretations. The interpretations offered are not the only possible meanings to be derived from the sayings. The reader is encouraged to contemplate the sayings to discover personal meaning and application.

*"Let the little children come to me, and do not stop them; for it is to such as these that the realm of God belongs. Truly I tell you, whoever does not receive the realm of God as a little child will never enter it." (Luke 18: 16-17, NIV)*

This statement has no obvious meaning. The statement raises questions with no definitive answers: Why does God's realm belong to *children*? What does it mean to receive it as a little child? What qualities does a child have that are not prominent in adulthood? One could hazard any number of opinions about childlike qualities: innocence, playfulness, openness, wonder, etc. Children may be more trusting than adults. Children probably use their imaginations more than adults. Children are unconcerned about money matters. Qualities that seem more prominent in children than adults do seem to express the kind of consciousness and behavior advocated in Jesus' philosophy.

Ultimately the "child mind" is complex, but with different prominent qualities than the "adult mind." The saying invites one to go within oneself and try to remember one's own childhood state of mind. In Jesus' time, children were generally thought to be inferior to adults; but here Jesus rejects that convention. There are at least two ways one can hope to discover the meaning of being like a child: by observing and trying to emulate the behavior of children and by looking within one's memory. The memory is subconscious for adults and so the statement could act as a catalyst to put one in touch with subconscious mentation.

I believe the farther back one goes in memory the closer one comes to a state of consciousness in which the world is seen as a whole rather than in terms of separate pieces; a state in which the world as a whole is nearly undifferentiated from "self." Such a state would be akin to the mystical consciousness of divine unity.

*"You must be sly as a snake and as simple as a dove." (Mt. 10: 16)*

Slyness or shrewdness is not a quality usually seen in children, so clearly Jesus was not simply advocating being childish or literally reverting to a child consciousness.

In Jesus' time the snake was associated with wisdom, shrewdness, deception and harm (e.g. Genesis 3: 13); the dove with innocence and being easily deceived (e.g. Hosea 7: 11). The command to be both sly as a snake and simple as a dove is a paradox. Later Christians would associate the serpent with evil and the dove with the Holy Spirit, which makes the saying even more obviously paradoxical.

The aphorism calls upon the audience to look at two sides or potentialities of their consciousness. Interpretations of "snake" and "dove" may vary from person to person. The "snake" may symbolize that in human consciousness which can discern and even employ deception. The ability to see through deception is obviously a very helpful ability. In some situations the ability to employ deception could be harmful, yet in other situations might be beneficial. Government intelligence agencies employ deception to protect national interests. Such deception could be beneficial, in the right circumstances. Jewish sympathizers employed deception to save Jews from the Nazis during World War II. Certainly the deceptions of Jewish sympathizers were on the right side of history and morality. People routinely tell "little white lies" to avoid hurting the feelings of others. It could be argued that such "white lies" are better in some circumstances than frank expression of opinion. Surprise parties can bring great joy, but deception is required to keep the surprise a secret. Deception to pull off a surprise party is harmless at worst and at best can contribute to a memorable and joyful experience.

The "dove" can symbolize that in human consciousness which is trusting, innocent and harmless. Such qualities can put a person at risk in interactions with untrustworthy people; yet trust and harmlessness are necessary for developing positive relationships and society as a whole. Some synthesis and balance of the "snake" and "dove" in character and consciousness could make one both effective and harmless in worldly interactions.

The serpent, because of its ability to shed its skin, was also a symbol for regeneration and transformation. The dove was also a symbol for peace and freedom.

Paradoxical aphorisms call upon the audience to reconcile the paradox, which cannot be done entirely through reason; only an intuitive or mystical insight can reconcile opposites in consciousness. That mystical insight transcends dualistic consciousness is affirmed in practically all mystical traditions. Mysticism is usually defined as seeking conscious oneness with God and is often described as an experience of pure unity in which all apparent separation is dissolved. The ultimate goal of all yogic systems is the conscious oneness with

God. Christian mystics seek the same experience. The Renaissance polymath and mystic Nicholas of Cusa spoke of God as the "coincidence of opposites."

Whether or not Zen Buddhism should be classified as a mystical tradition is controversial; it does not use the language of "conscious oneness with God," which is found in other mystical traditions. However, satori is sometimes described as a "non-dual" consciousness. Even if satori is not identical with mystical experience, satori in its transcendence of dualistic consciousness is at least akin to mystical consciousness.

If we accept the premise that Jesus was a mystic, it follows that he intended to convey mystical insight. If he intended to help others attain the mystical perspective, it would follow that his paradoxical sayings were intended as devices to provoke a consciousness transcending dualistic thinking, i.e. to provoke what is commonly called a "mystical experience."

If Jesus did not intend to help his disciples transcend dualistic thinking, then his paradoxical sayings could be seen as self-contradictory nonsense. Considering his impact on his own time and through the ages, it seems far more likely that Jesus had mystical insight than that he was just speaking nonsense.

Another example of Jesus' use of an obscure statement has been turned into an idiom meaning "give anonymously to charity" or "do good works without concern for praise." That idiomatic meaning is a result of a phrase that was probably added to the original saying. The phrase added by Matthew was "when you give to charity," which was followed by the instruction: *"don't let your left hand know what your right hand is doing." (Mt. 6: 3)*

On the other hand, the *Gospel of Thomas* records the same saying without the connection to giving to charity: *"Do not let your left hand know what your right hand is doing." (Thom. 62: 2)* If Jesus was *not* simply attempting to coin a new idiom and especially if the *Gospel of Thomas* has the original saying, then the saying is another example of an obscure and paradoxical sounding aphorism. Even if the saying is connected to the practice of giving to charity, the conventional interpretation is not obvious; "don't let your left hand know what your right hand is doing" is an odd way to say, "Give anonymously," if that was the intention.

Is there any significance in the "left hand" and "right hand" dichotomy of the saying? There does not appear to be any uniform association of "good and bad" or "clean and unclean" with handedness in the Hebrew biblical tradition. In "Proverbs," Wisdom is characterized as having "length of days in her right hand; and in her left hand riches and honor" (Proverbs 3: 16). The proverb indicates blessings in both hands. On the "other hand," Ecclesiastes contains a saying about the heart related to the hands: "A wise man's heart is at his right hand; but a fool's heart at his left." (Ecclesiastes 10: 2). However, there are no other biblical passages associating the right with wisdom and the left with foolishness. Most reference to right and left hands in the Hebrew Scriptures do not carry any connotative difference between right and left.

The New Testament only has a few passages making reference to the right and left hands. The mother of James and John asks Jesus "Grant that these my two sons may sit, the one on thy right hand, and the other on the left, in thy kingdom." (Matt 20: 21) Clearly she does not associate one hand with good and the other with evil. On the other hand, Matt. 25: 33 reports that on judgment day the King will separate the sheep from the goats (this is apparently figurative) with "sheep on his right hand and goats on the left." He then says to those on the left "Depart from me, ye cursed, into everlasting fire, prepared for the devil and his angels." (Matt 25: 41) The Jesus Seminar concluded that the "sheep and goat" passage did not originate with Jesus; it is found only in Matthew, so we should be wary of inferring that it represents the normative metaphorical understanding of right and left.

Overall, it appears that the left hand was generally thought of as *weaker* than the right, but the left hand was not necessarily usually associated with foolishness or evil. In our culture, the predominance of right-handed people and the prejudice of some right-handed people against left-handedness has resulted in a conventional interpretation of Jesus' saying in terms of "right hand, good; left hand, bad." Personally, as a "southpaw," I resent and reject such interpretations.

Regardless of the symbolic meanings of "right hand" and "left hand," there is the additional and more difficult issue of the meaning of one hand "not knowing" what the other is doing. How would one go about preventing the left hand from "knowing" what the right hand is doing? In what sense do hands "know"? If one focused all one's attention only on the activity of the right hand, one might be able to have "consciousness" in the right hand while becoming unconscious of the left hand, at least temporarily. Likewise, if one were to concentrate entirely on the left hand, one could become unconscious of the right hand.

Autogenic training uses the technique of concentrating only upon one hand in order to learn to produce a state of relaxed concentration. Autogenic training is "one of the most comprehensive and successful Western deep-relaxation techniques . . . which was developed by the German psychiatrist Johannes H. Schultz in 1932."[86] The first exercise in autogenic training is to repeat the phrase "My right [left] arm is heavy" (the subject uses "right" or "left" depending upon which hand is dominant).[87] The relaxed concentration can lead to an altered state of consciousness, which may be described as "autohypnotic" or "meditative."

While autogenic training is progressive and involves instruction on posture and attitude and Jesus' saying is only a paradoxical sounding command, the mental effect of both would be similar in one respect: both suggest concentrating attention on one hand to the listener.

There is a possibility that Jesus' statement was intended to help disciples get in touch with their power of concentration and help them open to the greater resources of the subconscious mind. That is not to say that Jesus would have had in mind the modern concepts of "concentration" and "subconscious resources." The saying suggests the possibility that Jesus practiced a form of meditation in which he learned to focus his attention upon parts of his body. Jesus' saying that the kingdom of God is within you and his predilection for thought provoking sayings strongly suggest that he was a man who practiced exploration of "inner space." He probably was expressing thoughts based upon his own contemplations and thought of the "trance state" as an experience of the realm of God. Regardless of how Jesus came up with his sayings and his intention in sharing them, the effect of thinking about the "right hand/ left hand" saying can be mental concentration on one's hand until one achieves an altered state of consciousness.

In any case, there is no one interpretation of the saying that can be considered definitive. With no definitive interpretation the saying becomes a catalyst for thought, inner experience and many possible interpretations.

One frequently used phrase in Hebrew Scriptures uses "right" and "left" in a way that has relevance for another of Jesus' catalytic aphorisms:

*"So be careful to do what the LORD your God has commanded you; do not turn aside to the right or to the left." (Deuteronomy 5:32)*

The idea of following God's commandments without turning to the right or left would have been familiar to Jesus' Jewish audience. A modern idiom reflects the same idea: "follow the straight and narrow." That phrase was probably derived from a saying attributed to Jesus: *"But small is the gate and narrow the road that leads to life, and only a few find it."* (*Matthew 7: 13-15*) This saying probably did not originate with Jesus, according to the scholars of the Jesus Seminar. The saying was probably added as an interpretation or extrapolation of another saying, which is about a *door*:

> *"Struggle to get in through the narrow door; I'm telling you, many will try to get in, but won't be able."* (*Lk. 13: 24*)

Jesus' Jewish audience might well have associated the "narrow door" with the idea of a "narrow road" from which they were not to turn right or left. Jesus' aphorism about the narrow door contains both an admonition and an observation. The two parts stand in a kind of tension with each other. First Jesus tells his disciples to do something; then he tells them that many won't be able to follow the instruction. The tension is another example of using conflicting "suggestions" which, as in Ericksonian hypnotherapy, could induce an altered state of consciousness.

"Many won't be able" *could* mean that Jesus expected only a few of his disciples to be able to obey the Laws of Moses. It also *could* mean that many of his disciples would be able to obey the Laws but that *many* would not be able.

However, the "door" could represent something other than obedience to the Mosaic Law. Considering the challenges Jesus made to conventional acceptance of Mosaic Law, there is no compelling reason to suppose that the "door" refers to strict adherence to Mosaic Law. The "narrow door" could mean living by Jesus' teachings, which, as we've seen, did not exactly advocate adherence to tradition. The narrow door could also mean "entering God's realm" which according to Jesus is "within." Since entering God's realm was the central idea in Jesus' mission, that "entry" is the most probable intended meaning of "getting through the narrow door."

The statement does not condemn the "many"; it only notes that many will fail – which could be true of practically *any* difficult enterprise. For example, many football teams will try to win the Super Bowl next year, but only one team will; many won't be able. Whatever the door is supposed to refer to, the aphorism is suggestive of maintaining focus and concentrating on a difficult task. The statement does not suggest that the listener (or reader) will fail – only that many will. The possibility of failure gives all the more reason to "struggle." The saying, in a way, is applicable to any difficult task. Any difficult task requires concentration and an awareness of the possibility of failure can act as a goad to keep a person "on task." The aphorism can be seen as a goad to what Buddhists call "right effort."

Traditionally, Jesus is thought to have established a "new covenant" in contrast to the "old covenant" of Mosaic Law. One catalytic aphorism contrasts old and new in a way that does *not* imply preference for the new.

> *"Nobody drinks aged wine and immediately wants to drink young wine. Young wine is not poured into old wineskins, or they might break, and aged wine is not poured into a new wineskin, or it might spoil."* *(Thom. 47: 3, 4)*

The passage on young and old wine in *Thomas* differs from this version in *Mark*:

> *"And no one pours new wine into old wineskins. Otherwise, the wine will burst the skins, and both the wine and the wineskins will be ruined. No, they pour new wine into new wineskins."* *(Mark 12: 22)*

*Mark's* version clearly emphasizes "new wine" and "new wineskins," probably because he wanted to suggest the "new covenant" of Christianity. *Thomas'* version may be closer to the original saying. In *Thomas* the saying acknowledges the aged wine as preferable to young wine and *then* points out the necessity of putting young wine in new skins and old wine in old skins. Hence the saying in Thomas is not about a "new covenant" superior to the "old" but rather is about a contrast between new and old in a general or abstract way.

What relevant meaning and application can be drawn from observation about the young and old wine? There are many references to wine in the Hebrew Scriptures. Wine was sometimes used to represent the negative consequences of drunkenness and sometimes to represent joy and merriment. "New wine" was generally used as a reference to abundant provision, while "old wine" was more likely to be associated with refined pleasure. The aphorism suggests that acceptance of new "abundance" requires the inner flexibility which characterizes new wineskins, while the old can be pleasant but pleasure from old ways cannot be sustained if one seeks new abundance with new flexible ways of thinking.

The saying seems to be pointing toward reflection on appropriateness: new skins appropriate for new wine, old skins appropriate for old wine. The wineskins may represent states of mind: attachment to old traditions vs. openness to new ideas. In that analogy, the wine would represent ideas or "spirits" (new vs. old). The point then could be something like "people who like old ideas won't be able to assimilate new ones; people who like new ideas won't be able to appreciate old ones." This interpretation is similar to but not identical with the "new and old covenants" interpretation.

In the Thomas version, the new is not recommended as superior, which probably means that it was *not* Jesus' primary intention to indicate the superiority of a "new covenant." To get the point of the saying is to understand something about the nature of the old and the new. The applications of such understanding would vary from case to case. Again, the aphorism serves as a catalyst for reflection rather than for specific advice or doctrine.

The wine and wineskin aphorism seems to imply "getting" something: new ideas or flexibility or understanding of the value of both old and new. Another aphorism says something about "having" and "getting":

*In fact, to those who have, more will be given, and from those who don't have, even what they do have will be taken away. (Mk. 4: 25)*

That aphorism about "having" was taken by singer-songwriter Billie Holiday to be about money. Her song "God Bless the Child" was inspired by the "having" aphorism and reflects a popular interpretation of the aphorism. The lyrics say in part: "empty pockets don't ever make the grade," "money you've got lots of friends . . . when you're gone and spending ends, they don't come no more," and "them that's got shall get, them that's not shall lose, so the Bible says and it still is news."

In *Mark*, the aphorism on "having" follows passages about not hiding light under a bushel and affirming that what is hidden will be revealed. *Mark* evidently took the aphorism as being about "letting your light shine." In contrast, *Matthew* uses the aphorism as an interpretation of the "parable of the talents," which on the surface is a parable about economics and "using your talents" rather than hiding them. Despite the different contextual settings, Matthew and Mark both indicate the saying is about *using* what you have – light or talents – not about merely "having or not having" per se.

Jesus clearly wanted people to "get" the importance of loving, trusting in God, and focusing on God's realm. He also clearly did not place much value on getting worldly wealth. In the context of what one should seek to get, Jesus' aphorism about "having" was probably not intended to be about having worldly wealth.

In the context of what Jesus taught, his disciples *could* have interpreted the passage as being a cynical statement about the economics of the world. Disciples could also have seen the aphorism as being about "entering God's realm," i.e. having "consciousness" of God, love, faith, and wisdom; in which case the saying would be about the importance of having that *consciousness*. In fact, the saying could be understood either way, both ways and other ways. The aphorism's ambiguity makes it another catalyst for reflection and insight.

Jesus' teaching on "asking and receiving" shows the "having" is not the only way of "getting" in his philosophy. A third way of "getting" in his philosophy is found in his emphasis on *producing*, which is seen in his seed parables. Related to his use of seed analogies is the simple observation that what is produced depends upon what is planted:

"*Since when do people pick grapes from thorns or figs from thistles?*" (Mt. 7: 16)

Figs and grapes were staples of the Mediterranean diet of that time; those fruits were valued for their pleasant flavor and, of course, grapes were also valued for wine. Why did Jesus relate the picking of figs and grapes to the unrelated idea of plants which produce thorns and thistles? That unusual conjunction is not at all an obvious idea, though the fact explicit in the question is obvious.

In *Matthew* and *Luke* the aphorism about figs and grapes is proximate to a saying about good trees bearing good fruit and bad trees bearing bad fruit. Relating the saying to "good and bad" trees is certainly a reasonable moral to draw from the saying. At the same time, one is left wondering about the figurative meaning of "good and bad" trees. What qualities of figs and grapes are supposed to be "good"? What qualities of thorns and thistles are "bad"? Are the trees supposed to refer to different kinds of *people* or to different kinds of *behaviors*? The answers to all such questions are left open to interpretation by the listener. Perhaps Jesus was saying that "prickly" people are not likely to bear "good fruit." Perhaps he was saying that "prickly" people are avoided by others.

Another possible interpretation is that the thorns and thistles represent ideas and teachings which lead to pain, while the grapes and figs represent pleasure. In other words, teachings and ideas which are painful to apply will not produce pleasure and fruitfulness. While Christianity has long emphasized the suffering of Jesus and Christian martyrs, Jesus himself thought of his teaching as producing love, joy, provision, and healing. Today more and more Christian ministries are emphasizing joy, "prosperity" and "positive thinking." Perhaps Christianity is ready to let go of emphasis on suffering and sacrifice and move on to the joy of finding God's realm.

In any case, the aphorism about grapes and figs is ambiguous; it can serve as a catalyst for reflection and insight.

Of course, Jesus' philosophy is not devoid of instruction regarding the nature of good. His advocacy of love and trust and his association of joy with entering God's realm make clear what his ideas of good are. Even so, it is up to the interpreter of his aphorisms to determine how Jesus' ideas of good are related to grapes and thorns and figs and thistles.

The ambiguity of Jesus' aphorisms is suggestive rather than didactic or specific regarding application. The specific applications of his catalytic aphorisms could in theory be as many as the individuals who seek to apply them. His sayings are relevant to common human desires, such as desire for friends, wealth, power, safety and fame. One aphorism in particular is relevant to the desires for fame, power and safety:

*A city built on a high hill and fortified cannot fall, nor can it be hidden. (Thom. 32)*

*Matthew* and *Luke* report only part of the saying found in *Thomas*; the two "synoptic" Gospels report Jesus saying, "a town on a hill cannot be *hidden*" (Matthew 5: 14), but say nothing about the town's invulnerability to *falling*. *Matthew* and *Luke* were both written after the fall of Jerusalem in 70 C.E. Jerusalem was a fortified city on a hill which fell, so perhaps *Matthew* and *Luke* recognized that Jesus was mistaken in the part of the saying they omitted: a fortified city on a hill *can* and *did* fall. In any case, both supposed qualities of a city on a hill are important for the effect of the saying.

Surely Jesus knew that Jerusalem had fallen several times in the past. In fact, Rome ruled Jerusalem during Jesus' lifetime. So why did he say a city on a hill cannot fall? Perhaps the key is the additional word "fortified." Yet surely Jerusalem was fortified in the times that it did fall. Perhaps Jesus was being ironic. Most of Jesus' sayings are intended figuratively rather than literally, so the saying about a city on a hill is probably not intended to be literally about building invulnerable cities.

Just to give one possible interpretation, suppose the saying to be about people of a certain type rather than literally about cities. If one supposes that the saying is about people, then a city on a hill could be about conspicuous and protected people. It may sometimes seem to us that very wealthy people and high officials in government and religion "cannot fall" (but of course, like cities on hills, they sometimes do) and they also cannot hide from the public. One of the biggest complaints of celebrities seems to be that it is difficult for them to go out in public. Celebrities have stalkers. There are disadvantages to being in the limelight. And while conspicuous power, fame and wealth usually offer some security in life, even the mighty *can* fall.

If one can accept the possibility that privacy and even anonymity can have advantages and prominence can have disadvantages, the saying suggests contemplation of that possibility. Such contemplation could lead to the realization that everything has its price; there are advantages and disadvantages to every position in life. Such a realization can help one accept with Stoic equanimity one's current conditions while at the same time remaining alert to risks and opportunities.

The city could also represent "consciousness." An interpretation of the saying in terms of consciousness would be: a high consciousness cannot be hidden nor can it fall. A high consciousness cannot be hidden – it naturally expresses through the one who has it. A high consciousness cannot fall – once one realizes God's realm, the lower consciousness loses all appeal.

While there can be disadvantages to fame, glory, wealth and power – and perhaps even to having a high consciousness - such attainments are often simply the result of people actualizing their potential. Some of Jesus' sayings promote actualizing one's potential. One example is this aphorism:

*"Since when is the lamp brought in to be put under the bushel basket or under the bed? It's put on the lampstand isn't it?"* (Mk. 4: 21)

This saying as found in Mark's Gospel is linked to the saying about "whatever is hidden is meant to be disclosed." However, in *Matthew* the same saying is linked to the sayings "You are the light of the world," "a town on a hill cannot be hidden" and "let your light shine before others, that they may see your good deeds and glorify your Father in heaven." The different contexts which Mark and Matthew use as settings for the "lamp" saying illustrate how freely Jesus' sayings were used and interpreted by early followers. Mark interprets the saying as being about revelation of what is hidden; Matthew sees the saying as an admonition to do good works to glorify God.

The saying is certainly about purpose: lamps are for the purpose of lighting a room so putting a lamp under a bushel defeats the lamp's purpose. The saying invites contemplation of one's purpose in life. The aphorism also raises a question with the uninterpreted symbol of the lamp and its light. What are the "lamp" and "lampstand" supposed to represent? What is the "light" which is meant to be shared?

Light is that by which things are seen. In terms of human experience, consciousness is analogous to light; consciousness is that by which things are seen. Lifting up one's consciousness to share what one sees is analogous to lifting a lamp up on a lampstand to share that by which things are seen.

Matthew's idea that the light represents "good works" is a reasonable interpretation; doing good works is a way of sharing one's consciousness. Mark's idea that the light is "revelation of the hidden" suggests the more common idiom of light as knowledge; sharing knowledge is a way of sharing one's consciousness. There is no good reason to reject one interpretation in favor of the other. There is also no good reason to prohibit any other interpretations. The quest for self-knowledge can be seen as a search for one's own "hidden light" which can be manifested in the world. That "light" can be shared in many ways.

Jesus and his disciples revealed their light by traveling from place to place, proclaiming the philosophy of God's realm. They were on a "road trip" to transform the world, just as Gautama and his disciples traveled to reveal the light of the Buddha. These dedicated spiritual travelers did not attempt to persuade everyone to adopt the life of the road. Householders could and did adopt the philosophies of Jesus and Gautama.

Some parts of Jesus' message were probably specifically meant for those who adopted the life of the road and may have had no relevance for householder disciples. For example, the following saying may have been meant as a description of the life of the spiritual traveler for those who considered adopting that life:

*Foxes have their dens and birds have their nests, but human beings have no place to lie down and rest. (Thom. 86: 1, 2)*

The saying may simply have been intended as information: if you adopt this way of living, you won't have a place to lie down; you won't have a home. There is an intriguing parallel to the saying in Plutarch's "*Life of Tiberius Gracchus*" describing the life of the homeless soldiers of Italy: "The wild animals that roam over Italy have every one a cave or lair to lurk in; but the men who fight and die for Italy enjoy the common air and light, indeed, but nothing else; houseless and homeless they wander about with their wives and children."[88]

Even though Jesus' saying *could* simply be a description of an adopted life-style, there are other possible ways of interpreting the saying. The saying is apparently counterintuitive: most human beings *do* have houses, usually more comfortable and well-appointed than the dens of foxes and nests of birds. On the other hand, human beings began as nomadic hunter gatherers and throughout history have exhibited a kind of restlessness. Tribes migrated. Armies of nations traveled to build empires. Today people frequently move to new locations. Even people who are the most settled, staying in the same house for decades, usually take time to vacate their homes for vacations. Many people stay at one job for most of their lives, hoping to eventually retire and *travel*.

From a spiritual perspective, human restlessness is a quest to "go home" to God. The idea of going home to God may mean for some their destination in the "after life." For the mystically inclined, "going home to God" means going within to find one's connection to the divine and to "live from" that center. From the mystical perspective, one is never truly alive until one finds one's center in God.

*"Follow me, and leave it to the dead to bury their own dead."* *(Mt. 8: 22)*

How can the dead bury the dead? The paradox is obvious in this saying, unless Jesus was talking about zombies. The only way to make sense of the saying is to interpret the "dead" figuratively. The "dead" could mean those who are not in touch with God's realm, those who are not alive to spiritual reality. Are the dead who are to be buried also those who are not spiritually alive or are they the literally dead? If both groups of the dead are understood to be not literally dead but figuratively spiritually dead, then what does it mean that the first group is to bury the second?

This catalytic aphorism calls for reflection upon what it means to be "truly" alive as well as upon what it means to be dead. It is also related to the quest for happiness. Happiness is not easy to define, but certainly happiness includes satisfaction with life. When people feel fully alive and live life to the fullest, they are happier than when they are simply resigned to tedium or are just going through the motions. A person obsessed with death is already dead in the figurative sense of "not fully alive." And so we come full circle, back to the saying which began this section:

*"Whoever discovers the interpretation of these sayings will not taste death." (Thomas 1).*

Any and all of the catalytic aphorisms of Jesus can be the basis for meditative experience, if you seek to know the interpretation by contemplating the saying, as a Zen student would contemplate a Zen koan.

Meditation is related to prayer. Prayer may be thought of as a starting point for meditation. Meditation may be thought of as deep prayer. Next we will consider what Jesus said about prayer and research related to the benefits of prayer, meditation, and hypnosis.

# Chapter Eight: Prayer, Meditation, and Hypnosis Research

## *Jesus on Prayer*

Jesus taught, "ask and you will receive." Prayer is one of the ways people ask for things. There are more ways of asking for things than prayer and prayer can be more than just asking for things.

There is a story about a young man who came to Socrates for guidance. The young man was contemplating marriage and wondered if it was wise. Socrates reportedly replied: "If you get a good wife, she will make you happy. If you get a bad wife, you will become a philosopher which is good for any man. Therefore by all means, get married."

But we all know that seeking a spouse for the sake of being married can make a person miserable without making them a philosopher. Likewise, a child can ask for harmful things such as too much candy. One can ask for things that are not ultimately beneficial to the seeker. One can ask for what seems good but proves to be troublesome.

Scientific studies of prayer in relation to healing indicate that the relation between prayer and healing is difficult to assess scientifically. Some experiments show that prayer can affect the health of humans and other organisms. Other experiments indicate no effect from prayer. Before reviewing some of the scientific evidence, let us review what Jesus taught about prayer.

Jesus offered guidance regarding what to request in prayer. Spiritual teachers almost inevitably create prayers, which are, in effect, guidance regarding what one ought to seek. This "ought" is connected to the teacher's idea of piety and morality. However, prayer can have a practical dimension as well.

Jesus' advice regarding prayer certainly can be seen as having dimensions of piety and morality. At the same time, his recommended prayer can also be seen as ultimately practical in the context of his whole philosophy. The prayer as rendered by the Jesus Seminar is a bit shorter than the liturgical "Lord's Prayer" found in Matthew (See Mt. 6: 9-13 and Lk. 11: 2-4). The following is my own slightly altered version of the Jesus Seminar version:

*"Father, let your name be revered. Let your realm arrive. Give us our daily bread. Forgive us to the extent that we have forgiven. Don't test us; deliver us from evil."*

Each sentence of the prayer can be thought of separately as a distinct request; actually, in terms of the mood of the verb, each "petition" is a *command*. In the context of Jesus' teachings, each "petition" can be understood as an affirmation of what Jesus held to be already true.

Why did Jesus pray for God's name to be revered (or "hallowed" in the normative English translation)?

In Hebrew the word for "name" in some contexts can refer directly to God. Generally a name was thought to refer to one's "reputation" and therefore to the very nature of the person named. The Hebrew word for "hallowed" signified that something was dedicated to God and was pure or "clean." Hence what is generally translated as "hallowed be thy name," here rendered "let your name be revered," suggests a description of God's nature: "Your nature is pure" (or "sacred"). The prayer "Father, let your name be revered" also suggests that "Father" is the appropriate name of God, describes God's character and is sacred. Thus the first prayer affirms God's nature as Father and sacred; in meaning it is roughly equivalent to simply saying "Holy Father." It is a way of bringing one's attention to the nature of God. In effect, Jesus was telling his disciples to ask for awareness of the "Holy Father."

"Let your realm arrive" ("thy kingdom come") is an invitation for God's realm or presence to enter the awareness of the one praying and/or the world in general. Since Jesus affirmed that God's realm is already present "within you," the prayer is an opening of one's *awareness* to that already present Divine Realm. In effect, Jesus was telling his disciples to ask for God's presence and rule to enter their consciousness, which is practically the same as the first "petition." The first two petitions or "commands" may be thought of as two ways to say the same thing or as one request which could be paraphrased as: *Holy Father, enter my consciousness* or *Holy Father, establish your realm in my awareness.*

As we will see, Jesus affirmed that entering God's realm (or having God's realm enter our awareness) is an experience of joy worth more than any earthly good. If we take it that all people in all their seeking are really looking for happiness, then this prayer is the ultimate practical prayer from Jesus' perspective. Find God's realm and you will find the joy you seek.

*"Give us our daily bread"* is a command that God give us all we need; "bread" figuratively refers to sustenance and life itself, as seen in the *Gospel of John* when Jesus refers to himself as "the bread" (John 6: 48). The figurative use of the word "bread" in the ancient world was similar to use in American slang, with "bread" and "dough" sometimes meaning "money."

In the context of Jesus' teachings, as we've already seen, Jesus believed that God supports our lives, provides for our need and for the needs of all creatures and even "clothing" for fields of grass. Hence the command is really *an acknowledgement of what Jesus took to be a truth* rather than a begging for some lack to be filled.

In much the same way "forgive us to the extent that we have forgiven" is affirmed elsewhere as a truth in Jesus' philosophy: "forgive and you will be forgiven." Again, in the context of Jesus' philosophy, the prayer is an "asking for" something that is already a "given."

What are we to make of the final "petition": *"Don't test us; deliver us from evil"?* Is it also a petition for something already given? The only "testing" ("tempting") that occurs in the gospels is the story of Jesus being tested/tempted by *Satan*. Nowhere does he suggest that *God* tests us. Perhaps the *Letter of James* gives us a window into Jesus' own belief on this point: *"When tempted, no one should say, "God is tempting me." For God cannot be tempted by evil, nor does he tempt anyone; but each person is tempted when they are dragged away by their own evil desire and enticed."* (James 1: 13-14) Furthermore, in Jesus' philosophy, God is consistently portrayed as loving Father who provides all we need, even if we are "evil" or "unjust." The most probable interpretation of the "petition" "don't test us; deliver us from evil" is that it is again an asking for what Jesus takes to be a given: God does not test us; God delivers us from adversity.

To summarize: the "Lord's Prayer" may be taken as guidance to *request or "command" God to do what God already does.* The prayer, though in the imperative mood, can be understood as being in the declarative mood, i.e. as a series of affirmations of what is already true. The best things to ask for are what the Father already gives. The prayer can be understood as saying:

*"Holy Father, your realm and rule is present. You give us all we need. You forgive us to the extent that we forgive others. You do not test us; you deliver us from evil."*

Is there therapeutic value in praying as if one is affirming God's will in contrast to praying as if one is petitioning God to do one's own will? There is in fact a spiritual tradition which does treat prayer as affirmation of the truth about God. The related traditions of Christian Science, New Thought, Religious Science and Unity all teach "affirmative prayer," i.e. affirm the Divine Truth, such as that God is good and all that comes from God is good. The adherents of all those traditions claim that affirmations are therapeutic spiritually, psychologically and physically. They further claim that one can use affirmations to help achieve success and prosperity. This approach is known to the general public as "positive thinking." The evidence that affirmations "work" is primarily anecdotal, but the anecdotes are myriad, consisting of thousands of testimonials which can be found in the literature of the different organizations.

The claim here is not that Jesus taught people to use affirmations. A more accurate way to state the case is that Jesus incorporated into prayer what he believed to be true about God and God's realm/rule. Hence the prayers he taught were, in *effect* if not in form, affirmations of what he already believed. In effect, he did not teach prayer as a way of *persuading* God to be good; rather, he taught prayer as a way of *acknowledging* that God is good.

The phrase in the prayer that expresses the spirit of the whole prayer is (in the usual translation of *Matthew*): "thy kingdom come, thy will be done on earth as in heaven." Seen as an affirmation, this is the prayer of a mystic, the prayer of one who believes or perceives that God is already present, already good, and that all we need is to perceive that God's realm is already present. "Father, your realm and rule has already arrived, your will is already done on earth as in heaven." This is a "non-directed" prayer, a prayer that asks only the realization of God's presence. Prayer research indicates that non-directed prayer is often more effective than "directed" prayer, which seeks specific results.

Having considered how Jesus' approach to prayer and how his sayings could induce meditative states, we need to consider some of the research that has been done on prayer, stress, hypnosis and meditation to understand how Jesus' philosophy could have had a healing effect.

## Prayer Studies

Jesus taught his disciples to pray. His fundamental approach was to "pray for" what he already perceived to be true: that God is to us as an unconditionally loving Father; that God's realm is already present; that our Father can be trusted to provide for our daily needs; that we are forgiven to the extent that we forgive; and that God does not test us. His prayers for others may be understood as his holding an intention that they be healed and a beholding of the presence of God in and all around them. We are told that his prayers healed not only those who were within his physical reach, but even, in at least one case, a person far distant from him (Luke 7: 1-10, John 4: 45-54).

Can prayers and thoughts of healing intention have a healing effect? I suspect that the question cannot be answered definitively by scientific method. First of all, while prayers can be spoken aloud, prayer is fundamentally *internal*; it is a mental or "soul" action which cannot be directly observed in the way physical events can. If "faith" is necessary, that introduces another unobservable element. How could the faith of those praying be objectively determined? Secondly, there are many ways to pray and some may be effective and others ineffective. In any given experiment some participants may pray effectively and others may not; the mixture of effective and ineffective prayers would hinder obtaining optimal results. Thirdly, conditions for effective prayer may not be limited to the ones who are praying; it may be that recipients of prayer must also be receptive to results. There may be "unconscious," "cosmic" and "spiritual" factors unknown and inherently unobservable to us which affect the outcome of prayer.

On the other hand, despite the obstacles to precise scientific measurement of effects of prayer, experiments have been constructed which indicate that prayer can have scientifically measureable effects. One physician-philosopher, Larry Dossey, has made a career of bringing to public awareness scientific studies indicating that prayer can indeed affect people near and far. The studies cited by Dossey also indicate that prayer can affect plants, bacteria, and cells.

Dossey was especially impressed with the experimental approach of the Spindrift organization. Bruce and John Klingbeil, the founders of Spindrift, devised a number of controlled double-blind experiments in which participants prayed for mold, seeds and other simple organisms. Researching prayer for simple organisms has experimental advantages over researching prayer for humans: possible effects on simple organisms are directly observable and simple organisms are less physically complex than humans. Also, I presume, simple organisms do not have the psychological complexity of humans. The results of the experiments indicated that simple organisms thrived more quickly and fully when prayed for.

Spindrift also tested two approaches to prayer, labeled "directed" and "nondirected." "Directed" prayer uses words and visualizations to intentionally direct the outcome. "Nondirected" prayer does not seek a specific outcome but instead attempts to maintain a "pure and holy qualitative consciousness of whoever or whatever the patient may be."[89] "Nondirected" prayer focuses on the presence of the divine, with an attitude of "thy will be done," as exemplified in the prayer of Jesus. Spindrift experiments found that the nondirected approach worked significantly better than the directed approach. The outcome of nondirective prayer "is always in the direction of 'what's best for the organism.'"[90]

Prayer practitioners of the metaphysical movement (New Thought, Christian Science, Spindrift, et al.) do not regard distance as an obstacle to effective prayer. That is also true of many who call themselves "psychic healers" and "non-contact therapeutic touch healers." Because of their denial of distance as a hindrance, researchers have frequently bundled together these different approaches to healing when studying "distant healing." For example, in his article "Prayer and Healing" Dossey cited experiments on distant healing performed by William Braud and Marilyn Schlitz. The Braud-Schlitz experiments used practitioners of different systems. Dossey summarized the results of the Braud-Schlitz research:

"In thirteen experiments, the ability of sixty-two people to influence the physiology of 271 distant subjects was studied (William Braud and Marilyn Schlitz, 1983, 1988, 1989). These studies suggested that (1) the distant effects of mental imagery compare favorably with the magnitude of effects of one's individual thoughts, feelings, and emotions on one's own physiology; (2) the ability to use positive imagery to achieve distant effects is apparently widespread in the human population; (3) these effects can occur at distances up to twenty meters (greater distances were not tested); (4) subjects with a greater need to be influenced by positive mental intent − i.e., those for whom the influence would be beneficial − seem more susceptible; (5) the distant effects of intentionality can occur without the recipient's knowledge; (6) those participating in the studies seemed unconcerned that the effect could be used for harm, and no such harmful effects were seen; and (7) the distant effects of mental intentionality are not invariable; subjects appear capable of preventing the effect if it is unwanted."[91]

Several things should be noted about this summary of results: (1) positive mental imagery seems to have been the primary method used, indicating that "nondirected prayer" was not significantly tested; (2) distances over 20 meters were not tested; metaphysical healers claim that there are *no* distance limitations on prayer; and (3) effects can occur without recipients knowing that they are being treated, but recipients can also prevent unwanted effects. Those three facts indicate some of the difficulties in testing the effects of prayer, especially when "prayer" is bundled with other approaches described as "distant healing."

A meta-analysis of research on the efficacy of "distant healing" provides another example of bundling different approaches and drawing conclusions from the bundling. The authors of the study made no distinction between approaches and also bundled in experiments with design flaws. As a consequence of the research the authors included in their meta-analysis, their review in effect showed that some experiments yielded significant effects and others did not. The authors concluded that there was not sufficient evidence to prove the effectiveness of distant healing. However, because 57% of the investigations they reviewed showed "statistically significant treatment effects," the authors also concluded that the "evidence merits further study." A more useful approach would have been to separate out the different types of "distant healing" and examine only well-designed studies to see which approaches were most effective.[92]

Overall, research on prayer and "distant healing" indicates that: prayer has some measurable positive effects and so it can be practical to pray; our mental intentions may affect others, including non-human organisms; and prayer without specific goals can still have positive effects.

Besides the effects that may occur for those who receive prayers, prayer affects the one who is praying. I have no studies to cite for this claim; however, from personal experience and the reported experiences of hundreds of my students and congregants, I know that prayer can bring peace and reduced stress to those who pray.

## *Anxiety Reduction and Health*

Stress is a contributing factor to a wide range of human illnesses. Discovering ways to regulate and defuse excessive stress is an important area of health research. Dr. Theodore VanItallie, Professor Emeritus of Medicine with the Columbia University College of Physicians and Surgeons, wrote that "despite all the problems involved in this area of investigation, evidence continues to accumulate that stress – particularly chronic stress – may give rise to, or worsen, a number of illnesses."[93]

The same article lists some of the illnesses to which extreme or chronic stress can be a contributing factor. Dysregulation of the stress system is known to be a contributive causative factor in a variety of illnesses, including: depression, post traumatic stress disorder, diabetes, Grave's disease, fibromyalgia, rheumatoid arthritis, peptic ulcer, hypertension, atherosclerosis, osteoporosis, and immune dysfunction.[94] Clearly, it is important for effective health care to find ways of coping with and reducing stress.

A study titled "Don't Worry, Be happy" reported that "increased positive affect was protective against" coronary heart disease. The study was a large population (1739 participants) 10 year survey of coronary heart disease incidents as related to positive and negative emotions (affect). "Positive affect" was defined as "the experience of pleasurable emotions such as joy, happiness, excitement, enthusiasm, and contentment."[95] "Negative affect" was defined as emotions such as depression, anxiety, and anger.

The authors wanted to know if worry and depression were related to incidence of heart disease and if being able to experience positive affect helped prevent such incidents. The authors concluded that their results indicate that "preventive strategies may be enhanced not only by reducing depressive symptoms" ("don't worry") "but also by increasing positive affect" ("be happy").[96]

Stress, worry, and anxiety are interrelated; it is just not yet clear *how* they are interrelated. Are "worry" and "anxiety" two words for the same psychological state? Precise clinical definitions can probably technically discriminate between the words "worry" and "anxiety" as referring to different psychological states or habits. However, "worry" and "anxiety," insofar as both involve thoughts and feelings of negative expectancy associated with physical tension, are similar enough to be considered interrelated factors contributing to what are generally regarded as stress related illness.

Do worry and anxiety cause stress or are they effects of stress? Even if worry and anxiety were often *effects* of stressful *conditions*, it is undoubtedly true that worry and anxiety exacerbate stress. What is more, since different people respond to the same conditions in different ways, stress is probably a result of both conditions and of how individuals involved respond mentally and emotionally to those conditions. What is stressful for one person can be exhilarating to another. Worry, anxiety and stress are best thought of as interrelated in a "feedback loop."

The worry-anxiety-stress "feedback loop" is counterproductive to health, and methods are needed to diminish or break the "loop" to improve health and cure illness. One way to counter "negative" feelings would be to find methods to increase the opposite "positive" feelings. Perhaps drugs provide a partial solution, but drugs usually have negative side effects; approaches which do not involve drugs would be preferable.

A number of different types of therapies for stress have been shown to be effective. The technology of biofeedback, the spiritual practice of meditation, physical exercise, dietary changes and even laughter have all shown promise for coping with stress.

Jesus was not a meditation teacher or hypnotherapist in the modern sense; yet there is reason to believe that his way of expressing his philosophy induced "meditative states" in his followers. The style and content of Jesus' sayings indicate similarities with some methods of hypnosis, and reflection on his sayings might have induced states similar to those produced by meditation methods.

Jesus' philosophy counseled "do not worry" and promised supreme joy as a result of following his way to enter the realm of God. Jesus' sayings show evidence of humor, which could also have provoked stress relieving laughter. His was a philosophy likely to induce "positive affect": faith, optimism, peace, love, and joy.

## Therapeutic Effects of Hypnosis and Meditation

Research on meditation practices indicates that they have significant effect on reduction of stress and anxiety. Research on hypnosis and autohypnosis indicates similar results. Meditation and hypnosis have similar effects on brainwaves and physiology. Meditation generally aims also at promoting spiritual values. Hypnosis generally has specific psychological aims, but also has proven therapeutically effective for some somatic and psychosomatic symptoms. Research indicates that there is no significant difference between meditation and hypnosis in associated physiological and subjective states.[97]

Supposing his sayings could induce meditative or hypnotic states and that the content of his sayings "suggested" positive affect, what could Jesus' sayings accomplish?

To see the possibilities, we need only consider what is known about what modern hypnotherapy has accomplished. We now know, for example, that some forms of blindness are psychosomatic and can be cured with hypnotherapy.[98] There are several early stories of Jesus curing a blind man. Consequently, it does not stretch credulity to suppose that Jesus cured a psychosomatic case of blindness by means of suggestion.

In fact, the category of psychosomatic "conversion disorder" can result in symptoms which were reportedly healed by Jesus. Conversion disorder occurs when psychological stress results in physical symptoms. According to the Mayo Clinic:

> "In conversion disorder, your leg may become paralyzed after you fall from a horse, even though you weren't physically injured. Conversion disorder signs and symptoms appear with no underlying physical cause, and you can't control them. Signs and symptoms of conversion disorder typically affect your movement or your senses, such as the ability to walk, swallow, see or hear. Conversion disorder symptoms can be severe, but for most people, they get better within a couple of weeks."[99]

The Mayo Clinic site also lists seizures or convulsions, inability to speak and hallucinations as possible symptoms of conversion disorder. Practically every illness cured in the healing stories about Jesus could have been caused by conversion disorder and so could have been cured, in theory, by hypnosis. One exception is found in resurrection stories such as that of Lazarus. Conversion disorder does not cause psychosomatic coma or psychosomatic death.

Beyond the case of conversion disorder, hypnotherapy has been used effectively in many ways. It is well established that in general terms hypnotherapy "can be used to relieve anxiety and pain during childbirth, as an anesthetic during surgery, to reduce stress, to promote healing, and to control habitual behavior."[100]

Research indicates that hypnosis can help with pain reduction and control for obstetrics, surgery, dentistry, metastatic breast cancer, and in laboratory experiments.[101] Hypnotherapy has also been used effectively on: atopic dermatitis in adults and children[102]; asthmatic patients[103]; migraine sufferers[104]; warts[105]; and at least one study indicated the possibility that hypnotherapy can have a positive effect on the immunological system.[106]

An article in the *American Journal of Clinical Hypnosis* pointed to evidence that hypnotic suggestion can: block skin reaction of poison ivy-like plants; give rise to localized skin inflammation with pattern of previously experienced burn; cure warts; ameliorate congenital ichthyosiform erythrodermia ("fish skin disease"); and stimulate the enlargement of the mammary glands in adult women.[107] (I doubt that last result would have been even considered in Jesus' time.) Many of the skin conditions that can be cured with hypnotherapy would have been called "leprosy" in Jesus' era.

It is probable that, besides inducing brief trance states, the content of the sayings and stories of Jesus invited extended contemplation of his sayings by his original followers to discern meaning and acquire understanding. Such contemplation is likely to have resulted in meditative and altered states of consciousness for some.

Jesus' stories and sayings "stuck with" people, which is why we still have records of the sayings today. Considering the innumerable different interpretations of Jesus' sayings that have been published since the beginning of Christianity, it is clear that Christian clergy and Christian mystics have done extensive contemplation of his sayings. The likelihood of Jesus' followers experiencing meditative states is sufficient reason to consider the known benefits of meditation.

A 2003 meta-analysis of meditation research defined "meditation" as "a family of practices that train attention and awareness, usually with the aim of fostering psychological and spiritual well being and maturity."[108] The family of practices uses a variety of focal points for training attention and awareness: passages from scripture, sacred names, points within the body, riddles (Zen), and the "flow of mind" itself. Hypnosis also "trains attention and awareness with the aim of fostering psychological" well being, if not "spiritual well being" and is in that way very similar to what is called meditation.

The 2003 meta-analysis of meditation research provides a description of the benefits of meditation supported by research. Among the benefits cited in the report are:

> "effective intervention for: cardiovascular disease (Zamarra, Schneider, Besseghini, Robinson, & Salerno, 1996); chronic pain (Kabat-Zinn, 1982); anxiety and panic disorder (Edwards, 1991; Miller, Fletcher, & Kabat-Zinn, 1995); substance abuse (Gelderloos, Walton, Orme-Johnson, Alexander, 1991); dermatological disorders (Kabat-Zinn, Wheeler, Light, Skillings, Scharf, Hosmer, & Bernhard, 1998); reduction of psychological distress and symptoms of distress for cancer patients (Speca, Carlson, Goodey, & Angen, 2000); and reduction of medical symptoms in both clinical and non-clinical populations (Reibel, Greeson, Brainard, & Rosenzweig, 2001; Williams, Kolar, Reger, and Pearson, 2001; Kabat-Zinn, Lipworth, Burney, & Sellers, 1985)."[109]

The article also mentions studies indicating that meditation can "produce improvements in" self-actualization, empathy, happiness, improvements in reaction time, school grades, learning ability, recall and creativity.[110]

Many of the cited studies probably require better experimental design and further research to be considered "conclusive." However, the sheer number of possible benefits indicates that accessing human potential through altered states of consciousness has a significant upside with untapped therapeutic possibilities.

The 2003 study also cited the physiological effects of meditation including: improvement in immune system functioning, relaxation, reduced respiration rate, increased skin resistance, and enhanced alpha theta EEG power.[111] Measured effects of meditation have consistently shown an increase of alpha wave amplitude in the brain.[112]

Even if contemplation of Jesus' sayings was not a discipline as formalized as meditation and hypnosis, there is reason to believe that such contemplation produced altered states of consciousness. Still today people contemplate Jesus' sayings, trying to understand what they mean. When a story "sticks" with a person, it indicates that the person has thought about the story to some extent. In my experience, remembering a clever story or thinking about a surprising saying can lead to a relaxed "meditative" state as easily as contemplating a sacred mantra or prayer.

If, as seems likely, Jesus' sayings induced meditative or "self-hypnotic" states in some of his listeners, that supports the hypothesis that his philosophy had a healing effect.

## The Practice of Meditation

Jesus noticed a principle of expansion at work in the universe, which he described in the parables/metaphors of seeds and leaven. In interpreting those metaphors, we must think of seed and earth and leaven and flour all as symbols of the idea and energy of God's realm and rule. All the ideas Jesus spoke of or symbolized are part of God's realm, i.e. the universe, which may also be conceived of as the universal energy field and laws which govern it. The laws that govern the universe are the equations/ideas which give direction and form to the universal energy.

One of the most practical applications suggested by interpretation of Jesus' philosophy is focusing mental energy on ideas, as the earth focuses energy on seeds. Like seeds, ideas expand in mind when we focus the energy of our thoughts and attention upon them. Creative individuals in any field – politics, business, invention, the arts – are individuals who focus their attention on ideas related to their fields. They succeed because they use imagination and reason to build up an idea and then do the work necessary to bring the idea into expression. If the idea appeals to a significant segment of the population, the creative work results in an increase of wealth for the creator.

Likewise, focusing mental energy on ideas of health can help those ideas expand in mind and body to increase vitality and even cure illnesses. Studies of hypnosis, biofeedback and meditation have provided evidence for the therapeutic value of focusing on ideas of health.

Recall the statement of Elmer Green on the placebo effect: "Humans, through visualization, are able to self-trigger physiological behaviors . . . . The placebo, by definition, is something false by means of which a patient is tricked into using his or her own visualization powers for physiological manipulation."

Vivid visualization triggers physiological changes. We need not think of hypnosis, visualization and meditation as "false" and "trickery." The use of mind for healing the body is well established; we just do not yet have a mechanistic explanation. The explanation may be that the universe consists of an information system and that, when we think, we are sending information to receptors in the body. It is also possible that a biological feedback loop involving brain and nervous system will ultimately provide a "physical" explanation for mind-body cause and effect. Whatever the explanation, there are well-established techniques for using mind to heal the body. We can apply that "technology" even if we do not yet have a full physical or metaphysical explanation.

Recall a situation in which you experienced a strong emotion, and you will to some degree re-experience the emotion; the emotion involves corresponding physiological changes such as change in heart beat, blood rushing to the face, etc. The imaginative recall of previous emotional experiences is the most common way people experience the effect of imagination on physiology. The more vividly and frequently you imagine something, the more you experience the corresponding physiological changes.

In yoga, chakras are thought of as energy centers which are associated with the various organs and functions in the body and also with a process of illumination. There is a similar system in the teachings of Charles Fillmore, co-founder of the Unity School of Christianity. Fillmore developed a "Twelve Powers" system with chakra-like physiological centers associated with spiritual qualities such as love, faith, wisdom, etc. Other mystical and esoteric schools have similar systems. These systems are used to focus mental energy on ideas and into body centers.

Jesus did not teach a "chakra" like system, but his affirmation that God's realm is within us and his comparisons of that realm to seed growing in soil is suggestive of inward focus. Jesus' philosophy suggests that God's realm is within us as seeds which expand when properly nurtured. We nurture these divine seeds by focusing the energy of our attention and thoughts upon them. Where in the body are these divine seeds? We may think of the divine seeds as potentials present behind or within *every* point in the body. In effect, applying what is suggested in Jesus' philosophy, we may choose any point in the body as a point of focus and associate that point with any idea we choose.

I have been practicing meditation since 1975 and have experimented with a number of techniques, including Fillmore's system and yogic chakras. My experience in the inner realm tells me that, since the divine potential is everywhere, we may use any developed meditative system and get satisfying results. By "developed meditative system" I simply mean a system developed within an established spiritual or esoteric tradition. Such systems have provided satisfying results for many generations of students and so may be considered reliable.

Here is a simple form of meditation which can be used by anyone to focus mental energy for health in the body. The meditation utilizes ideas suggested by Jesus' philosophy.

## Sit

Most traditions that have prayer or meditation also have traditional postures for prayer or meditation. Some of the asanas of Hatha-Yoga, such as the lotus position, are intended as postures for meditation. There is no recommended posture for prayer in the philosophy of Jesus, so a disciple of Jesus can use any posture that feels appropriate for contemplation of ideas. Jesus' original disciples may have contemplated his sayings while praying in the traditional prayer postures of the time, while sitting and listening to him, while sitting alone in a quiet place, or even while walking.

Since meditation involves an extended period of concentrated attention, the important thing about posture is that it is comfortable and not distracting to the mind, yet not so comfortable that one simply falls asleep. It is also possible to meditate while one is walking, as long as one is walking in a familiar space which has minimal distractions. If you have never practiced meditation, the simplest thing to do is sit upright in a comfortable chair with your hands on your lap in a comfortable position. At the start, in order to stay alert, it is probably best to use a straight back chair rather than an easy chair. Put your feet flat on the floor.

## Breathe

It is helpful at the outset of meditation to focus your attention on your breathing. In this way you can easily begin to focus your attention inward, not only into the body but also into the mind itself. While meditation teachers offer a variety of methods of breathing to begin meditation ("take three deep breaths" etc.), I have found that I can enter a relaxed state by simply observing my breathing for a few moments and *allowing* it to take on a natural rhythm and depth. Jesus did not give breathing directions to his disciples (as far as we know); so if they did pay any attention to their breathing, they would have done what felt natural for them.

## Focus

Once you feel relaxed and comfortable, think about the idea that God's realm is within you as centers of energy and light or as seeds of limitless Divine Potential. You may find it helpful to simply form an image of seeds growing into "trees of life" within you. Or you may prefer to imagine tiny spheres of energy and light within your body and think of those points as radiating light and energy into every part of your body. As you visualize your body filling with light, think of yourself as having an aura of divine light all around you. I would recommend focusing only on one "divine seed" or "energy-light sphere" at a time. If you do not have a preference regarding where to begin, you might choose one of the traditional centers taught in Yoga, Unity and other systems, such as the solar-plexus, heart, throat, or center of the brain.

The healing stories about Jesus suggest giving directions to your body or using affirmations. You can imagine a point of light within your body and think into the point of light: "Be whole and clean" or "I am whole and clean." You can repeat "the Lord's Prayer" or parts of it as a way of focusing your attention. You can simply affirm "The realm of God is within me." You need not stick to words literally spoken by Jesus. You can use statements such as: "The Infinite Energy of the Universe flows through me." Or even more simply, use a short phrase you associate with divinity, such as "Divine Love." In the beginning just repeat one phrase thoughtfully, as if to let it unfold its meaning, light and power within you.

Using this simple method for about 15 or 20 minutes per day, you will eventually experience meditative states which involve health supporting physiological changes. It should not take more than three weeks to notice these inner states and begin reaping their benefits.

The best way to learn to meditate is to take classes, where a meditation practitioner can offer you support and instruction. However, I am confident that the method described above provides sufficient instruction for most people to begin meditating in a way that brings satisfying and healthful results.

# Chapter Nine: Self Knowledge and Transformation

When we consider Jesus' philosophy in its entirety, it becomes clear that his philosophy aimed at personal and social transformation. That Jesus had a transforming impact on individuals and society is simply a historical fact. His disciples were transformed from fishermen, farmers and tax collectors into spiritual teachers and "community organizers." His disciples started a new religion which eventually became the primary religion of the Western world and then spread to have a significant impact in Asia. The fact that the "Jesus Movement" became a world religion rather than a school of philosophy does not negate the concept of Jesus as "philosopher," as will be seen in the discussion of parallels between Jesus' teachings and those of philosophers of his era.

Historically the social aspect of Jesus' philosophy has been more widely discussed than the philosophy's therapeutic value for the individual. Emphasis on Christian charity, involvement in political causes, and various theories about Jesus' "social gospel" over the centuries all attest to the attention given to the social aspect of Jesus' philosophy.

The New Testament describes Jesus and his disciples as practicing a communal economy. They shared "all things in common" (see Acts 2: 44 and 4: 32). The first recorded such communal economy was the Pythagorean community (ca. 500 BCE). Later (ca. 150 BCE) the Essenes had a similar system. Unlike the communalism of the Pythagoreans and Essenes which required initiations and were merit based, Jesus promoted an egalitarian communalism which shared food and resources with all who chose to participate. Jesus is described as having meals with a variety of people on numerous occasions. He is described as consorting with people who were classed as inferior or "unclean": lepers, prostitutes, tax collectors, and "sinners" of all sorts.

Although Christian communal meals were eventually reduced to the sacrament of the Eucharist, at least in the first generation the movement was practicing and modeling a democratic and egalitarian communalism. The communal model provided by early Christians was difficult to implement beyond a limited local level and ultimately survived only in the form of monasticism and occasional communal

Christian experiments. The Greeks invented democracy as a form of government; the spirit of inclusive love and egalitarianism in Jesus' philosophy was compatible with democracy, even though the church has not always supported that spirit "in his name."

The fact that Jesus had a transformational effect on individuals and cultures shows that his philosophy was transformational. This is not to deny that his consciousness, personality and life were important elements of his impact on the world; it is only to affirm that his message expressed his consciousness and had effects on his followers. Jesus' philosophy of personal and social transformation was coherent with his metaphysics and ethics. In fact his metaphysics and ethics were important aspects of his transformational impact.

First, the ontological and cosmological implications of Jesus' teachings would fundamentally change a disciple's *"ontological self-image."* A shift in self-image is inherently transformational. By *"ontological* self-image" I mean what one believes about one's ultimate being and possibilities, in contrast to *personal* self-image which is what one believes about one's current human expression and conditions.

Self-image determines to a great extent the individual's feelings and behaviors. Successfully changing one's self-image can have a truly transformational effect.[113] The self-image suggested by Jesus' teachings is fundamentally positive and differs radically from the self-image suggested by the prevailing religion of his place and time.

The ontological self-image suggested by most of the religious and some philosophical systems of Jesus' era is that of a very vulnerable self at the mercy of fate or the stern judgment and painful punishment of a demanding Creator. That type of religious belief has, to a great extent, prevailed in Christianity up to this day due to the inability of later generations of Christian converts to entirely release the older beliefs. Some disciples of Peter's and Paul's generation were, for the most part, able to adopt Jesus' concepts of God and self and thought of themselves as having a powerful and benign "holy spirit."

Jesus' teaching that God is our "Father" implies that we must be essentially divine and spiritual. If we are in some essential way offspring of the divine, then there must be a "divine core" present in our nature. As God unconditionally loves and accepts us, according to Jesus' teaching, we must also have the capacity to love as "the Father" loves. The self-image suggested by those ideas is a self embraced by divine love and imbued with divine power and limitless possibilities. The certainty of early Christians, reflected in Paul's letters, that they had spiritual power and were loved by God reflects the original teaching of Jesus. To the extent that Jesus' ideas of the Fatherhood of God and "the Kingdom within" took hold in his listeners, their ontological self-images would have been transformed in an empowering and comforting way.

The self-image suggested by Jesus' philosophy was different from the self-image suggested by the era's prevailing views of God. While the idea of God as Father did not originate with Jesus, it was also not the *primary* idea of God in the Judaism or philosophy of Jesus' time. Judaism was focused on God as *King* and *Judge* and humans as *subjects* of God's rule and judgment. Some philosophies of the era also emphasized God as judge of human souls, ready to inflict punishment. The concept of God as *unconditionally* loving in Jesus' philosophy does not appear in other major belief systems of the era; the God concept of the era demanded obedience in order to receive the blessings of divine benevolence.

Jesus' disciples ultimately could not shake the idea of divine wrath and consequently portrayed Jesus in the Gospels as speaking of divine retribution. However, scholarly analysis of the Gospels indicates that Jesus himself did not speak of judgment day; such sayings are not well attested and contradict the logic of sayings that can reliably be attributed to Jesus.

Jesus' ethical teachings were also transformational. The adoption of Jesus' ethical ideas would involve a transformation of a disciple's character, thinking, and acting. Jesus taught an ethic distinctly different from both the Jewish legalism and the various Greek philosophies of his era. The ethics of the era either involved following a set of rules or cultivating a set of virtues. His ethic did not reject rules but he did rationally critique them, indicating that the rules were not the absolutes of moral goodness. The only ethical virtue emphasized in Jesus' ethic was universal benevolence. The ethic was simple, clear, uncomplicated and probably psychologically liberating in a way that knowing and obeying a list of rules cannot be.

His ethic set disciples free to be egalitarian, inclusive and democratic in their associations. The new ideal for relationships was put into practice by Jesus and his followers and had a transformative effect on society. Though the transformative effect may have diminished with each passing generation, the ideals remained alive and have acted as catalysts for social reform over the centuries.

Jesus "converted" people to a different way of perceiving the world and being in the world. Conversion – whether to a religion or a philosophy – usually results in character and moral transformation in some sense (for better or for worse). The effects of conversion on a person's character, state of mind and behavior is amply illustrated in the numerous cases of different types of conversion collected by William James for his 1901 lectures on the varieties of religious experience.

Jesus' philosophy also included practical suggestions for psychological and material well-being. He emphasized *faith* in God's benevolence, mercy, and generosity. The healing power of faith is verified by the placebo effect and is probably the reason that "relics" and pilgrimages sometimes seem to produce cures.

Jesus emphasized various aspects of love. The health benefits of love and forgiveness were noted in Chapter 6, "Ethics and Healing." If Jesus had only effectively taught love and faith to people it would have been sufficient to have some therapeutic value for those who adopted his philosophy. However, there were other important transformational elements in the philosophy of Jesus.

## Five Keys to Transformation

In addition to thinking of oneself as God's offspring, practicing love and trusting God, Jesus' philosophy also indicated at least five other keys to personal transformation. The five keys are:

(1) Focus on God first;

(2) Use of catalytic aphorisms;

(3) Pursuit of humble self-knowledge (e.g. *"get the log out of your own eye"*);

(4) Cultivation of non-attachment (e.g. *"it is easier for a camel etc."*); and

(5). Use of one's gifts (e.g. *the parable of the talents*)

The first two keys, "focus on God first" and catalytic aphorisms, have already been discussed in chapters three and seven, respectively. Here the other three keys will be discussed.

### Pursuit of Humble Self-Knowledge

*"When you know yourselves, then you will be known, and you will understand that you are children of the living Father. But if you do not know yourselves, then you live in poverty, and you are the poverty." (Thomas 3: 2)*

The above saying, recorded in *Thomas*, was not chosen by the Jesus Seminar as being an authentic saying of Jesus. I quote it here because it reflects one of the primary concerns of philosophy after Socrates: pursuit of self-knowledge. Even if Jesus did not make this reference to the importance of self-knowledge, I believe the nature of his catalytic aphorisms demonstrates that facilitating self-knowledge was one of his aims. If Jesus had simply intended to convey information or rules for living, his style would have been didactic. Instead, his style was elusive and allusive; his sayings provoke questions and reflection. His sayings generally direct his disciples' attention inward to their own minds. I suspect that there are many more authentic sayings of Jesus in the *Gospel of Thomas* than scholars have supposed; but even if one rules out *Thomas* as a source of authentic sayings, the canonical Gospels contain most of the catalytic aphorisms.

At least one saying of Jesus' is clearly a call to his disciples to know themselves:

*"Why do you notice the sliver in your friend's eye, but overlook the timber in your own? How can you say to your friend, 'Let me get the sliver out of your eye,' when there is a timber in your own? You phony, first take the timber out of your eye and then you'll see well enough to remove the sliver from your friend's eye."* (Mt. 7: 3-5)

This passage calls upon people to stop trying to "fix" others and instead focus upon "fixing" themselves. "Taking the timber out of your eye" may be taken to mean "clear out of your mind what is obstructing your perception of God's realm."

The passage is a clear example of Jesus' sense of humor. Exaggeration is one of the primary ways humans express their sense of humor. Exaggerated imagery surprises and often provokes laughter. The image of having a timber in one's eye while trying to remove a sliver from another's eye is a classic example of humorous exaggeration.

The word translated as "phony" is the Greek word for actor from which the English word "hypocrite" is derived. It is likely that he used the word for humorous effect rather than as an insult. He was inviting people to look at the "acting" they were doing to hide their true nature.

Jesus recognized that people play roles in public life. He recognized that just because a person had a particular station or office in life did not necessarily indicate that the person was trustworthy. His awareness of the deceptiveness of position is expressed in a saying about "scholars":

*Look out for the scholars who like to parade around in long robes, and insist on being addressed properly in the marketplaces, and prefer important seats in the synagogues and the best couches at banquets. (Mk. 12: 38, 39)*

The scholars or scribes were the educated class who sustained the industry of preserving literature and letters. They performed a crucial function for government, religion and business. In his warning Jesus did not condemn people for being scholars. He did not even criticize scholars in general. The warning is specific: watch out for *ostentatious* scholars who expect special treatment. Why should we be wary of ostentatious people who expect special treatment? Perhaps we should be wary because their behavior indicates self-seeking rather than seeking the public good.

The saying can also be taken as a warning to notice one's own behavior. In that sense, it can be taken as a guide to self-knowledge. The saying suggests questions to ask oneself: am I self-seeking? Do I "parade around" to show off? Do I expect people to address me properly? Am I a pompous blowhard?

The quest for self-knowledge is psychologically and often physically therapeutic. The whole endeavor of psychoanalysis is a quest for self-knowledge; the hope of psychoanalysis is that the patient will be helped or cured by becoming conscious of unconscious material. Psychosomatic symptoms are sometimes cured by the psychoanalytic process. Likewise, hypnotherapy can be a tool for self-knowledge for psychological and psychosomatic therapeutic purposes. Jesus' catalytic aphorisms may well have been therapeutic in the same way that psychoanalysis and hypnotherapy can be therapeutic.

The warning to watch out for status conscious people also reflects the social purposes and inclusive spirit of Jesus' philosophy. The antithesis of an inclusive spirit is elitism. Elitism is inherently exclusive; when there are elite people there are classes. Once hierarchical classes are established, "lower" classes are often excluded from access to wealth and power. Status conscious people thrive in elitist systems. Consequently, communities seeking to have an inclusive spirit need to be cautious about the motives of people who relish and seek status.

## Cultivation of Non-Attachment

Like status, wealth and poverty are relative to each other and to culture. A person considered wealthy in one culture might be considered impoverished in another. A "poor" American might well be considered "rich" by people in impoverished lands. The wealth required to acquire a 2,000 square foot home in Manhattan is usually at least ten times as much as is needed for 2,000 square feet in Missouri. The struggling American "middle class" could be considered "poor" relative to America's upper 1%. Whether one considers oneself "rich" or "poor" might well be at least partly a matter of personal perspective. And that perspective *can* be that "money isn't everything; I am rich in other ways."

In Jesus' time there was practically no "middle class"; there were a few very wealthy people while the vast majority lived at a subsistence level or worse.    First century Palestine was an "under-developed, agrarian economy based primarily on the production of food through subsistence-level farming by the peasantry." Peasants made up 90% of the population.   City-dwelling absentee landlords were common.[114]   It is well to keep this in mind when considering Jesus' sayings about the "rich" and the "poor."   At least 90% of his audience would have been "poor" in economic terms.

*"How difficult it is for those who have money to enter God's realm! It's easier for a camel to squeeze through a needle's eye than for a wealthy person to get into God's realm." (Mk. 10: 25)*

In Christian circles a couple of explanations have circulated regarding the expression "camel to squeeze through a needle's eye." One explanation that circulates is that the "needle's eye" was a name for a low gate into Jerusalem.   That interpretation is baseless; there was no "needle's eye" gate in Jerusalem's walls.   Another less well known explanation is that "camel" is a copyist error; the original word was "rope," which in Aramaic is very similar in spelling and pronunciation to "camel."   That explanation is more plausible than the "Jerusalem gate" theory.   Both explanations fail to note that Jesus was simply using humorous exaggeration to make a point.   Even if he said "rope," he was using a humorous image; personally, I find "camel" funnier than "rope."

The saying's main point remains, regardless of which explanation one accepts:   it is very difficult, nearly impossible, for wealthy people to "enter God's realm."   Perhaps human desire for wealth is behind attempts to divert attention from the main point of the saying by focusing on the camel and needle's eye.

Why should it be so difficult for wealthy people to enter God's realm?   We have seen that, according to Jesus, entering God's realm is a matter of focusing on love, generosity, trusting in God instead of in wealth, and putting God before greed.   Focusing on getting rich distracts attention from spiritual efforts. We have seen that in Jesus' philosophy God's realm is not a future place but an inner state. God's realm is a state of mind rather than a state of money.

In the history of philosophy and religion there have been many movements which emphasized rejection of the worldly value of wealth. The Pythagoreans, Essenes and early Christians had the economic equality of communal property. In a society in which wealth is shared there are no rich or poor in the relative quantitative sense. Another way to characterize members of commune is that all are "poor" in the sense that none own personal property. All could also be characterized as "rich" since each owns the property of all; the cumulative economic resources of 100 "poor" people would increase the resources of each member. A saying (which probably did not originate with Jesus) summarizes the nature of a communal situation in terms of wealth:

*"And everyone who has left houses or brothers or sisters or father or mother or wife or children or fields for my sake will receive a hundred times as much . . ." (Matthew 19: 29)*

Cynic philosophers and early Christian hermits practiced independent self-reliant voluntary poverty as a means to spiritual freedom. Some Hindu yogis, Buddhist monks and Christian monastics reject worldly wealth in favor of spiritual advancement. Jesus' comments about wealth are in alignment with the attitudes of all these philosophical and religious perspectives.

On the other hand, neither Judaism nor Christianity espouses voluntary poverty as *necessary* for spiritual well-being. In fact many modern Jews and Christians interpret acquisition of wealth as a sign of God's favor. Somehow Christians have justified worldly success as desirable and communal living as undesirable despite sayings and example of the founder. Jesus' philosophy encourages detachment from and sharing of wealth and discourages pursuit of wealth for its own sake.

Nevertheless, some of Jesus' sayings appear to provide keys to worldly success. His saying about "asking and receiving" does not place limits upon "how much" one can request from others or from God. His "parable of the talents" seems to advocate using what one has as a way to increase one's wealth. Furthermore, a few of his parables hold up the generosity of rich men as being admirable: the father of the prodigal son; the generous vineyard owner; the master who (initially) forgives the equivalent of a ten million dollar debt; and the man who invites people off the street to a feast. How could one emulate the behavior of those wealthy men without first becoming wealthy? How can one "give to one who begs" if one has nothing to give?

Although he adopted a Cynic-like lifestyle, Jesus does not appear to have insisted upon that lifestyle except for the disciples who went out to proclaim the "good news" of God's realm. The voluntary poverty of Jesus and some of his disciples was relative to their wandering preaching mission; they relied upon the resources and generosity of householders in the towns to which they traveled. They may also have had a community treasury, as suggested by passages describing Judas as the keeper of the funds (John 12: 6).

According to Acts, Jesus' disciples held all things in common. The early followers of Jesus probably adopted a communal approach to property, similar to the systems of the Pythagoreans and Essenes. Those who traveled with the message probably organized such groups in the towns they visited. Those who had no personal property because they were part of a communal property arrangement would also be "poor." Hence, a dedicated rich person could give his or her property to the community and thereby become one of the "poor" while increasing the wealth of the community as a whole.

Jesus' attitude toward wealth was probably ultimately more like the Stoic than the Cynic attitude. The Cynics disparaged wealth; the Stoics attempted to practice non-attachment to wealth, even if they happened to be wealthy. The Stoics did not value accumulation of riches; on the other hand, they affirmed that one's life work could result in wealth. By Stoic standards the point was to be *detached* from worldly wealth, even if you could not help becoming rich. They believed one could use wealth and power for good as long as one was not attached to wealth and power.

The vast majority of Jesus' audience would have been, relatively, the "poor." He may have had a few wealthy followers. The "poor" who might have felt stigmatized by their relative poverty might well have felt some relief in hearing that they were "blessed" while the rich would have difficulty entering God's realm. There may have been some "therapeutic value" in whatever relief, uplift or encouragement the "poor" might have felt from Jesus' sayings about the rich and poor. If the early movement shared wealth, that also might have had an anxiety and stress relieving effect on the relatively poor.

In order to persuade people to non-attachment, Jesus had to point out the "downside" of attachment to wealth and the "upside" to non-attachment to wealth.

In one short parable Jesus points out the futility of placing too much confidence in one's wealth:

*"There was a rich person who had a great deal of money. He said, 'I shall invest my money so that I may sow, reap, plant, and fill my storehouses with produce, that I may lack nothing.' These were the things he was thinking in his heart, but that very night he died."* (Thom. 63: 1-3)

The saying "you can't take it with you" is an appropriate moral for the parable of the rich man who died. The abrupt ending of the parable is shocking and the abrupt surprise could be considered an ending either tragic or humorous, depending upon one's point of view. Ordinarily, it is not funny when a person dies; but when the person is fictional and not particularly a sympathetic character, the fictional death *could* provoke laughter. Effective humor is as much a matter of timing of delivery as of content. A slight pause before saying, "he died" could be enough to surprise the audience and provoke (perhaps uncomfortable) laughter.

Regardless of how one responds to the story emotionally, the point seems to be that accumulated wealth has no lasting value. The story raises the question of ultimate value: is there *any* pursuit in life that has lasting value? One answer given by Jesus or his early followers is to "store up treasures in heaven" through acts of love and generosity:

*"Do not store up for yourselves treasures on earth, where moths and vermin destroy, and where thieves break in and steal. But store up for yourselves treasures in heaven, where moths and vermin do not destroy, and where thieves do not break in and steal. For where your treasure is, there your heart will be also."* (Matthew 6: 19-21)

Luke's version of the saying emphasizes specifically giving to the "poor" as a way to store up heavenly treasures:

*"Sell your possessions and give to the poor. Provide purses for yourselves that will not wear out, a treasure in heaven that will never fail, where no thief comes near and no moth destroy. For where your treasure is, there your heart will be also."* (Luke 12: 33-34)

Since accumulation of wealth was a low priority or "non-priority" in the philosophy of Jesus, one might expect parables in which characters pursue wealth to end badly for those characters. Sometimes that expectation is fulfilled; sometimes not. The following parable ends badly for a character seeking wealth:

> "*A person owned a vineyard and rented it to some farmers, so they could work it and he could collect its crop from them. He sent his slave so the farmers would give him the vineyard's crop. They grabbed him, beat him, and almost killed him, and the slave returned and told his master. His master said, 'Perhaps he didn't know them.' He sent another slave, and the farmers beat that one as well. Then the master sent his son and said, 'Perhaps they'll show my son some respect.' Because the farmers knew that he was the heir to the vineyard, they grabbed him and killed him." (Thom. 65: 1-7)*

The parable as found in *Thomas* is the simplest version and so probably closest to the original. *Mark's* expanded version of the same parable concludes with Jesus saying, "*What then will the owner of the vineyard do? He will come and kill those tenants and give the vineyard to others.*" (Mark 12: 9)

In both *Matthew's* and *Luke's* versions, Jesus asks the same question, but it is the audience that gives the reply: "*He will bring those wretches to a wretched end, and he will rent the vineyard to other tenants, who will give him his share of the crop at harvest time.*" (Matt. 21: 40-41) *Matthew* and *Luke* probably used a version recorded in *Q*, since their versions are practically identical with each other, but differ slightly from *Mark's* version. The implied conclusion to be drawn from the Synoptic versions is that Jesus is the son who will be killed and those who kill him will be punished.

However, it should be noted that the parable does not support the theology developed by the church about Jesus' death. First of all, the father is not like Jesus' or the later church's concept of God: the father in the story is not compassionate, generous, all-knowing or all powerful. He is unable to impose his will, short-sighted, and doesn't seem to care about the suffering of others. Secondly, the theology of the church is that Jesus' death was redemptive; his death was a payment for sins so that people could be forgiven. The parable does not have a redemptive conclusion. The son is not resurrected and no one is forgiven. In the synoptic versions, the story ends with death and then in a conversational epilogue the *punishment* of those responsible for the son's death. However, the ending of Thomas' version is stark and shocking: the "wicked farmers" apparently get to keep the land!

All versions of the parable agree in basic outline: a landowner sends out servants to collect crops; the servants are beaten; the landowner sends his son to collect, thinking the farmers will respect his son; but the farmers kill the son.

In the parable's literal content, the landowner cares more about collecting his crops than he does about the safety of his own son. The parable is a tragedy for both son and father, partly caused by the cruelty of the farmers, but also partly caused by the father's obsession with collecting his profits. The parable is structured like a classic tragedy: the main character has a fatal flaw, in this case an obsession with collecting profits regardless of possible costs; the fatal flaw results in tragic consequences. The parable as originally told probably was not a theological allegory but a tragedy, intended to make a point about consequences of heedless profit seeking. The man's persistence does not gain him what he wants; instead he suffers loss of something precious – his son. This is a parable about misplaced priorities. It demonstrates that making wealth as one's top priority can result in tragic consequences.

According to Jesus' teaching, non-attachment to wealth helps one avoid tragic consequences. His teaching on non-attachment aims at shifting people's perspectives from the view that wealth is a blessing to the view that having a consciousness of owning nothing is the ultimate blessing. By thinking of oneself as owning nothing, one gains everything: the entire realm of God, the universe itself. This, at any rate, is a plausible interpretation of the beatitude of poverty: *"Fortunate are you poor! God's realm belongs to you."*

*Luke* follows this beatitude with two more surprising blessings: *"Fortunate are you hungry! You will have a feast. Fortunate are you who weep now! You will laugh." (Luke 6: 20-21)*

The blessing on the hungry is perfectly logical from one point of view: only someone who is hungry *can* have a feast; those who are full *cannot* have a feast. Jesus' audience may have understood the blessing as a future promise, but that does not mean he intended it that way. He may have intended it as a simple observation: only the hungry can have a feast and in that sense the hungry are fortunate.

Jesus may also have had spiritual meanings in mind for these sayings. Matthew's version of the "Beatitudes" speaks of hungering and thirsting for righteousness or justice (5: 6). Matthew may have modified the original simpler versions of the Beatitudes to help readers understand the spiritual meanings. Instead of the stark "those who weep shall laugh," Matthew gives a possible spiritual interpretation: "those who mourn shall be comforted" (5: 4).

The blessing on those who weep could also have been a simple observation: those who weep now will also laugh – at some point. A study of the relationship between crying and laughing would be interesting and possibly revealing about human nature. A link between laughing and weeping is suggested by the fact that it is difficult to tell from sound alone whether someone is laughing or sobbing. Laugh hard enough and you can end up shedding tears. Both crying and laughing may be cathartic if they involve physiological release of pent up emotions. Since the psychological and physiological effects of crying and laughing are similar, there could be a deeper emotional link between the ability to laugh and the ability to cry. Mark Twain claimed that the secret source of humor is sorrow, so he certainly saw a psychological link between laughing and crying. Perhaps Jesus intuitively grasped such a link too and meant to suggest the link in his blessing for those who weep.

The sayings can be understood as reflecting the fleeting nature of temporary conditions: sometimes we are hungry and sometimes we feast; sometimes we weep and sometimes we laugh. This alternation of temporary experiences is in fact part of the Jewish wisdom tradition found in Ecclesiastes:

> *"For everything there is a season, and a time for*
> *every purpose under heaven:*
> *a time to be born, and a time to die;*
> *a time to plant, and a time to pluck up what is*
> *planted;*
> *a time to kill, and a time to heal;*
> *a time to break down, and a time to build up;*
> *a time to weep, and a time to laugh . . ."*
> *(Ecclesiastes 3: 1-4)*

Since conditions including wealth are temporary, it is not wise to be emotionally attached to conditions. This is the essence of non-attachment in spiritual and philosophical teachings: there is something more important than temporary earthly conditions and possessions. That "something more important" varies from one religion and philosophy to another. Estimates of the something of greater value have included happiness, virtue, enlightenment, and knowledge of God. In Jesus' philosophy "entering God's realm" is the "something more important" than temporal conditions; and entering God's realm brings joy.

The practice of "non-attachment" includes the idea of "letting go" or "emptying oneself" of worldly thoughts. A parable found only in the Gospel of Thomas expresses that perspective of "emptying oneself":

*The Father's rule is like a woman who was carrying a jar full of meal. While she was walking along a distant road, the handle of the jar broke and the meal spilled behind her along the road. She didn't know it; she hadn't noticed a problem. When she reached her house, she put the jar down and discovered that it was empty. (Thom. 97:1-4)*

The Jesus Seminar concluded that the parable of the woman with the jar was an authentic saying of Jesus, even though it is only found in *Thomas*. The parable fits the style of Jesus, illustrated for example in the "mustard seed" parable: a giant tree as the common metaphor for divine power was reversed by representing divine power with a common shrub. In the woman and jar parable images in biblical stories are reversed. The parable reverses the imagery of the popular stories about poor widows' jars miraculously filling up because of the words of Elijah and Elisha. Instead of jars filling up, Jesus compares God's realm to a woman's jar emptying.

A parable about "emptying" from the Cynic tradition provides insight into the meaning of Jesus' parable about the woman with the jar:

*"It's like this. Some merchants ran their ship aground on a reef. Since they could not budge it in any way, they went away lamenting. So, when robbers, without understanding the problem of these men, sailed up with an empty ship, they freely loaded cargo, and at once transferred the cargo from the strange ship, unaware of the calamity as they made the transfer. For as the one ship emptied, it started to float and become seaworthy. But the ship taking on the other's cargo quickly sank to the bottom because of the robbery of foreign goods. This can always happen to the person who has possessions. But the Cynics have stood apart from all of these things. All of us possess the whole earth."[115]*

Emptying one's life of possessions was seen by the Cynics as a way to freedom and to being "godlike." For the Cynics, since God needs nothing, to be free from needs and anxieties about possessions is to be godlike. For the Cynics, only by owning nothing can one possess everything. The parable of the woman with the jar fits perfectly with the Cynic philosophy regarding possessions, which suggests that Jesus wanted to convey a similar philosophical idea with his woman and the jar parable.

Jesus' philosophy of non-attachment to biological family, old traditions, and wealth extends even to non-attachment to ideas of self: *"Whoever tries to save his soul will lose it, but whoever loses his soul will save it."* *(Lk. 17: 33)* This is a shockingly paradoxical saying, and fits the category of "catalytic aphorisms," which was discussed in chapter 7.

Jesus spoke of losing one's *soul* (*pseuche*); traditionally the word "pseuche" in the saying has been translated as "life." In all New Testament passages translated as "soul" the Greek word is "pseuche." A different Greek word ("zoe") is usually translated as "life."

The conventional translation of the saying misleads the reader into thinking Jesus was talking about martyrdom. The conventional translation encourages a radical shift in consciousness; willingness to give up one's life would certainly involve a radical shift from the instinctive desire to preserve one's life. The self-preservation instinct is very strong and not easily "overridden" by willing self-sacrifice.

In historical retrospect, because many early Christians were martyred, it is understandable that the church interpreted the saying as being about martyrdom. However, the overall philosophy of Jesus is optimistic and non-violent; his original audience would have little reason to believe that following Jesus would result in martyrdom. Nor is there a call for martyrdom as a way to "enter God's realm" in other authentic sayings of Jesus.

The saying is about a radical shift in consciousness, but not necessarily the shift from pursuit of self-preservation to pursuit of martyrdom. The concept of martyrdom was not foreign to Jesus' original audience, but neither was it a primary theme of any of the major religious sects of the time. Neither the authentic message nor historical context of Jesus' sayings suggests that he was calling his disciples to martyrdom. It is therefore reasonable to consider alternative ways of seeing the saying about "losing and saving one's soul."

Even translating "pseuche" as "soul" probably does not convey the original meaning to the modern mind since the meaning of the word "soul" has changed over the years. In Greek and Hebrew the word "soul" encompasses all aspects of perception and feelings. In Greek philosophy going back at least to Plato, the soul was also thought to include rational thinking. Originally the concept of soul referred to individual awareness or what we today usually call "consciousness" or "self." In Hebrew and Greek the "soul" is that in humans which could feel sorrow, fear or joy; in soul resided the powers to see, hear, love, "sin" or do good works. One could "say" something to the soul, indicating the "self" as distinct from "consciousness," yet in some contexts "soul" means roughly the same as "self."

What could it mean then to try to save the soul and lose it or lose the soul to save it? The word "save" means "preserve" or "hold on to." To try to preserve one's consciousness would be to hold on to one's usual ways of perceiving, feeling and acting. To "lose" one's consciousness would be to let go of habitual ways of perceiving, feeling and acting. In other words, hanging onto one's soul is resistance to changing one's consciousness; letting go of one's soul is willingness to change one's consciousness. "Letting go of consciousness" can be understood as ceasing to rely exclusively on conscious rationality and will to cope with life, thereby opening to a "Higher Mind." Most forms of mystical meditation seek such a "letting go," as does the use of hypnosis to unlock "unconscious resources." Interpreted this way, the saying encourages an attitude of openness to radical internal change. The way to "save" one's "soul" or consciousness is to remain open to change.

It is also worth noting that the saying contains a kind of circular paradox. "Whoever seeks to save his soul will lose it." Yet having lost his soul, that person would meet the criteria in the saying to save his soul: "whoever loses his soul will save it."

### Using Your "Talents"

The English word "talent" has an etymology linking it to one of Jesus' parables and before that to a specific measure of weight. Jesus did not use the word "talent" to mean "ability" or "special gift"; nevertheless, the parable of the talents is about the use of abilities. Influenced by the parable, the modern use of the English word "talent" originated sometime in the late Middle Ages.[116]

The value of a "talent" has significance for understanding the parable and there are a couple of ways to get a sense of the monetary value of the talent. In Jesus' time the Roman talent was a weight equal to about 71 pounds; in Palestine it was equal to about 130 pounds. In Jesus' parable of the talents, a talent would have been about 130 pounds of silver. In the parable three servants are given talents; one receives five talents, another gets two and the last gets one. To get a sense of the value of silver today, I looked up the value of a pound of silver on the internet on July 18, 2012. The estimate given was about $435. Hence a Palestinian talent of silver today could be worth around $56,550; two talents could be worth $113,100 and five talents could be worth $282,750.

Another measure of the value of a talent in Jesus' parables would be to estimate its value to the people who lived in that time. In Jesus' time a silver coin was equivalent to a day's working wage and a talent was the equivalent of about 6,000 silver coins. The silver coin was basically the daily minimum wage of its time. In 2013 Federal minimum wage was $7.25/ hour. Hence minimum wage for 8 hours would be about $58. A talent of silver in Jesus' time would mean as much to the workers of his time as $348,000 (58 x 6,000 = 348,000) would to a worker today. Two talents would be worth $696,000 and five talents would be the equivalent of $1,740,000.

The point is that the parable involves large amounts of money. The servant who buried his talent in effect buried somewhere between $56,000 and $350,000, depending upon the method you use to assess its worth. The large amount he buried in the ground helps us understand why his master gave the coins to a more competent servant. The translation of the parable which follows simply uses the amount of silver coins involved rather than attempting to estimate the values in dollars.

*"You know, it's like a man going on a trip who called his slaves and turned his valuables over to them. To the first he gave 30,000 silver coins, to the second 12,000, and to the third 6,000, to each in relation to his ability, and he left.*

*Immediately the one who received 30,000 silver coins went out and put the money to work; he doubled his investment. The second also doubled his money. But the third, who had received the smallest amount, went out, dug a hole, and hid his master's silver.*

*After a long absence, the slaves' master returned to settle accounts with them. The first, who had received 30,000 silver coins, came and produced an additional 30,000, with this report: 'Master, you handed me 30,000 silver coins; as you can see, I have made you another 30,000.' His master commended him: 'Well done, you competent and reliable slave! You have been trustworthy in small amounts; I'll put you in charge of large amounts.'*

*The one with 12,000 silver coins also came and reported: 'Master, you handed me 12,000 silver coins; as you can see, I have made you another 12,000.' His master commended him: 'Well done, you competent and reliable slave! You have been trustworthy in small amounts; I'll put you in charge of large amounts.'*

*The one who had received 6,000 silver coins also came and reported: 'Master, I know that you drive a hard bargain, reaping where you didn't sow and gathering where you didn't scatter. Since I was afraid, I went out and buried your money in the ground. Look, here it is.' But his master replied to him: 'You incompetent and timid slave! So you knew that I reap where I didn't sow and gather where I didn't scatter, did you? Then you should have taken my money to the bankers. Then when I returned I would have received my capital with interest. So take the money away from this fellow and give it to the one who has the greatest sum.'" (Mt. 25: 14-28; cf. Lk 19: 12-24)*

The moral of this parable is pretty obvious: use your abilities to make the most of what you have or you might lose what you have. It is reminiscent of Jesus' saying, *". . . to those who have, more will be given, and from those who don't have, even what they do have will be taken away. (Mk. 4: 25)* A shorter expression of the moral of the story could be "use it or lose it."

The style of the parable reflects Jesus' style. The large amounts of money involved reflect his penchant for hyperbole, as seen for example in the large amount of debt forgiven in the parable of the "unforgiving slave" (Matthew 18: 23-34). Jesus liked to surprise his audience and there are a couple of surprising turns in the parable. The comical foolishness of a slave burying a large sum of money in the ground is surprising. The master taking the money from the "incompetent slave" is a bit of a surprise; it makes "business sense" but seems harsh. The master in the parable is not forgiving or generous as are some characters in Jesus' other parables. Jesus' listeners might have expected more compassion at the end of the parable.

It would be a mistake to think that all fathers, rich men, and masters in Jesus' parables represent God the Father. Jesus portrayed the Father as forgiving and generous. When a character reflects the "heavenly" nature of God the Father, it is reasonable to interpret the character as illustrating the heavenly character. When a character does not reflect Jesus' descriptions of the Father, the character must represent something else.

Jesus' parables can be thought of as sometimes being illustrations of the way the world is and sometimes as being illustrations of the realm of God. The distinction is important and not that difficult to discern. The parable of the judge who is reluctant to give a widow justice is far different from the father who embraces his prodigal son. The judge is worldly; the father is "heavenly." Or again, the master who is willing to forgive a million dollar debt is markedly different from the master who takes money from an incompetent slave. The forgiving master is like the forgiving father, heavenly; the master who takes money away is worldly. The master in the talent parable probably represents something like the way of the world rather than the heavenly Father.

There is a theme of "fruitfulness" or "usefulness" in Jesus' philosophy. The parable of seed sown on different kinds of soil (Mark 4: 3-8) focuses upon the relative fruitfulness of the different soils. The parable of the talents fits this theme in a different way. The theme of fruitfulness seems to be aimed at encouraging the audience to be productive, to make use of their abilities. This aspect of Jesus' philosophy could be called "motivational."

There are two other sayings which are related to the theme of "usefulness":

*"Since when is the lamp brought in to be put under the bushel basket or under the bed? It's put on the lampstand isn't it?"* (Mk. 4: 21)

*"Salt is good. But if salt loses its zing, how will it be renewed? It's no good for either earth or manure. It just gets thrown away."* (Lk. 14: 34-35)

It is unlikely that Jesus intended the saying about lamps to be *just* about lamps. Light is universally understood as a symbol for knowledge and enlightenment. The saying suggests that hiding your knowledge, abilities and resources is useless to you and everyone else, while sharing that "light" makes it useful to you and everyone else. The saying fits with Jesus' admonition to not be timid as well as with his parable about using your "talents."

The symbolic meaning of salt is not as universally recognized as the symbolism of light. Salt was seen as adding enjoyment to life from its use as a seasoning. Ritual food for holy feasts often included salt and food offered to divinities was enhanced with salt to make the offering pleasing to the deities. Salt was used ritually in Egyptian, Greek and Roman religions as part of offerings to deities; Judaism, Hinduism, Jainism and Shintoism also have some rituals which use salt.

Regardless of what symbolic meaning we might ascribe to salt, the saying equates goodness with usefulness. In that way, like the lamp illustration, the saying stands as another example of the idea that what makes something relatively "good" or "bad" is its *usefulness*. Taking into account the talent parable, the lamp example and the salt example Jesus' philosophy is salted with a definite Utilitarian flavor.

# Chapter Ten: Jesus on Human Potential and On Himself

*Jesus on Human Potential*

The idea of humans being offspring of God implies a divine potential in humanity. Jesus' ideas about the nature of that potential are implied in his teachings. He taught that we have the potential to love universally and unconditionally, like "our Father." His parables suggested potential for enlightened usefulness. Sayings attributed to Jesus suggest that through faith *anything* is possible.

There are many sayings attributed to Jesus which indicate that there is "light" within the children of God (human beings in general). Light is archetypally representative of enlightenment and divine presence. To have light within oneself suggests having a divine potential. The Jesus Seminar scholars do not consider most of the "light" sayings as original to Jesus, for a variety of reasons. The only saying involving light that the scholars agreed was authentic is the saying about putting a lamp on a lampstand.

However, there is good reason to believe that Jesus made some other references to "inner light" even if we cannot be certain about the form of the sayings. In addition to the saying about the lamp discussed previously, there are at least 13 other sayings about inner light ascribed to Jesus in the Gospels of Matthew, Luke, John and Thomas:

*"You are the light of the world." (Matt. 5: 14)*

*"Let your light shine before others." (Matt. 5: 16)*

*"The eye is the lamp of the body. So, if your eye is healthy, your whole body will be full of light." (Matt 6: 22 and Luke 11: 34, probably from Q)*

*"He was a burning and shining lamp, and you were willing to rejoice for a while in his light." (Jesus referring to John the Baptist, John 5: 35)*

*"I am the light of the world." (Jesus referring to himself, John 8: 12 and John 9: 5)*

*"While you have the light, believe in the light, so that you may become children of light." (John 12: 36)*

*"I have come as light into the world." (John 12: 46)*

*"When you are in the light, what will you do?" (Thomas 11: 3)*

*"There is light within a person of light, and it shines on the whole world." (Thomas 24: 3)*

*"If they say to you, 'Where have you come from?' say to them, 'We have come from the light, from the place where the light came into being by itself, established itself, and appeared in their image." (Thomas 50: 1)*

*"If one is whole, one will be filled with light, but if one is divided, one will be filled with darkness." (Thomas 61: 5)*

*"I am the light that is over all things." (Thomas 77: 1)*

*"Images are visible to people, but the light within them is hidden in the image of the Father's light." (Thomas 83: 1, 2)*

Of the above sayings, the saying most likely to be authenticly from Jesus (though not so designated by the Jesus Seminar) is: *"The eye is the lamp of the body. So, if your eye is healthy, your whole body will be full of light; but if it is not healthy, your body is full of darkness"* (Luke 11: 34). The saying in *Matthew* and *Luke* is from *Q*. *Thomas* has a similar saying (61:5), the only differences being *Thomas'* version does not include "the eye is the lamp of the body" and speaks in terms of being "whole" or "divided" rather than in terms of "healthy/not healthy eye." Note that the word "healthy" can be and has been translated as "single," which is closer in meaning to *Thomas'* "whole." The double attestation of *Q* and *Thomas* indicates that some version of the saying was very early and could have originated with Jesus.

The saying about the eye has some markers of Jesus' style. Jesus typically used concrete imagery and the passage refers to the eye, which is a concrete image; the "whole" and "divided" of Thomas is abstract and probably is a modification for the purpose of interpretation. Modification for interpretation is typical of Gospel authors, as for example when Matthew added the phrase "in spirit" to the beatitude "blessed are the poor," which was retained in the original form by Luke. Also Jesus generally spoke figuratively rather than literally. The saying about a "healthy eye" could easily be seen as figurative, since a "body full of light" is not easily understood literally. "Eye" could represent the way you "see" and "look at" things *mentally*. In that case, the saying is about mentally "seeing" things in "healthy" or "unhealthy" ways.

What could be the meanings of "a body full of light" and "a body full of darkness"?

Perhaps some of the sayings in *Thomas* shed light on the meaning of the "healthy/unhealthy eye" saying. Either Jesus or some of his early followers believed that *"we have come from the light, from the place where the light came into being by itself."* In other words, our true being is self-existent divine "light."

The notion that we are really "beings of light" has an interesting parallel in the modern scientific understanding. From a scientific viewpoint there is a sense in which we are made of light. Our bodies are *potentially* light, for if our bodies were accelerated to the speed of light they would become pure energy and light, according to the formula $E = mc^2$.

Jesus or some of his early followers believed that there is "light" behind visible images; that inner light is "hidden" in "the image of the Father's light." The image of the Father's light can be understood as humanity itself, since the creation story in Genesis established the belief that humanity is made in the image and likeness of God. These statements from *Thomas* are ontological affirmations: we come from the light of God, we are the image of that light, and the light that illuminates the visible world is within us. "Light" in these passages seems to mean something like "divine conscious being."

The light sayings can be understood as being about divine potential in humanity. They can be interpreted as meaning:

God is the Source of Light: knowledge, enlightenment, talents, consciousness and being itself.

Humanity is the "image and likeness" of that light.

How we mentally look at things (represented by the "eye") determines our health (the light or darkness in our bodies) and our experiences in general.

"You are the light. Let your light shine." Use your talents and they will increase. Share your wisdom and knowledge. Then what you have within you will be useful to you and useful to others. Then you will be healthy, happy and prosperous – full of light.

Jesus may very well have, on one or more occasions, told people that he was "light" and told them that they were light.

Jesus' sayings also affirm the human potential to experience a divine joy. In fact, joy seems to be the primary potential he explicitly associates with his primary objective of entering God's realm. There are five authentic sayings which speak of finding the joy of God's realm. These sayings have typically been interpreted as being about "saving souls" because Christianity has placed so much emphasis on proselytizing. However, we have seen that Jesus had a philosophy which emphasized attaining a consciousness of love, wisdom, and God's presence. Since Jesus' concept of entering God's realm was about consciousness, the sayings about finding joy are as likely about finding that consciousness as about "saving souls."

*"What do you think of this? If someone has a hundred sheep and one of them wanders off, won't that person leave the ninety-nine in the hills and go look for the one that wandered off? And if he should find it, you can bet he'll rejoice over it more than over the ninety-nine that didn't wander off." (Mt. 18: 12-13)*

*"Is there any woman with ten silver coins, who if she loses one, wouldn't light a lamp and sweep the house and search carefully until she finds it? When she finds it, she invites her friends and neighbors over and says, 'Celebrate with me, because I have found the silver coin I had lost.'" (Lk. 15: 8-9)*

One can understand how, with their emphasis on evangelism, early Christians saw the above two parables as being about saving lost souls. On the other hand coins and sheep can be interpreted in ways other than as signifying "lost souls." The people in the story were searching for possessions they had lost. There is no reasonable sense in which a "lost soul" can be seen as the rightful *possession* that *previously* belonged to an evangelist or a church. If one says the shepherd and the woman represent "God" and God rejoices over lost souls who are found, there is the problem of the implication that the omniscient God can somehow lose track of "His" possessions.

Viewed without the evangelical spectacles of the later church, a simpler and more obvious interpretation of the man and woman in the parables is that they represent human beings in general. Human beings lose things, search for what they have lost, and rejoice when they find what they've lost. This interpretation also fits well with Jesus' admonition to seek and his affirmation that those who seek will find.

Then the question becomes: what is it that we lose, search for, find and rejoice in finding? It is not unreasonable to suppose that Jesus meant the lost sheep and coin to represent something that we once had and can have again, something that will bring great joy to us when we recover it. That supposition opens the sayings to a wide variety of interpretations, which, as we have seen, is typical of his sayings. The something lost could be innocence, the "child mind," "buried talents," faith, self-control, happiness or a host of other elements of consciousness or even "God's realm" itself. The value in the ambiguity is that individuals can interpret the saying in terms of reflection upon their own experience and conditions. Such reflection can lead to therapeutic insight. Finding what we have "lost" can infuse renewed joy into our lives.

The connection of joy to finding God's realm within us and "spread out on the earth" is explicit in the following parable:

*"Heaven's realm is like treasure hidden in a field: when someone finds it, that person covers it up again, and out of sheer joy goes and sells every last possession and buys that field." (Matt 13: 44)*

In this analogy, "heaven's realm" is hidden and can be "accidently" found when one goes "digging." Digging how and where? In the context of philosophical thinking of Jesus' time, one should "dig" into one's own mind for self-knowledge. As a result of self-exploration one could "accidently" discover hidden potential or attain a mystical experience. Discovery of self-knowledge was equated with enlightenment not only in Greek philosophy but also in Chinese and Indian philosophy. As we have seen, Jesus indicated the importance of self-knowledge. If the realm of God is within you, you could discover it by searching within yourself.

Thomas' Gospel contains a variation on the "hidden treasure" parable:

*"The Father's realm is like a person who had a treasure hidden in his field but did not know it. And when he died he left it to his son. The son did not know about it either. He took over the field and sold it. The buyer went plowing, discovered the treasure, and began to lend money at interest to whomever he wished." (Thomas 109: 1-3)*

This extended account of the parable seems to imply that previous generations had the "treasure" within them but did not know it. That notion of "unknowing" generations is another idea that Jesus might have expressed. Alternatively, the previous generations who did not know about the hidden treasure could represent previous phases in the life of an individual. The ending of Thomas' version might be an extension of the original parable to emphasize the "profit" of finding the Father's realm. It does not include the response of joy that is found in Matthew's version. The versions found in *Matthew* and *Thomas* have in common that God's realm is a hidden treasure to be found by digging.

Another theme of the buried treasure parable in *Matthew* is that the treasure is worth more than all of the finder's worldly possessions; he sells all he owns to get the treasure. The ideas of the great value of "heaven's realm" and of finding the realm are also found in the parable of "the pearl of great price":

*"Again, Heaven's realm is like some trader looking for beautiful pearls. When that merchant finds one priceless pearl, he sells everything he owns and buys it." (Matt 13: 45-46)*

The potential to heal by spiritual means was a prominent feature in the New Testament tradition about Jesus and his disciples. Assuming that his reputation as a healer has a historical basis, the potential to be healed by spiritual means and to be a spiritual healer may be considered other aspects of human potential. Jesus did not teach directly about healing, but his philosophy contains therapeutic elements. It was not a philosophy about healing but a philosophy that had healing effects.

## What Jesus Said about Himself

According to the synoptic gospels, the *Q* Gospel and the *Gospel of Thomas*, Jesus rarely made self-referential statements. According to the *Gospel of John*, Jesus spoke incessantly about himself and referred to himself as mediator between God and humanity. The most probable reason for the startling difference between *John* and the rest of the Gospels is that John had a different agenda than the other gospel authors. *John*, the last of the Gospels to be written, is a Gospel expressing what the church came to believe about Jesus over the course of about 70 years. The other gospels, at least in part, were attempts to record what his first generation followers remembered of Jesus' sayings. The synoptic gospels had the additional agendas of creating a narrative of Jesus' life and expressing what disciples believed was the meaning of his death.

Because the *Gospel of John* is now regarded by most scholars as being a development of church "Christology," the unique sayings attributed to Jesus found in John are regarded as having little or no value for discerning what the historical Jesus actually said. Consequently, John probably doesn't tell us much, if anything, about what Jesus said about himself.

There are a few sayings in the other Gospels which are probably authentic and which are self-referential. From these sayings we may be able to gain some insight regarding how Jesus saw himself.

*"I have cast fire upon the world, and look, I'm guarding it until*

*it blazes." (Thom. 10: 1)*

Jesus saw himself as an agent of change. "Setting the world on fire" is today a common idiom meaning "having a great transformational impact on the world." As fire has long been an archetypal representation of change and was used by the "process" philosopher Heraclitus as a symbol of the changing nature of the world, Jesus may have used "fire" in the saying to suggest changing the world. Jesus' philosophy was unconventional and countercultural, no doubt intentionally so and, in that sense aimed at "setting the world on fire."

*"I was watching Satan fall like lightning from heaven." (Lk. 10: 18)*

This saying is found only in Luke, but the Jesus Seminar scholars believed it was an authentic saying of Jesus. Since Jesus habitually spoke in figurative and non-literal ways, we should be cautious about taking this saying as proving that Jesus "believed in Satan" in a literal and ontological way.

The saying sounds like a comment about something Jesus was doing: "I was watching." The language suggests that Jesus was having a vision and then afterward told some disciples what the vision was. The saying suggests that Jesus occasionally had vivid subjective visions, probably while in a trance state.

In early church writings there are several references to another saying which sounds like a description of a subjective vision. Even though that saying is not included in the canonical gospels or in the Jesus Seminar "canon," it is relevant to the discussion of Jesus having subjective visions. The saying was quoted by Origen and Jerome:

*"Just now my mother, the holy spirit, took me by one of my hairs and carried me to Tabor, the great mountain."[117]*

Origen and Jerome claimed that this saying of Jesus was recorded in a lost book titled *"The Gospel according to the Hebrews."* Some early Christians thought of the "holy spirit" as "mother," a feminine aspect of God. This saying indicates that Jesus may have likewise. On the other hand, there are no other "authentic" sayings that make reference to "the holy spirit" so we do not know if Jesus even spoke about "the Holy Spirit." The two sayings, taken together, offer a tantalizing glimpse of a possibility that Jesus occasionally had visions. Unfortunately, it is only a glimpse of a possibility rather than compelling proof.

Jesus may have quoted the proverb *"Those in good health don't need a doctor" (Mk. 2: 17)*. If so, it indicates that he saw himself as a "doctor," a healer in some sense.

Jesus may have believed that his disciples represented him and that he was "sent by God" in some sense. While the Jesus Seminar did not accept the following quote as authentic, it is one of several from different sources which suggest Jesus' view of having a divine mission:

*"The one who accepts you accepts me; and the one who accepts me accepts the one who sent me." (Mt. 10: 40)*

Mark contains a similar saying:  *"Whoever welcomes one of these little children in my name welcomes me; and whoever welcomes me does not welcome me but the one who sent me." (Mark 9: 37)*

Luke sounds the same theme, but again in different wording: *"Whoever listens to you listens to me; whoever rejects you rejects me; but whoever rejects me rejects him who sent me." (Luke 10: 16)*

A saying in *John* is fairly close in wording to Matthew's version: *"Whoever accepts anyone I send accepts me; and whoever accepts me accepts the one who sent me." (John 13: 20)*

The presence of the same basic idea attributed to Jesus in all four canonical gospels suggests a very early and widespread tradition. The tradition may have originated with Jesus, but just exactly what he said is obscured by the different wordings in the Gospels. Based not only upon these sayings but also upon the fact that Jesus traveled around delivering a message and had a following of enthusiastic disciples, I think it is highly probable that Jesus saw himself as having a divine mission and encouraged his disciples to participate in that mission.

Christianity has emphasized that Jesus came to sacrifice his life to pay for our sins and to give eternal life to those who believed in him. Yet the historical Jesus does not appear to have said anything about those ideas; they seem to be later interpretations of his mission. As has been shown in previous chapters, Jesus' sayings can be understood as expressing a philosophy including ontological, cosmological and ethical concepts as well as strategies for provoking reflection and self-knowledge.

Even though "eternal life" does not appear to have been a major theme of Jesus' philosophy, he may have made reference to the possibility of "not tasting death." This idea was discussed in the section on "Catalytic Aphorisms." Jesus may have seen himself as one who had transcended fear of death and as having the ability to convey that transcendence to others through his sayings. The idea of "not tasting death" is compatible with the belief that death is an illusion; that life and consciousness continue beyond the appearance of dying. After all, if a person does not experience death, wouldn't that mean when the person eventually *seems* to *others* to be "dead," nevertheless, the person continues in a consciousness of being alive?

Jesus may have seen himself as "possessing" all things in some way:

*"My Father has turned everything over to me."* *(Mt. 11: 27 - also see Lk. 10: 21; John 3: 35; Thom. 61: 3)*

The best way to understand his perspective is to think of his saying that God's realm (the whole universe) belongs to the poor (*"blessed are you poor, for yours is God's realm"*). Jesus had a mentality similar to that of the Cynics, who eschewed possessions and at the same time thought of themselves as possessing all things. The logic of the Cynics is compatible with Jesus' philosophy: we are children of God; all things in the universe belong to God; as children of God we are heirs to all that God has; therefore, we possess all things. The Cynics and Jesus thought of personal possessions as burdensome and yet also thought of all things belonging to them as children of God. This seems to be a paradoxical position; it requires a mystical perspective to make sense.

Finally, Jesus may have seen himself as someone who had the intention of helping to unify humanity and of helping people realize their unity with God. His emphasis on inclusive love and entering God's realm attest to that self-image.

*Luke* and *Thomas* both tell a story of someone asking Jesus to settle a dispute. In *Luke 12:14*, Jesus responds by asking: *"Who made me a judge?"* In *Thomas 72:2*, Jesus responds to the request with an ironically haunting question: *"Mister, who made me a divider?"* The irony of course is that Jesus' followers eventually became divided over him into many factions, sometimes bitterly and with tragic consequences. Since *Luke* and *Thomas* independently tell the same story, it may reflect a very early memory of Jesus.

It is my hope that the day will come when, instead of using the religion *about* Jesus as an instrument of division, humanity will use the philosophy *of* Jesus as an instrument for unity. It is my hope that through the philosophy of Jesus people will discover their own innate

God-like capacity for compassion, forgiveness, understanding, and healing. It is my hope that the day will come when people will stop waiting and looking to the sky for "Judgment Day," and instead see that God's realm is within us and all around us.

# Chapter Eleven: Jesus as Philosopher, Humorist, and Healer

Throughout its history, philosophy and religion have interacted because they cover some of the same territory and both claim to have truth. Both seek the truth about God, morals, and structure of the universe. Some philosophers have argued against religion and some religious preachers have preached against philosophy. Some religious people have been philosophical and some philosophers have been religious.

Jesus of Nazareth was religious in the sense that he believed in God and morality and probably participated in some practices of Judaism, but what has not been widely recognized is that he was also philosophical. His philosophy is similar at certain points to some philosophies of his era and also can be differentiated from those philosophies. In this chapter the philosophy of Jesus will be compared to the Western philosophies of the Cynics, Stoics and Pythagoreans, all of which preceded Jesus and were popular during Jesus' life. This chapter also includes a comparison of Jesus' philosophy with the Chinese philosophies of Taoism and Moism, to further illustrate Jesus' place in world philosophy.

Classifying Jesus as a philosopher does not imply a complete characterization of him, but his historical place as a philosopher has been almost entirely neglected. He can also be accurately categorized as a "mystic" and "healer." The categories of "philosopher," "mystic" and "healer" are not mutually exclusive. Both philosophers and mystics devote themselves to quests for truth and insight through contemplation of ideas. Many philosophers have also been mystics, e.g. Pythagoras (probably), Plotinus (undoubtedly), St. Augustine of Hippo and Ralph Waldo Emerson. Nearly all the earliest philosophers of India were mystics. Pythagoras and Empedocles are two philosopher-mystics who also had reputations as healers.

Within the Judaism contemporary with Jesus, some Jews saw their religion as philosophical.

*"The Jews had for a great while three sects of philosophy peculiar to themselves; the sect of the Essenes, and the sect of the*

*Sadducees, and the third sort of opinions was that of those called Pharisees.* " – Flavius Josephus[118]

Flavius Josephus was a first century C.E. Galilean Jew who wrote extensively on the history of Judaism. He referred to the different sects of Judaism as "philosophies" which indicates that religion and philosophy were not as strictly differentiated in the first century as they are today.

Another first century Jew, Philo Judaeus of Alexandria (20 BCE – 50 CE), was a philosopher and also thought of the different sects of Judaism as being "philosophies." In fact, he thought of Moses as being a philosopher: "Moses, who had early reached the very summits of philosophy."[119]  Philo had some familiarity with Pythagorean and other Greek philosophies as well as with Jewish "philosophies." Philo's approach to interpreting scriptures was Pythagorean and Platonic. When commenting on the Ten Commandments, Philo wrote an extended explanation of why there were *Ten Commandments* using Pythagorean numerology:

> "... *one must at once admire the number, inasmuch as they are completed in the perfect number of the decade, which contains every variety of number, both those which are even, and those which are odd, and those which are even-odd. ... it comprehends likewise all the proportions .... It also contains the harmonic proportion ... the visible peculiar properties of the triangles, and squares, and other polygonal figures.*"[120]

Philo even had some acquaintance with Persian Magi and with Indian philosophers, whom he referred to as "gymnosophists," i.e. "naked wise men."

The fact that first century Jewish intellectuals thought of Judaism as one of the philosophies of their time indicates that the term "philosopher" would have been aptly applied in that time to any person advocating beliefs about God, nature, and how people ought to live. According to the *Gospel of Thomas* when Jesus asked his disciples to tell him what he was like one disciple replied: "You are like a wise philosopher."[121]

## The Cynic Jesus

At some point, Antisthenes (ca. 445-365 BCE), a disciple of Socrates, concluded that human culture was an unnatural contrivance; merely relative to societies and without absolute truth or value. He came to believe that nature provides an ethical norm that is in most respects superior to human values. In particular, he considered the pursuit of wealth and the social restraints on individual freedom to be "unnatural" and a major cause of human unhappiness. Discussing Antisthenes' perspective on wealth, modern philosopher Anthony Long wrote: "Antisthenes defends the claim that, although he is penniless, he prides himself on his wealth. True wealth and poverty, he argues, are possessed in people's souls."[122]

Antisthenes is considered the first Cynic by some and by others a forerunner of the Cynics. Diogenes of Sinope lived in the same era and location as Antisthenes and is generally regarded as either the iconic model for the Cynic philosophy or the first true Cynic. Here I shall not be concerned with the controversy about who was the first Cynic, but shall consider both philosophers to be representative of the Cynic philosophy. I shall also refer at a couple of points to later Cynics. The Cynic philosophy began in the era of Antisthenes and Diogenes and continued to be adopted and practiced for nearly a thousand years.

Some modern New Testament scholars have speculated that Jesus was strongly influenced by the Cynics and may even be considered a Jewish Cynic.[123] There are in fact significant indications that Jesus was similar to the Cynics in "life-style" and thought.

One expert on the Cynic philosophy characterized Diogenes' main ideas as follows:

"The central ideas of Diogenes' Cynicism are: (1) nature provides an ethical norm observable in animals and inferable by cross-cultural comparisons; (2) since contemporary Greek society (and by implication any existing society) is at odds with nature, its most fundamental values (e.g. religion, politics, ethics, etc.) are not only false but counterproductive; (3) human beings can realize their nature and, hence, their happiness only by engaging in a rigorous discipline (*askēsis*) of corporeal training and exemplary acts meant to prepare them for the actual conditions of human life – all the ills that mortal flesh is heir to; (4) the goal of Cynic 'discipline' (*askēsis*) is to promote the central attributes of a happy life, freedom and self-sufficiency (*autarkeia*); (5) while Cynic freedom is 'negative' . . . – 'freedom from' rather than 'freedom to' – it is also active, as expressed in the metaphor of 'defacing' tradition (by parody and satire) and in provocative acts of free speech meant to subvert existing authorities (e.g. Plato, Alexander the Great, et al.)."[124]

With regard to the list of Diogenes' central ideas there are points of similarity with Jesus. On point (1), Jesus used nature as a model for human behavior, specifically regarding human means of food and clothing production.[125] On point (2), Jesus felt free to critique some of the practices of the Jewish religion, for example kosher rules and Sabbath practices.[126] On the other hand, it would not be accurate to characterize Jesus as being opposed to all fundamental religious values. On point (3), Jesus clearly considered "entering" or "finding" "God's Kingdom" to be an occasion of great happiness, as indicated in the parables of found treasure, found pearl of great price, found lost coin, et al. The role of self-discipline is indicated in his instructions to his disciples for their behavior (see especially the section on "Ethics") and travels (discussed below). On (4), Jesus' freedom to travel wherever he chose, violate customs and speak his views regardless of conventions is similar to the freedom advocated by the Cynics. His emphasis on joy has already been noted in connection with point (3). His self-sufficiency is indicated by the counter-cultural nature of his message and behavior as well as his independence from religious, familial and political entanglements. On point (5), Jesus also used parody and provocation in his speech (note section on humor in this chapter).[127]

Jesus' "lifestyle" and ways of self-expression are also comparable to the Cynic lifestyle and ways of self-expression. The Cynics were easily recognizable in the context of their culture by what they possessed as well as by their behavior. Their possessions consisted of a rough cloak, a knapsack (also sometimes called a "bag," "wallet" or "purse"), and a staff. Cynics were "homeless beggars" and evangelizing preachers. The minimalism of their possessions and their beggar/preacher lifestyle were important elements of their "*askēsis*", intentionally using hardship to develop a state of happiness independent of external social and natural conditions.

The "homeless lifestyle" of the Cynics and of Jesus is reflected in the following quotations:

*"Diogenes liked to proclaim himself, 'Without a city, without a home, bereft of fatherland,*
*A beggar and a vagabond, living from day to day.'"[128]*
Jesus said, *"Foxes have dens and birds have nests, but the son of man has no place to lay his head."[129]*
According to the Gospels, Jesus sent out disciples with instructions even more minimalist in terms of "luggage" than the customary Cynic possessions. The tradition reflected in Mark's Gospel has Jesus instructing his disciples: *"Take nothing for the journey except a staff – no bread, no bag, no money in your belts. Wear sandals but not an extra shirt."[130]* This description reflects familiarity with the Cynic "uniform," referring specifically to the staff, knapsack (bag), sandals, and clothing. The Cynics carried a bag; Jesus instructs his disciples to be even less burdened on that point. He has them carry the Cynic staff and not carry an extra shirt (Cynics carried no extra clothing); on these points his disciples would resemble the Cynics. The only point on which Jesus allows his disciples to be more "burdened" than the Cynics is by allowing them to wear sandals. The upshot of the instructions may be stated as "be *like* the Cynics, but not *exactly* like them."

There were other similar traditions regarding what Jesus told his disciples which is reported in Matthew's and Luke's Gospels. The instructions in *Matthew* and *Luke* make reference to the well known elements of the Cynic uniform but again with differences. In *Matthew*, Jesus instructs the disciples to take "no bag for the journey or extra shirt or sandals or a staff, for the worker is worth his keep."[131] In *Luke*, Jesus says, "Take nothing for the journey – no staff, no bag, no bread, no money, no extra shirt."[132] Both these traditions emphasize the difference from the Cynics. The emphasis on difference suggests that at some point early on Jesus and his followers were similar enough to the Cynics that they needed to emphasize their difference by means of an even more rigorous rejection of possessions than was practiced by the Cynics.

The movement started by Jesus became a mass movement cutting across lines of nationality, gender, and ethnicity. The same was true of the Cynic philosophy which began hundreds of years before Christianity. "Cynicism was unique among classical intellectual traditions in becoming something like a 'mass movement.'"[133]

*"But the appeal of the Cynic ideology was too contagious to contain and control, as we see if we consider how disparate were the positions, both social and intellectual of those who took a serious interest in it:*

*Philo Judaeus, the early Christians, Roman aristocrats
. . . satirists, Greek sophists, imperial educators and
moralists, the Church Fathers . . . a pious emperor . . .
and the urban poor, both free and slaves.*[134]

Notice that the list of those interested in the Cynic philosophy includes early Christians and Church Fathers; the interest was partly a result of the similarities between the original activities of the Cynics and of Jesus and his disciples.

Recall the parables of Jesus and the Cynics about "emptying," discussed in the section on non-attachment:

*"The Father's kingdom is like a woman who was carrying a jar full of meal. While she was walking along a distant road, the handle of the jar broke and the meal spilled behind her along the road. She didn't know it; she hadn't noticed a problem. When she reached her house, she put the jar down and discovered that it was empty."*[135]

*"It's like this. Some merchants ran their ship aground on a reef. Since they could not budge it in any way, they went away lamenting. So, when robbers, without understanding the problem of these men, sailed up with an empty ship, they freely loaded cargo, and at once transferred the cargo from the strange ship, unaware of the calamity as they made the transfer. For as the one ship emptied, it started to float and become seaworthy. But the ship taking on the other's cargo quickly sank to the bottom because of the robbery of foreign goods. This can always happen to the person who has possessions. But the Cynics have stood apart from all of these things. All of us possess the whole earth."*[136]

In both cases a surprising parable is used to express the philosophy; both parables emphasize the process of "emptying" as key to the respective philosophies. Recall that Jesus said the kingdom of God belongs to the poor (the Greek word essentially means "beggars") and we find a paradox similar to the claim at the end of the Cynic parable: "the Cynics have stood apart from all of these things (possessions). All of us possess the whole earth."

A man named Crates was a wealthy landowner who became a Cynic. He sold all his land and distributed the proceeds to fellow citizens.[137] Crates said: "I don't have one country as my refuge, nor a single roof, but every land has a city and house ready to entertain me."[138]

Note the striking parallel to a saying attributed to Jesus: "No one who has left home or brothers or sisters or mother or father or children or fields for me and the gospel will fail to receive a hundred times as much in this present age: homes, brothers, sisters, mothers, children and fields . . ."[139]

By referring to God as "your Father" and "the Father" Jesus implied a divinity in humanity. That idea of divinity in humanity was found among the Cynics long before Jesus.

The Cynic self-image as found in ancient texts can be summarized in these terms: "The gods, who are man's benefactors, provide a paradigm for Cynic self-sufficiency; the Cynic himself is godlike, friend of the gods, their messenger, their agent, and, in being *agathos daimōn* ('tutelary god,' 'guardian angel'), he is himself virtually divine."[140] There is here a similarity and a difference. Jesus' way of speaking of the Father implied that we are already divine in some sense; the Cynic way implied that one could *become* divine by adopting the Cynic philosophy. Christians fairly quickly shifted from the inherent divinity in humanity implied by Jesus to a divinity attained by "adoption" through joining the Christian movement.

Jesus' idea of his followers as God's children, sharing all things in common and in some mystical sense "owning" God's kingdom finds a parallel in a syllogism of Diogenes: "Everything belongs to the gods. Wise men are the friends of the gods. The goods of friends are held in common. Therefore everything belongs to the wise."[141] Jesus spoke of God's kingdom as already present, inside and outside, spread out on the earth; in other words, the *cosmos* is governed by God. Diogenes said: "The only good government is that in the cosmos."[142]

There are two important differences between Jesus' philosophy and the Cynic philosophy: (1) Jesus' philosophy adds emphasis on community to the rugged self-sufficiency of the Cynic philosophy and (2) Jesus' philosophy includes a theological-metaphysical-ethical dimension which is for the most part absent from the Cynic philosophy. One especially noteworthy difference is that Jesus emphasized inclusive shared meals, while Cynics tended to eat their meals alone, anytime and anyplace they were hungry. The community ideas present in Jesus' teachings are directly related to the theological-metaphysical-ethical dimension. I hyphenate "theological-metaphysical-ethical" because the three categories are intimately interwoven in Jesus' philosophy. With respect to the theological-metaphysical-ethical dimension, Jesus' philosophy is more like the Stoics than the Cynics of his era. The community ideas in Jesus' philosophy have some similarity to the Pythagorean philosophy. In addition, Pythagoras used a strategy similar to one used by Jesus to provoke contemplation in his disciples and Pythagoras had a reputation as healer and wonder-worker very much like that of Jesus.

## The Stoic Jesus

The founder of Stoicism was Zeno, a Phoenician philosopher. Zeno and later Stoics were strongly influenced by the Cynics. Bertrand Russell noted regarding Zeno that "the views of the Cynics were more congenial to him than those of any other school, but he was something of an eclectic."[143]

The similarities between Jesus' philosophy and Stoicism are immediately apparent in Russell's description of views of Epictetus, a Stoic philosopher nearly contemporary with Jesus. According to Russell, Epictetus (ca. 60-100 CE) held that "God is the father of men, and we are all brothers,"[144] and that we should love our enemies.[145] Because Christianity is commonplace today, those ideas seem commonplace to us. However, when Jesus and the Stoics were pronouncing the Fatherhood of God and the related ethical idea loving one's enemies, those ideas did not reflect the prevailing consciousness.

As has been discussed, Jesus' metaphysics consisted primarily of the following ideas: (1) God's love and power are universal, (2) God's rule of nature operates by a law of reciprocity ("the measure you give will be the measure you receive") and by a principle and process of expansion, (3) God's rule is also characterized by bountiful benevolence, and (4) as children of God we freely determine our experience by our use of the law of reciprocity. The ethical values he advocated are directly related to the consequences of the law of reciprocity: forgive and you will be forgiven, love your enemies, be "good Samaritans" (as we now generally think of the moral of the parable), etc.

Jesus' sayings and parables express a concept of justice. The parables sometimes juxtapose the value of justice/fairness with the value of forms of benevolence (another primary value of the ancient world). For example, he told a story about a vineyard owner who paid a day's wage to all the workers, no matter if they worked all day or only an hour. The "fair" response of the owner would have been to pay those who worked shorter hours less than those who worked the full day. Those who worked the full day objected to the owner's generosity, leaving the listener with the question: which is better, fairness or generosity? The Prodigal Son parable raises basically the same tension between forgiveness and fairness with the father forgiving the younger son and the elder son questioning the justice of the father's behavior.

The Stoic philosophy expressed ideas very similar to those in Jesus' philosophy. Bertrand Russell's description of Stoic ideas reveals some of those similarities:

"The course of nature . . . was ordained by a Lawgiver who was also a beneficent Providence."[146]

"God is not separate from the world; He is the soul of the world, and each of us contains a part of the Divine Fire."[147]

"As a principle, the Stoics preached universal love."[148]

The Stoics believed the world was ruled by Law or Reason and that Law, Right Reason, Zeus, Mind, Destiny, and God are one and the same thing.[149] The idea that the universe is ruled by general laws is a metaphysical concept affirmed in science and in spiritual teachings, e.g. the law of karma. Identifying the ruling law or reason with God is a theological as well as metaphysical concept. The ethical ideas of both Jesus and the Stoics are directly related to the theological concept of imitating the nature of God and the metaphysical concept of a universe ruled by law.

Even a famous Stoic prayer is similar to the way of prayer taught by Jesus. The Stoic philosopher Cleanthes devised this prayer: "Lead me, O Zeus, and thou, O Destiny, lead thou me on. To whatsoever task thou sendest me, lead thou me on."[150] The spirit of the prayer is practically the same as the prayer of Jesus: "Father . . . your kingdom come, your will be done." These prayers do not ask for favors for self, family, or nation; they affirm a willingness to "flow with" the will of God, whatever that might be.

One significant difference between Jesus and the Stoics is that the Stoics were more intellectually oriented; they tried to solve classic philosophical problems such as: is the universe deterministic or do we have freedom? If God is good and all-powerful, from whence is evil? What is the substance of things? Jesus did not formulate rigorous rational answers to such questions; he was more concerned with how best to live and with proclaiming the "hidden treasure" of the presence of God within humanity and nature.

Philosophically, Jesus seems a hybrid of Cynicism and Stoicism.

He lived and frequently talked like a Cynic. His theology, metaphysics and ethics are similar to the Stoic philosophy. He was more "community oriented" than the Cynics; he had less to say about metaphysics than the Stoics.

Before moving on to comparison of Jesus' philosophy with the Pythagorean philosophy, I should mention that there are hints in Jesus' philosophy for thinking about the type of philosophical questions with which the Stoics were concerned.

Greek philosophers' speculation about the substance of the universe produced a wide range of proposals: water, air, earth, mind, number, fire, etc. As far as is known, Jesus never explicitly proposed a theory of substance. On the other hand, one of his favorite metaphors for the universe (God's kingdom) was seed and earth: the mustard seed; seed sown in different kinds of soil; the seed that unfolds first the blade, then the ear, then the full grain in the ear. The metaphors involve potential "packed" into a point (the seed), a *process* which forms something larger and very different from the original seed, and a "field" in which the seeds are buried. These metaphors are apt for "process metaphysics" as advocated by Heraclitus (*fl.* 500 BCE) and Alfred North Whitehead (1861-1947) and the process philosophers who followed him.

Regarding the question of "whence evil?" one would think this would be an important issue for Jesus considering his idea of a universe ruled by a benevolent Father, but he did not directly address it. His parables indicate that he was aware that people can be greedy, unforgiving, dishonest and violent; but he offered no explanation for such behavior. His parables assume that people choose their own thoughts and behaviors; he simply assumed humans have free will and their choices are the cause of good or ill.

Another possibility is that he believed, as one saying attributed to him states, that God alone (presumably including "God's government" of the universe) is good (Mark 10: 18). If that was his view, then he may well have thought of "good and evil" in the human context as merely relative concepts – no person can be completely good because only God is completely good. In that way of thinking, there is no problem of evil in an absolute sense; good and evil are relative to human perception. That view is roughly equivalent to the view of the philosopher Spinoza. That Jesus gave no definitive answer to "the problem of evil" is clear from the history of Christian thought, in which a wide range of theories have been proposed.

The philosophy of Jesus was clearly more concerned with

helping people flourish and find joy than with answering deep philosophical questions. His reputation as a healer reflects his convictions regarding divinity in humanity, the prodigious benevolence of God, and his conviction that as children of God we can have whatever we ask for.

Some of Jesus' practices and methods are reminiscent of a philosopher who also had a reputation as a healer: Pythagoras (*fl.* 570 BCE).

## The Pythagorean Jesus

The Pythagorean philosophy has been summarized in the following terms:

*"Man realizes the divine by knowing the universal and divine principles which constitute the cosmos . . . . To know the cosmos is to seek and know the divine element within, and one must become divine and harmonized since only like can know like."* [151]

I may as well note at the outset that the Pythagorean philosophy in its best known features appears unrelated to the message of Jesus. The Pythagoreans focused upon the idea that "all is number," by which they meant something like "all things can be described mathematically or geometrically." The Pythagoreans were mathematicians, musicians, and developers of music theory. Jesus had no apparent interest in mathematics or music.

On the other hand, there are at least five significant ways in which Jesus and Pythagoras were very much alike: (1) as mentioned, both were probably healers; (2) both founded communities in which the members shared all property in common and which were open to both men and women; (3) both believed in a divinity in humanity; (4) both believed in friendship extended to all; and (5) both used concrete aphorisms with obscure meaning as a teaching device.

Aphorisms ascribed to Jesus tend to use concrete imagery which has no obvious application. His disciples had to interpret the meanings. Here let us recall just a few examples:

*"You must be sly as a snake and as simple as a dove." (Mt. 10: 16, SV)*

*"Since when do people pick grapes from thorns or figs from thistles?" (Mt. 7: 16, SV)*

*"Do not let your left hand know what your right hand is doing."* *(Thom. 62: 2, SV)*

*"Struggle to get in through the narrow door; I'm telling you, many will try to get in, but won't be able." (Lk. 13: 24, SV)*

Pythagoras taught by means of enigmatic commands, which disciples contemplated for deeper meaning. Pythagoreans also contemplated "number" i.e. geometry and music theory. Iamblichus was one of the few ancient writers to record information about the Pythagoreans. He asserted that "All Pythagoric discipline was symbolic, resembling riddles and puzzles, and consisting of maxims."[152]

Pythagoras' sayings included:

*"Eat not the heart."*

*"Do not sit upon a bushel basket."*

*"Do not walk in the public way."*

What do these sayings mean? I ask the reader to reflect for a moment to interpret the above sayings before reading any further.

The meanings of the sayings according to Porphyry were:

*"Eat not the heart* signified not to afflict ourselves with sorrows."

*"Do not sit upon a bushel basket* meant not to live ignobly."

*"Do not walk in the public way* meant to avoid the opinions of the multitude, adopting those of the learned and the few."[153]

The meanings ascribed to the sayings are not obvious nor the only possible interpretations. Porphyry's explanations were probably his own conclusions or what he heard from previous teachers. In all probability, Pythagoras used such sayings to provide memorable images and to provoke his disciples to turn inward not merely to interpret the sayings but to explore the depths of their own consciousness. Jesus probably spoke his aphorisms for the same purpose.

The similarities between Jesus' ideas and the Greek philosophies of his era suggest that he may have encountered some of the philosophical ideas of the time and been influenced by them. He certainly encountered the Jewish philosophies of his era and was influenced by Judaism as a religion. We cannot know which philosophers and Judaic writings influenced Jesus, but clearly he had a philosophical turn of mind which resulted in teachings with strong similarities to Cynics, Stoics and Pythagoreans.

Some have speculated that Jesus was influenced by ideas from Asia. While that is possible, it is unlikely for two reasons: (1) it would have been very difficult for a Galilean to travel to Asia and to communicate with Asians and (2) there would be no particular reason for Gospel writers to neglect or suppress mention of Jesus traveling to Asia. There are Eastern philosophies which have similarities to Jesus' philosophy, but the similarities are no stronger than to the ideas Jesus could have encountered in the Mediterranean world.

We know that Zen Masters use obscure riddles (koans) for the purpose of helping disciples reach a higher consciousness; it is not improbable that the sayings of Pythagoras and Jesus had a similar purpose and effect. With the possible parallel between methods of Western philosophers and Eastern philosophers in mind, I turn now to briefly describe two Chinese philosophies with similarities to the philosophy of Jesus.

## The Taoist Jesus

Taoism began with the *Tao-Te-Ching*, traditionally attributed to a philosopher named Lao-Tzu. I will use the book title *"Tao-Te-Ching"* and *"Lao-Tzu"* interchangeably, as is customary. In China Taoism developed in two directions: a religion and a philosophy. The religion interpreted the texts in terms of magic-thinking and folk beliefs. The philosophy interpreted the texts in terms of ethics, metaphysics and mysticism. I've long thought that the mentality of the author of the *Tao-Te-Ching* is very similar to the mentality of Jesus. It is beyond the scope of my purpose to provide a full description of Taoism. Instead, I simply want to point out a few passages with ideas similar to Jesus' philosophy.

Jesus suggested that his students rediscover the "child mind": *"Truly I tell you, anyone who will not receive the kingdom of God like a little child will never enter it."* (Mark 10: 15, NIV)

The *Tao-Te-Ching* also points to children as models of the Way (Tao):

*"Can you concentrate your vital forces and achieve the highest degree of weakness like an infant?"*[154]

*"He who possesses virtue in abundance may be compared to an infant."*[155]

As discussed above, Jesus modeled a "Cynic" simplicity of life. He saw abundance of possessions as obstructive to "entering the Kingdom":

*"How difficult it is for those who have money to enter God's*

*government!  It's easier for a camel to squeeze through a needle's eye than for a wealthy person to get into God's government." (Mk. 23, 25, SV)*

Similarly the *Tao-Te-Ching* advocates simplicity:

*"Let people hold on to these: manifest plainness, embrace simplicity, reduce selfishness, have few desires."*[156]

*"I alone am inert, showing no sign (of desires), like an infant that has not yet smiled.  Wearied, indeed, I seem to be without a home."*[157]

*"Elegant clothes are worn, sharp weapons are carried, food and drinks are enjoyed beyond limit, and wealth and treasures are accumulated in excess.  This is robbery and extravagance.  This is indeed not Tao."*[158]

Like Jesus and Pythagoras, the *Tao-Te-Ching* makes use of paradoxical sounding aphorisms:

*"To yield is to be preserved whole.  To be bent is to become straight.  To be empty is to be full.  To be worn out is to be renewed.  To have little is to possess.  To have plenty is to be perplexed."*[159]

Like Jesus, the *Tao-Te-Ching* affirms the omnipresence and benevolence of the Source of the universe: *"The Great Tao flows everywhere. . . . It clothes and feeds all things but does not claim to be master over them."*[160]

Like Jesus, Lao-Tzu advocated universal benevolence:

*"I treat those who are good with goodness, and I also treat those who are not good with goodness.  Thus goodness is attained."*[161]

*"The sage does not accumulate for himself.  The more he uses for others, the more he has himself.  The more he gives to others, the more he possesses of his own.  The Way of Heaven is to benefit others and not to injure.  The Way of the sage is to act but not to compete."*[162]

One primary difference between Jesus and Lao-Tzu is that Lao-Tzu was much concerned with political science: how to be a good ruler and how to govern society. Jesus' philosophy is concerned with personal ethics and God's rule of the universe (roughly equivalent to one meaning of "Tao" as the "Way" of the universe), but does not directly offer advice for temporal human rulers.

## The Mo-ist Jesus

Moism, named after its founder Mo-Tzu, for a time rivaled Confucianism and Taoism in China. Though Moism faded from popularity, the philosophy has been preserved as part of the history of Chinese thought. The central message of Moism was love and its teachings on love are consistent with that aspect of Jesus' philosophy. A few quotations should suffice to make the point:

> *"But how do we know that Heaven loves all the people in the world? Because it enlightens them all. How do we know that it enlightens them all? Because it possesses them all. How do we know that it possesses them all? Because it feeds them all."[163]*

> *"When all the people in the world love one another, the strong will not overcome the weak, the many will not oppress the few, the rich will not insult the poor, the honored will not despise the humble, and the cunning will not deceive the ignorant. Because of universal love, all the calamities, usurpations, hatred, and animosity in the world may be prevented from arising."[164]*

> *"If the rulers of the world today really want the empire to be wealthy and hate to have it poor, want it to be orderly and hate to have it chaotic, they should practice universal love and mutual benefit. This is the way of the sage-kings and the principle of governing the empire, and it should not be neglected."[165]*

Moism, while not containing other elements found in the philosophy of Jesus, is perfectly compatible with Jesus' philosophy insofar as love is a central, if not *the* central idea.

Soon after his crucifixion, Jesus of Nazareth was proclaimed by his disciples to be the resurrected Messiah ("Christ" in Greek). However, during his life before his crucifixion, Jesus could have been seen by some as a philosopher and his way of life and message fit that categorization.

In terms of his way of life and philosophy, Jesus was more like the Cynic philosophers than any other schools of philosophy or of Judaism. One important tactic shared by Jesus and the Cynics was use of humor. Their use of humor was not simply a matter of personality or the desire to entertain; rather humor was used to shift the perspectives of their listeners.

Philosopher R. Bracht Branham described this tactical use of humor by Diogenes and other Cynics:

"In addition to being pragmatic and improvisational, a third feature of Diogenes' performance stands out and in my view is the most fundamental: that is its humor. . . . The violation of the countless rules both tacit and explicit that govern our behavior, beginning with our use of language, is basic to any form of humor. As Mary Douglas has argued, the form of a joke 'rarely lies in the utterance alone' and can only be understood with reference 'to the total social situation.' The Cynics' innovation consists of exploiting this fact polemically as a way of defining themselves in opposition – not to this or that rule or this or that group, but to the authority of society to dictate thought and behavior."[166]

Like the Cynics, Jesus used humor as a way of defining himself and his ideas in opposition to the status quo. Beyond that, his humor aimed at liberating his listeners from their anxieties and encouraging them to have faith. That he used humor becomes clearer when we understand his words in the context of the "total social situation."

## Jesus as Humorist

*"Don't put all your eggs in one basket." – Proverb (ca. 1600 C.E.)*

*"Behold, the fool saith, 'Put not all thine eggs in the one basket'—which is but a manner of saying, 'Scatter your money and your attention'; but the wise man saith, 'Put all your eggs in the one basket and—WATCH THAT BASKET!'"* – Mark Twain, from *Pudd'nhead Wilson's Calendar*

I have pointed out in the previous chapters many sayings of Jesus which have characteristic forms of humor. Humor can provoke laughter, and laughter is generally good for psychological and physical health. Before turning to a discussion of research on laughter and health a brief discussion of the nature of humor and Jesus as a humorist is in order.

Mark Twain's aphorism about eggs and baskets is amusing at least in part because it turns conventional wisdom upside down, reversing the common way of looking at investment of money and time. There can be wisdom in the idea "don't put all your eggs in one basket." On the other hand, under certain circumstances or for certain people it may well be wiser and more productive to focus attention and energy in one area of life than to scatter one's attention and energies in many directions.

Humorists and comics look at the world in unconventional ways and say unconventional things. One of the ways they provoke laughter is by setting up expectations and then saying the unexpected. The humorous twist in a saying or story helps us see experience in new ways. Often, seeing experience in new ways helps us get in touch with joy and may even stimulate creativity.

Humor is relative to context. When we are removed from or do not relate to the context of a humorous saying or joke we won't "get it." An ethnic joke, told by a member of the ethnic group, can be funny. The same joke, told by someone outside the group, is likely to be offensive. When it comes to humor, one person's "funny" is another person's "offensive."

Humor does not age well. Political humor usually needs to be timely to get laughs; jokes about President Millard Fillmore's policies aren't likely to be funny to anyone today. Even Shakespeare's jokes don't get the laughs they used to.

Because humor is relative to time and context, people today do not think of Jesus as funny. Even the gospel authors - writing 40 to 100 years after Jesus' time in a different context than that of Jesus' original sayings – may not have seen the humor in Jesus' sayings.

On the other hand, even humor removed from time and context can be recognized by its *form* and an understanding of its *time* and *context*. So even if an old joke doesn't make us laugh, we can still recognize the intent of the saying and understand why people at one time may have seen humor in a saying.

We have seen that Jesus' sayings were characterized by surprising reversals of ordinary expectations. The use of shocking and surprising images in sayings and parables can serve a three-fold purpose: (1) it makes the sayings memorable, (2) it shifts perspective from the "ordinary" and may even induce meditative states and (3) it creates the possibility of laughter. The sayings needed to be memorable because Jesus was teaching in spoken form, with no written text for disciples to consult. The second point, the perspective shift, can produce in the one who contemplates the story a meditative state, which can be beneficial to health and give access to deeper levels of consciousness.

The third point about laughter is not obvious. Yet if one thinks about how surprising and shocking statements of modern comics provoke laughter *even when the audience members would be offended in other contexts*, the claim that Jesus was sometimes humorous may not seem so far-fetched. Modern comics say unconventional things about politics, relationships, society, and religion. Satirists in earlier times did the same. The *form* and *content* of some of Jesus' sayings are like satire past and present.

The modern comedian George Carlin once did a routine that was similar in perspective to the views of Jesus and the Cynics regarding possessions. Carlin cleverly mocked the human propensity to collect and be attached to stuff. He noted:

"That's all you need in life, a little place for your stuff. That's all your house is: a place to keep your stuff. If you didn't have so much stuff, you wouldn't need a house. You could just walk around all the time. . . . That's what your house is, a place to keep your stuff while you go out and get . . . more stuff."

Carlin unintentionally described the intentional freedom of Jesus and the Cynics: because they did not have a lot of "stuff," they could freely "just walk around all the time."

It is reasonable to surmise that the humorous form of Jesus' sayings would have been the same then as the effect of humor today: laughter.

A review of some of Jesus' sayings in terms of their context and form may help the reader see more clearly that Jesus had a sense of humor and may have provoked therapeutic laughter for some of his followers.

## Context and Form of Jesus' Humorous Sayings

To understand the humor in Jesus' sayings, it is helpful to consider specific context and conventional opinions of his time, and to contrast the conventional opinions with Jesus' unconventional sayings.

Conventional opinion: *we must earn our living by the sweat of toil.*

Jesus: *Why do you worry? Birds of the air do not farm, yet your Father feeds them. The fields do not slave away weaving clothes, yet your Father clothes them in lilies – clothing more grand than Solomon in all his glory. Won't your Father even more feed and clothe you, who worry about everything?* (Paraphrase of Matthew 6: 25-32 and Luke 12: 22-28)

The saying is a *satire* of human tendency to strive and worry.

Conventional opinion: *widows are defenseless and oppressed by the powerful.*

Jesus: *Once there was a judge in this town who neither feared God nor cared about people. In that same town was a widow who kept coming to him and demanding, "Give me a ruling against the person I'm suing." For a while he refused; but eventually he said to himself, "I'm not afraid of God and I don't care about people, but this widow keeps pestering me. So I'm going to give her a favorable ruling, or else she'll keep coming back until she wears me down."* (Luke 18: 2-4)

The form of the parable is effectively a "joke": it is set up with two stock characters and reverses expectations about where the power is in their relationship.

Conventional opinion: *Pharisees are righteous men, obedient to the Law and blessed by God; toll collectors are sinners and traitors to God's people.*

Jesus: *Two men went up to the temple to pray, one a Pharisee and the other a toll collector. The Pharisee stood up and prayed silently as follows: "I thank you, God, that I'm not like everybody else, thieving, unjust, adulterous, and especially not like that toll collector over there. I fast twice a week, I give tithes of everything I acquire." But the toll collector stood off by himself and didn't even dare to look up, but struck his chest, and muttered, "God, have mercy on me, sinner that I am." Let me tell you, the second man went back to his house righteous but the first one did not.* (Luke 18: 10-14)

In effect the form is a "joke": set up with two stock characters and reversing expectations about who turns out to be righteous.

Conventional opinion: *God's Kingdom is like a mighty cedar of Lebanon, with branches reaching up to heaven.*

Jesus: "*It's like a mustard seed. It's the smallest of all seeds, but when it falls on prepared soil, it produces a large plant and becomes a shelter for the birds of the sky.*" (Thomas 20: 2-3)

The form is a *parody* of a conventional simile.

Conventional opinion: *God blesses the righteous, who are honest in all their ways.*

Jesus: "*There was this rich man whose manager had been accused of squandering his master's property. He called him in and said, 'What's this I hear about you? Let's have an audit of your management, because your job is being terminated.'*

*Then the manager said to himself, 'What am I going to do? My master is firing me. I'm not strong enough to dig ditches and I'm ashamed to beg. I've got it! I know what I'll do so doors will open for me when I'm removed from management.' So he called in each of his master's debtors. He said to the first, 'How much do you owe my master?'*

*He said, 'Five hundred gallons of olive oil.' And he said to him, 'Here is your invoice; sit down right now and make it two hundred and fifty.'*

*Then he said to another, 'And how much do you owe?' He said, 'A thousand bushels of wheat.' He says to him, 'Here is your invoice; make it eight hundred.'*

*The master praised the dishonest manager because he had acted shrewdly.*" (Luke 16: 1-8)

The parable is a *parody* of stories and sayings about men who are rewarded for their honesty or punished for dishonesty. At the same time, the parable suggests the practical value of forgiving debts.

Conventional opinion: *correct your brother when he goes astray.*

Jesus: "*Why do you notice the sliver in your friend's eye, but overlook the timber in your own? How can you say to your friend, "Let me get the sliver out of your eye," when there is a timber in your own? You phony, first take the timber out of your eye and then you'll see well enough to remove the sliver from your friend's eye.*" (Matthew 7: 3-5)

The form of humor used is *exaggerated image*. No one could literally have a timber in their eye. The saying also expresses an unconventional perspective: deal with your own faults before you try to fix others.

Conventional opinion: *a person is defiled when that person eats food God has declared unclean.*

Jesus: *"It's not what goes into a person from the outside that can defile; rather it's what comes out of the person that defiles."* (Mark 7: 15) *"Do you not see that whatever goes into the mouth enters the stomach, and goes out into the sewer?"* (Matt. 15: 17, NRSV)

Besides expressing an unconventional perspective, the sayings makes reference to natural body functioning that is usually not referred to in "polite company," let alone religious discourse. Such references are unexpected and, if made with some wit, can provoke laughter.

Conventional opinion: *The wealthy are fortunate and blessed by God.*

Jesus: *"How difficult it is for those who have money to enter God's realm! It's easier for a camel to squeeze through a needle's eye than for a wealthy person to get into God's realm."* (Mark 10: 25)

The form of humor is *exaggerated imagery* (camel trying to squeeze through a needle's eye) with a reversal of expectations, asserting that the rich are not necessarily blessed by God.

Conventional popular story: *Through the prophet Elijah, God miraculously filled a widow's jar with meal to prosper her until a famine ended. Through the prophet Elisha, God miraculously filled a widow's jars with oil to prosper her.*

Jesus: *The Father's rule is like a woman who was carrying a jar full of meal. While she was walking along a distant road, the handle of the jar broke and the meal spilled behind her along the road. She didn't know it; she hadn't noticed a problem. When she reached her house, she put the jar down and discovered that it was empty. (Thom. 97:1-4)*

The parable is a *parody* of stories about God filling jars, reversing the usual association of God filling a woman's jars.

The observation that Jesus' sayings contained elements of humor goes back at least 40 years. Theologian Elton Trueblood wrote a discerning book entitled *"The Humor of Christ"* on that very subject in 1975.[167] The scholars of the Jesus Seminar agreed that Jesus' sayings and parables were characterized by humor. If indeed Jesus was humorous and sometimes strategically provoked laughter, his sense of humor could well have had a therapeutic effect in some cases.

## The Therapeutic Effects of Humor and Laughter

To the extent that humor relieves us of stress and helps us get in touch with joy, it is therapeutic. The laughter provoked by humor has physiological effects that help us release for a few moments the stress of daily life. Humor and laughter can provoke psychological liberation. There are undoubtedly electrochemical changes occurring in the brain when we hear a joke or humorous saying: those physiological changes correspond to the mental act of perceiving humor and the physical act of laughing. Research indicates that the physiological changes that accompany laughter can relieve stress, boost the immune system, and even momentarily improve respiration and circulation. Beyond whatever positive health effects may occur with laughter, witty sayings and stories can also help us discover new wisdom.

One of the best known cases of the effect of laughter on health is that of Norman Cousins who rationally and intuitively created his own therapy for an illness which had no known cure. Cousins' doctors said there was no effective cure for his particular illness, which they diagnosed as *ankylosing spondylitis*. Cousins believed that large doses of vitamin C and positive emotions, particularly the joy of laughter, might help him overcome the illness. He decided to take more control of his treatment, in which he included regularly watching films that made him laugh. Cousins' self-prescribed treatment proved effective and he wrote about his experience, which brought to public awareness the therapeutic potential of laughter.[168] Cousins' remarkable experience stimulated some research into the effects of laughter.

An article on the "CancerConnect" website refers to a couple of studies indicating the healing power of laughter. The article cites a study conducted at the Indiana State University Sycamore Nursing Center in which 33 healthy adult women were divided into two groups. The treatment group watched a humorous video, while the control group viewed a tourism video. All participants completed questionnaires regarding their stress and humor levels before and after watching their videos. In addition, blood drawn before and after treatment was tested for natural killer cell levels.

Compared to the control group, the laughter group reported a significant decrease in stress following treatment. Participants with high scores on the humor questionnaire also had significantly higher numbers of natural killer cells after treatment. The laughing participants' natural killer cell levels were significantly higher than those of the control group too. The researchers concluded that laughter appears to reduce stress and improve activity of natural killer cells, which may benefit cancer patients.[169]

One study demonstrated that laughter raises the "discomfort threshold" (i.e. ability to withstand discomfort) in participants who were subjected to pressure induced discomfort.[170] Another study of laughter published in the Japanese journal *Biomedical Research* indicated that laughter has a measureable chemical stress relief effect as well as a subjective uplift effect.[171]

Most people would probably agree that humor and laughter make them feel better subjectively. The possible medical benefits of humor and laughter are still being studied and not yet accepted by the medical community. Even so, the popularity of comedy in the human arts indicates that in some sense laughter is like "a medicine," even if it is not literally "the *best* medicine."

# Chapter Twelve: A Philosopher-Healer Goes to Jerusalem

Jesus' work after his baptism by John was as a teacher, philosopher, and healer. Most of the Gospel stories of Jesus healing the afflicted have precedents in "miracle stories" found in Hebrew Scriptures. Consequently many healing stories in the gospels could be imaginative constructions based upon stories from older Jewish sources. Nevertheless, a number of healing stories in the Gospels are most likely based upon memories of actual events.

At least one healing story in the Gospels almost certainly records an accurate memory of a healing involving Jesus. That healing could have been the basis for word spreading among the people that Jesus had healing power or a special connection to God. Once a person gets a reputation as a healer, desperate people will flock to that person. Many will experience healing, if only of a psychosomatic kind or from a so-called placebo effect.

The story of healing that likely reflects authentic memories involves Jesus' encounter with Simon Peter's mother-in-law:

"They left the synagogue right away and entered the house of Simon and Andrew along with James and John. Simon's mother-in-law was in bed with a fever, and they told him about her right away. He went up to her, took hold of her hand, raised her up, and the fever disappeared." (Mark 1: 29-31, SV)

There are several reasons this story is likely true. The story lacks a precedent in Hebrew miracles stories, so it was not merely a result of borrowing a tale from Jewish lore. Unlike in other healing stories, Jesus does not give a command, such as "be healed." Unlike in other healing stories, the illness cured was not a severe enough case to be considered a "miraculous" event. A fever can break suddenly without drugs or other treatments; it is a fairly common occurrence.

Once when one of my daughters was about 2 years old she had a serious fever. The fever was high enough and lasted long enough that we decided to take her to see a doctor. The doctor took a blood test. While we were in the office, I was holding her in my arms. I meditatively focused upon feelings of love and visualized her as well and happy and eating (she wouldn't eat while she had the fever). By the time we got home she no longer had a fever and was happy and readily ate her dinner. The next day the doctor called and said we needed to take her back in because she had an infection and needed antibiotics. She seemed fine, but we took her in for another test. The doctor was surprised because there was no sign of infection. He said the first blood sample must have gotten contaminated. I believed she had been healed through prayer. Whatever the explanation, few today would call the healing "miraculous." Nevertheless, we were grateful that our daughter was well and relieved of her suffering.

Simon's mother-in-law experienced her healing just when Jesus arrived and took her hand. The healing might be explained as a coincidence: her fever just happened to break when Jesus came to the house. The healing might have been a result of a silent prayer by Jesus. Whatever the explanation, once the word spread, the healing certainly would have been enough to begin attracting others seeking healing.

There were no hospitals or doctor's offices in those days. People relied primarily upon folk remedies, prayer and individuals supposed to have special powers. Anyone reputed to have performed a cure would attract public attention, especially in a relatively small fishing town like Capernaum. The incident of the healing of Peter's mother-in-law might well have been the beginning of Jesus' reputation and work as a healer.

Many Galileans had a positive response to Jesus' message and healing work. He gathered a group of disciples around himself, some of whom would begin the religion of Christianity in his name. We are told in the Gospels that Jesus had an inner circle of twelve disciples, but the number twelve was probably used by the gospel writers as symbolic of the twelve tribes of Israel. Early traditions indicate that he had women disciples, including Mary of Magdala, as well as the twelve men usually named. The lists of the twelve give various names and the church has asserted that some of the twelve disciples were known by more than one name, e.g. Nathaniel in the *Gospel of John* is identified with Bartholomew in the synoptic Gospels. Jesus probably had more than twelve disciples, men and women, who followed him and then went out to proclaim his message.

We are also told in the Gospels that Jesus attracted large crowds and on at least one occasion provided food for a crowd of 5,000 or more. The truth is that we do not know how large a following Jesus had in Galilee, but it seems likely that he had enough followers to stand out from other teachers in the area.

The fundamental focus of this work is the healing philosophy of the historical Jesus. As such, the crucifixion and resurrection stories are not essential to my purpose here. However, Christianity has placed so much emphasis on the final week of Jesus' time on earth that addressing those events seems irresistible and unavoidable.

Once Jesus had achieved significant success as a teacher and healer in Galilee, he had a number of options.

He could have settled in a town such as Capernaum and continued his work as a respected philosopher and healer. Jesus attracted both Jewish and Gentile disciples, according to both the gospels and the Jewish historian Josephus. Since Capernaum was near a busy trade route, it is likely true that he attracted Greek speaking followers along with native Aramaic speakers.

Or Jesus could have continued traveling from town to town in Galilee, teaching those who were attracted to him and building up a larger following. Had Jesus stayed in Galilee, he might have lived to a ripe old age, honored and respected in his native land.

Jesus also had the option to take his philosophy and work into Judea and Jerusalem. Because of his success in Galilee, he had good reason to expect similar success in Judea. His message was relatively unthreatening to the power of Rome, so it may have seemed possible to Jesus that the Roman overlords would not oppose him and his followers.

Of these available options, Jesus chose to go to Jerusalem. The Gospels, looking at that choice in retrospect, take the view that this was a divinely predetermined event; that what happened in Jerusalem was an inevitable result of God's will.

Events often seem predetermined when viewed retrospectively. But when we look forward and try to foresee events, we see only possibilities and are often surprised by what actually happens.

Historians are obliged to try to understand the past in terms of human choices, circumstances, and historically reliable evidence. The historian's duty is to try to discern what most *probably* happened from a naturalistic perspective, not what could *possibly* have happened from a predetermined or supernatural perspective. What follows is an attempt to describe what probably happened from a historical perspective.

Jesus intended to go to Jerusalem to participate in a Jewish holiday, probably Passover. He intended to continue his work there; the Gospels report that he taught and healed while in Jerusalem. We cannot say how long Jesus originally intended to stay in Jerusalem.

It is *possible* that Jesus planned to cause a disturbance in the temple and thereby provoke authorities to execute him and make him a martyr to his cause. It is at least as likely that Jesus' words and actions in Jerusalem were spontaneous and the results unanticipated.

Taking Jesus' philosophy into consideration, we can gain some insight into his motivations and probable actions.

Jesus taught and practiced radical reliance on God to provide for every need. He optimistically proclaimed *"ask and you will receive; seek and you will find; knock and it will be opened to you."* He affirmed that we must become like little children to enter the realm of God, and so we may assume that Jesus was in touch with his inner child. He affirmed that finding God's realm within is like experiencing the joy of finding a great buried treasure. We may assume he was joyful. He advocated love and forgiveness even for enemies and "going the extra mile" with those who have worldly power. He coined the expression "turn the other cheek." In short, there is nothing in Jesus' philosophy to suggest that he would seek to provoke authorities with violence or that he sought martyrdom.

There was certainly some risk in going to Jerusalem with a large following, especially during a religious festival. Crowds gathered in Jerusalem during Passover, which made maintaining public order more challenging than usual. Soldiers and police would have been especially vigilant, on the lookout for any disturbance of public order. There were soldier watchtowers all around Jerusalem. Any large cohesive group would have been watched with suspicion as possible rebels or outlaws.

Pontius Pilate had shown he was willing to slaughter large groups of people who seemed a threat to the "Roman peace." Josephus reported an incident in which Pilate had soldiers slaughter a crowd of Jewish protestors.[172] This occurred probably not long before the time Jesus came to Jerusalem, since Josephus mentions Jesus just after the description of the slaughter of protestors. So a journey with a crowd into Jerusalem posed significant risk, especially if the group staged protests or stirred up any violence.

*"Tell the daughter of Zion, Behold, your king is coming to you, humble, and mounted on a colt, the foal of an ass."* (Matt. 21: 5; Zech. 9: 9)

Matthew, taking the Greek Septuagint translation of *Zechariah* literally, has Jesus riding in on *both* a colt *and* an ass. The other Gospel authors have Jesus riding only one animal.

Did Jesus ride into Jerusalem on a donkey to fulfill the prophecy of Zechariah and indicate that he was coming as a king? It is possible that Jesus decided to make a claim on kingship in Israel and that he rode into Jerusalem on an ass to symbolize that claim.

However, it is important to keep in mind that the Gospel narratives were written some 35 to 80 years after the fact, from the authors' perspectives that Jesus was the Messiah. The information around the last days of Jesus is not entirely reliable from a historical perspective. The Gospel authors appear to have taken details from *Psalms* and the prophetic books and inserted them into their narrative to present a picture of Jesus fulfilling prophecies. Therefore we cannot easily tell the difference between when events "fulfilled scriptures" and when scriptures were used to invent events for narrative and evangelical purposes.

It is also possible that Jesus rode in on a donkey not to fulfill *Zechariah* but to emulate Solomon. According to *I Kings 1: 38*, Solomon rode into Jerusalem on a mule to be anointed as king. This passage was probably the inspiration for Zechariah. Jesus entered Jerusalem with a large following, some of whom probably had messianic expectations for him. It is possible that to present himself as a Solomon-like sage and man of peace, Jesus chose to enter on a donkey or mule. It is also possible that he hoped to be anointed as a king by a temple priest. However, considering the suspect nature of the Gospel narratives, we cannot know for certain that Jesus had messianic intentions when he went to Jerusalem.

It is interesting that scholars accept the historicity of the story of Jesus entering Jerusalem on a donkey on the basis of the fact that it is recorded in all four Gospels. Yet such scholars usually do not claim that miracle stories appearing in all four Gospels are also historical on that basis.

Since all four Gospel authors knew of the *Zechariah* passage and probably also the story of David entering Jerusalem on a donkey, it is just as probable that the story was invented on the basis of the "prophecy" as that Jesus rode the donkey to fulfill the prophecy. After all, all of the Gospel writers wanted to show that Jesus was the Messiah and, if scholarly dating and authorship theories of the Gospels are correct, none of the Gospel authors were present with Jesus in Jerusalem.

Sometimes the story of Jesus' entry into Jerusalem is seen as the key to understanding him and his sayings. For example, in his popular book *Zealot: The Life and Times of Jesus of Nazareth*, Reza Aslan makes the following claim about that event:

"So revelatory is this single moment in Jesus's brief life

that it alone can be used to clarify his mission, his theology, his politics, his relationship to the Jewish authorities, his relationship to Judaism in general, and his attitude toward the Roman occupation. Above all, this singular event explains why a simple peasant from the low hills of Galilee was seen as such a threat to the established system that he was hunted down, arrested, tortured, and executed."[173]

Setting aside for the moment the question of the historicity of the entry into Jerusalem story, consider for a moment the logic of this claim. Can everything a person ever said truly be interpreted in light of a singular event in that person's life?

Consider the Greek philosopher Empedocles (c. 490-430 B.C.E.). Empedocles held a variety of influential theories, including that the universe consists of four elements: fire, air, water, and earth. He theorized that there are two primary forces: a force of attraction (love) and a force of repulsion (hate). His theory of how life formed anticipated the theory of evolution. He had theories about perception and knowledge. He had a reputation as a wonder-working healer. Legend has it that he leaped into a volcano, which caused his death.

Would it make any sense at all to claim that Empedocles' life and teaching should be interpreted in light of the legend that he jumped into a volcano? Such a claim would be analogous to interpreting Jesus' sayings and defining his life in light of the legend that he rode a donkey into Jerusalem.

As far as we can tell from Gospel stories, Jesus traveled on foot. It is just as likely that Jesus just *walked* into Jerusalem as that he rode a donkey. Jesus' message was philosophical and mystical; it was about God's *present* realm. As *Mark* emphasized, Jesus did not go around proclaiming "I am the Messiah." *Mark* shows Jesus as a person who withdrew when he attracted too much attention. He kept moving from place to place.

Unlike Jewish Messianic claimants such as Judas of Galilee (c. 6 C.E.) and Simon Bar Kokhba (c. 135 C.E.), Jesus did not build an army to revolt against the Romans. From the Maccabees (c. 160 B.C.E.) to Abu Isa (c. 750 C.E.), *every* Messianic claimant (there were at least ten such claimants in that period) sought to lead a *violent* military rebellion. None of them left behind memorable wisdom sayings, as Jesus did. Based upon consideration of Jewish Messianic claimants of the era, it is questionable that Jesus saw his work in messianic terms and therefore questionable that he would have planned to fulfill "messianic prophecies."

Jesus might even have been to Jerusalem earlier in his life. According to the *Gospel of John,* Jesus had gone to Jerusalem and had returned to Galilee *twice* before this final trip (John 2: 13; 5: 1). In other words, Jesus could have gone into Jerusalem more than once in his life. The synoptic gospels do not mention religious holidays that occurred during Jesus' time in Galilee. That is not sufficient reason to assert that his mission only lasted one year. Holidays listed in the *Gospel of John* indicate at least three years passed from the beginning of Jesus' teaching mission until his final journey; but his mission could have been longer than even the three years mentioned in *John.*

Jesus may have simply intended to visit the temple, do some teaching and healing, and then return to Galilee.

The Gospels tell us Jesus caused a disturbance in the Temple courtyard, disrupting the business of the vendors and money changers. The *Gospel of John* tells us this happened on Jesus' *first* visit to Jerusalem, not the final visit. The other Gospels place the temple incident at the end of Jesus' ministry. Had he done what the Gospels say, the temple police would have tried to arrest him immediately.

But did Jesus actually get violent in the temple courtyard? The doubt arises about the incident from what Jesus taught: love, forgive, turn the other cheek, go the extra mile. His philosophy does not reflect the thoughts of a violent man. His philosophy was an inspiration for Gandhi and Martin Luther King, neither of whom committed acts of violence and both of whom were assassinated.

If Jesus acted from the philosophy he advocated, he would not have reacted violently in the Temple. If Jesus overturned tables and drove people out of the temple area, it would have been out of character. But, of course, sometimes humans react to situations in unexpected ways; so it is *possible* that Jesus turned over some tables or drove some people out of the Temple courtyard. If so, it was the only such incident in his career. When we take into consideration Jesus' philosophy and character, it is reasonable to doubt the story of the Temple disturbance.

If Jesus did *not* physically create a disturbance in the Temple courtyard, there are other possible explanations for why Jesus was arrested and crucified. In fact, the *Gospel of John* provides an alternative reason for Jesus' arrest. According to the *Gospel of John,* after Jesus raised Lazarus, the priests were afraid that everyone would believe in

Jesus and that consequently the Romans would destroy the Temple and the nation (John 11: 45-50). According to John, the priests conspired to have Jesus killed because they feared the people would follow him (John 11: 53).

There is also another possibility. The Jewish historian Josephus, a contemporary of the Gospel authors, also mentioned Jesus in the context of describing events during Pontius Pilate's rule in Jerusalem. The brief passage in Josephus referring to Jesus is controversial, in that some scholars believe the whole passage was inserted by pious Christian manuscript copyists, while other scholars believe that at least part of the passage was written by Josephus. I am persuaded that Josephus included a passage about Jesus, which was modified by Christian copyists.

The passage is found immediately after Josephus' description of the slaughter of Jewish protesters by Pilate's soldiers.

"Now, there was about this time Jesus, a wise man, if it be lawful to call him a man, for he was a doer of wonderful works – a teacher of such men as receive the truth with pleasure. He drew over to him both many Jews, and many of the Gentiles. He was Christ; and when Pilate, at the suggestion of the principal men amongst us, had condemned him to the cross, those that loved him at the first did not forsake him, for he appeared to them alive again the third day, as the divine prophets had foretold these and ten thousand other wonderful things concerning him; and the tribe of Christians, so named from him, are not extinct at this day."[174]

Since Josephus was not a Christian, it is highly improbable that he would have said that Jesus "was the Christ." That sentence was almost certainly interjected or modified by a Christian copyist. In a later passage about James the brother of Jesus, Josephus wrote that Jesus was "called the Christ."[175] Josephus' passage about Jesus might have also said "he was *called* the Christ," which phrase would not commit Josephus to the belief that Jesus *was* the Christ.

It is also unlikely that Josephus would have been concerned about the "lawfulness" of calling Jesus a man, for Josephus, like other Jews, did not hold to a belief in divine humans. Nor would Josephus have believed in the resurrection appearances or that Jesus fulfilled the "ten thousand things" foretold by the prophets. Josephus did believe in and made reference to "wonder-workers" and so might have included the phrase "doer of wonderful works."

Josephus would have heard of the Christians, but probably did not know much about them. He barely mentions them and elsewhere Josephus goes into great detail about what he did know (or thought he knew) about the various religious movements of the early first century. Josephus may well have thought of the Christians as a *tribe*, i.e. a clan of relatives and allies, from Galilee. Josephus' last statement that the "Christian tribe" was not "extinct at this day" suggests that Josephus might have expected that the "tribe" would eventually become extinct. Josephus may well have thought that the Christians were not a new sect but an actual *tribe* from Galilee. Such a belief would not be contradicted by the claim that Gentiles followed Jesus, since Galilee had many "Gentiles" and many people of "mixed" ancestry.

On the other hand, it is unlikely that a Christian would use the term "tribe" to describe Jesus' followers or choose the words "wise man" and "teacher" as the most apt descriptions of Jesus. More likely descriptions by Christians would have been "a descendent of David" or "a man without sin" or possibly even "born of a virgin, the son of God."

When the words probably interjected by Christians are removed, the passage would look something like this.

> "Now, there was about this time Jesus, a wise man . . . a doer of wonderful works – a teacher of such men as receive the truth with pleasure. He drew over to him both many of the Jews and many of the Gentiles. . . . When Pilate, at the suggestion of the principal men amongst us, had condemned him to the cross, those that loved him at first did not forsake him . . . . and the tribe of Christians are not extinct at this day."

Josephus' passage indicates that Jesus had a widespread reputation as a wisdom teacher and wonder-worker who spoke to both Aramaic and Greek speaking people and who was executed by Pilate at the suggestion of some of the Jewish leaders. Josephus usually mentioned names of persons when he knew them, so he probably did not know which "principal men" suggested the crucifixion to Pilate. Since Josephus had sources about all the priests and their families and nearly always used their names, it could be that it was not the Jewish priests who spoke to Pilate. The "principal men" could have been Jewish aristocrats who disapproved of the class of people who reportedly followed Jesus: the poor, Gentiles, women, tax collectors and "sinners." They may also have been worried that Jesus and his multitude of followers were planning a rebellion to try to establish Jesus as King of Judea.

Jesus might have said something that was overheard by an influential person who was offended by what he said. Jesus said things about the wealthy that were less than complementary. While the gospels indicate that priests were involved in Jesus' arrest, Josephus asserts that "principal men" among the Jews suggested to Pilate that Jesus be arrested. In Josephus' writings, when a priest or official is involved in some event, Josephus usually gives the person's name or office, as he does in describing the death of James, brother of Jesus. But Josephus did not write "Priest So-and-so"; he wrote "some of the principal men among us." "Principal men" *could* mean priests, but could also simply mean persons of honored families, wealth or political influence.

The Gospels report that while Jesus was in Jerusalem, he said, *"Do you see these great buildings? There will not be left here one stone upon another that will not be thrown down."* (Mark 13: 2; Matt. 24: 2; Luke 21: 6) That saying could be authentic and certainly would have been perceived by aristocratic Sadducees as a threat to the Temple. Jesus might have simply been making an observation about the impermanency of human buildings, rather than predicting immanent doom. Jesus' saying about "throwing down" building stones might easily have evolved into a story about "throwing down" temple tables.

Based upon his teachings and works before Jerusalem, I have doubts about Jesus physically assaulting people in the Temple courtyard. However, Jesus certainly said and/or did *something* that offended the powerful in Jerusalem. That does not prove that before entering Jerusalem he planned upon or intended to offend the powerful. Socrates did not philosophize with the hope that he would offend people and be executed, but he was executed all the same. The case of Jesus was similar: he philosophized and healed and was crucified as a threat to the status quo.

## The Aftermath

The earliest written works we have from the followers of Jesus are from one who never met Jesus: Paul's letters. Paul had some familiarity with the general philosophy of Jesus, if not with actual sayings. Paul must have heard teachings of Jesus' followers, otherwise why would he persecute them? Paul's attitude toward Mosaic Law indicates an awareness of Jesus' less than rigid attitude regarding those laws. Paul knew about Jesus' God concept of the all-providing Father (Philippians 4: 19). Paul knew about the love ethic of Jesus (1 Corinthians 13). Paul knew about the importance Jesus placed upon giving (2 Corinthians 9: 7) and not judging others (Romans 14:10-13).

However, since Paul rarely directly quoted sayings of Jesus, it is probable that Paul did not have access to a list of Jesus' sayings. That is not surprising, since there were surely only a few of those lists in circulation in Paul's time, and those lists would have circulated in the communities established by Jesus' earliest followers rather than in the cities where Paul traveled to make converts. In fact, Paul apparently took some pride in proclaiming his own revelations, rather than having familiarity with the teachings of Jesus' followers.

> *"But when he who had set me apart before I was born, and had called me through his grace, was pleased to reveal his son in me, in order that I might preach him among the Gentiles, I did not confer with flesh and blood, nor did I go up to Jerusalem to those who were apostles before me, but I went away into Arabia; and again I returned to Damascus. Then after three years I went up to Jerusalem to visit Cephas (Peter), and remained with him fifteen days. But I saw none of the other apostles except James the Lord's brother."* - (The Letter of Paul to the Galatians, ca. 55 C.E.)

Notice three things about this passage. Paul spoke of God revealing his son *in* Paul. The Greek word in the passage is εη (en' which means "in," not "to" as it is conventionally translated in this passage. The "in" signifies that Paul's revelatory experience was an *inner vision* rather than an outer physically perceived experience. Note too that Paul did not speak to any of Jesus' disciples until three years after his experience, and then only for fifteen days. Finally, note that Paul met Jesus' brother James. This is another witness to the existence of the historical Jesus; a purely fictional character cannot have an actual brother.

Paul had disagreements with Peter and James, which indicate that Paul thought of his own opinions/"revelations" as more authoritative than the views of Jesus' brother and original disciples. Paul's letters are of great value for understanding the origins of the Christian religion, but his opinions are of minor value in the project of understanding the historical Jesus.

Two practically certain historical facts became central to the development of Christianity: (1) Jesus was crucified and (2) his disciples claimed that Jesus had appeared to them after his crucifixion. The nature of those "resurrection appearances" was eventually proclaimed by Gospel authors to be the resurrected physical body of Jesus. However, the evidence indicates that the "appearances" were inner experiences, possibly dreams or, in some cases, "visions." Judaism had a tradition of understanding dreams and visions as messages from God. Even if we consider visions to be hallucinations, such experiences can have a profound impact on those who have them.

We also find in Paul's letters the earliest written description of the resurrection appearances:

> *"For I delivered to you as of first importance what I also received, that Christ died for our sins in accordance with scriptures, that he was buried, and that he was raised on the third day in accordance with the scriptures, and that he appeared to Cephas, then to the twelve. Then he appeared to more than five hundred brethren at one time, most of whom are still alive, though some have fallen asleep. Then he appeared to James, then to all the apostles. Last of all, as to one untimely born, he appeared also to me." (1 Corinthians 15:3-8)*

There are a number of odd things about this passage.

Paul does not say that Jesus was raised "according to eye witnesses" but "according to scriptures." Paul does not say which scriptures, apparently assuming the Corinthians would know. The passage shows that by the time Paul wrote, Jesus' followers were already searching the scriptures for proof that Jesus was the predicted Messiah. However, there are no passages in the canonical Hebrew Scriptures which state clearly that the Messiah would die for our sins and be raised on the third day. There is a passage in Hosea (6: 2) which says "on the third day he will raise us up," but the passage does not refer to a Messiah; it refers to the Israelites collectively. There is also the story of Jonah being in the belly of the fish for three days, but it is a stretch to call that incident a Messianic prophecy.

The Greek word translated as "appeared" in the above passage is "ὀπτάνομαι" (optanomai). This word is not used for passive physical sight. Rather "optanomai" indicates gazing at something remarkable and is the word from which the Greek "ὀπτασία," meaning "vision" or "apparition" is derived. When Paul wrote of something seen physically with the eyes, he used the Greek "βλέπω" (blepo). The use of "optanomai" in the passage regarding post-crucifixion appearances of Jesus indicates that Paul and the others had "visions" of Jesus rather than that they saw a physical form with their eyes. Remember that Paul never saw the physical historical Jesus, and therefore would have no idea of what Jesus looked like. If Paul saw a physical man, how would he know it was Jesus?

Another oddity in the passage is the list of names of those to whom Jesus appeared. Cephas (Peter) is listed as first. Next were the "twelve." Who were the twelve? The Gospels list twelve disciples, *including* Peter and Judas; but Peter was named separately from the twelve by Paul and Judas supposedly died before the resurrection.

Who were the "five hundred" of whom Paul speaks? No such event was mentioned in Acts or anywhere else. One would certainly think that of five hundred witnesses to an appearance of a resurrected man, at least one would have left a written record. One would expect that such an event would be even more widely known than an appearance to twelve people. Yet other than this passage from Paul, there is no record of the supposed "five hundred." Based upon these considerations, it is unlikely there was an appearance to five hundred. Paul didn't necessarily simply make up the event; he may have heard the story from someone and simply repeated it.

"Then he appeared to James, then to all the apostles." There is no mention of Jesus appearing to his brother James in the Gospels, in Acts or in the *Epistle of James*. Even more puzzling than the appearance to five hundred at once is Paul's assertion that Jesus appeared to "all the apostles." This *could* mean that "the twelve" had experienced a second appearance. However, Paul refers to apostles other than the traditional twelve, e.g. Andronicus and Junias (Romans 16: 7). We do not know how many followers of Jesus came to be known as "apostles," but evidently there were more than the traditional twelve and, according to Paul, Jesus "appeared" to all of them. Perhaps at the time a dream or vision of Jesus was necessary for one to be given the title "apostle."

Another passage in Paul's letters indicates that the appearances of Jesus to Paul should be understood as visions. Paul wrote:

> "*I must boast . . . I will go on to visions and revelations of the Lord. I know a man in Christ who fourteen years ago was caught up to the third heaven – whether in the body or out of the body I do not know, God knows. And I know that this man was caught up to Paradise.*" (2 Corinthians 12: 1 – 3)

Based upon the context in the letter, "the man in Christ" is undoubtedly a self reference. Paul's reference to his visions and revelations supports the hypothesis that his experience of Jesus was one of his visions, possibly the same vision in which he was "caught up to Paradise." The description sounds like a mystical experience. The "14 years" is probably an approximate and symbolic number (14 = 2 x 7) rather than a literal period of time.

Further evidence that Paul did not see Jesus' *physical* body is found in his description of the resurrected body. Paul spoke of the resurrected body as a spiritual body, different from the physical: "*It is sown a physical body, it is raised a spiritual body.*" (1 Corinthians 15: 44)

If Paul's vision of Jesus was a spiritual vision and was accepted by Jesus' original followers as authentic, those followers probably also had spiritual visions rather than physical sightings of Jesus after the crucifixion.

The earliest copies of *Mark*, which is the earliest Gospel, end with the empty tomb and an announcement to some women that Jesus will be seen by his disciples in Galilee. Later versions of *Mark* have a few different endings which include appearances. *Matthew*, following *Mark*, has Jesus appearing to the disciples in Galilee. Luke places the first appearance to two unnamed disciples as they were on their way to Emmaus, near Jerusalem; then Jesus is said to appear to "Simon" and other disciples in Jerusalem. John has the first appearance to Mary Magdalene in Jerusalem, then to the disciples in Jerusalem.

Chronologically in New Testament writings, the trajectory of Jesus appearance stories begins with inner visions or spiritual experiences (Paul's letters) to *no* recorded visions in Mark, to differing stories of appearances in Matthew and Luke, to a resurrected physical Jesus who eats fish in the *Gospel of John*. The chronological trajectory of the stories is from inner apparitions to external visions to a physical body capable of eating.

From the passages in Paul and the chronological trajectory of New Testament writings, the most probable conclusions are: that Jesus' disciples had inner experiences and possibly dreams and visions of Jesus after the crucifixion; that those experiences convinced them that Jesus had been raised up to heaven and was the Messiah; that later disciples, like Paul, also had similar "resurrection experiences"; and that reports of the inner experiences of the early disciples gradually evolved into the stories that Jesus literally and physically arose from death.

Ultimately the atonement and resurrection of Jesus are matters of faith.  It cannot be historically or scientifically proven that Jesus' death was redemptive.  It cannot be proven historically or scientifically that Jesus physically arose from death.  Either you believe these things or you do not.

It should be noted that belief in miracles is not necessary for believing that Jesus arose physically after the crucifixion.  It is naturalistically possible that Jesus came back to life after the crucifixion; there are modern authenticated incidents of people appearing to be dead and then reviving.[176]  However, considering the above passages from Paul, it is more probable that the resurrection appearances were psycho-spiritual experiences in the minds of the beholders.

The fact that the execution of Jesus did not end his movement and influence, but rather increased them, can be partially explained by the resurrection appearances (whatever their nature).  The appeal of Jesus' philosophy and healing work were undoubtedly equally important in spreading the movement, for it was that philosophy and healing work that initially attracted followers.  The resurrection experiences of the early disciples of Jesus, whatever the nature of those experiences, gave them hope of everlasting life.  Hope moves us forward when we are dissatisfied with our lives.  Hope of everlasting life helps people feel that life has meaning.  Hope of everlasting life is not an insignificant matter.  Hope matters.

# Chapter Thirteen: The Experiment

I conducted an experiment to see how individual's emotional and physiological states might be affected by listening to sayings of Jesus. I wanted the sayings they heard to be as close as possible to what the historical Jesus actually said. For those sayings I have relied to a great extent upon the judgment of the Jesus Seminar Scholars, as discussed in Chapter 1. In addition, I wanted to compare such effects with effects of sayings attributed to Jesus, but not originating with the historical Jesus. For convenience I have labeled sayings probably originating with the historical Jesus "authentic" and those probably not originating with him "attributed."

A discussion of how the Gospels were written and chosen is necessary for the reader to understand how I chose the two types of sayings. In the course of identifying what the historical Jesus probably *did* say ("authentic sayings"), the Seminar also identified things Jesus probably did *not* say ("attributed sayings").

## Recovering the Unique Voice of Jesus

It may be shocking to the average Christian that New Testament scholars do not believe Jesus said everything reported in the Gospels. Nevertheless, historical research frequently discovers new documents and errors in the work of previous historians. We should not be too surprised that historical analysis reveals errors in even the most sacred books, especially considering that ancient sacred texts were written for religious purposes and not to provide accurate histories in the modern sense.

New Testament scholars, especially those associated with the Jesus Seminar, have uncovered a unique perspective and voice within the New Testament: the perspective and voice of Jesus of Nazareth. It is a voice that says things in a style different from those of the New Testament authors. It is a voice that says things which contradict the views of other New Testament authors, including authors of the Gospels. It is a voice that can be distinguished in style and substance from other New Testament voices. It is a voice the Gospel authors often had difficulty interpreting.

Examining the style and content of that unique voice and perspective, we have seen that Jesus' philosophy had ideas which are consistent with modern ideas about healing. Jesus saw the world as ruled by divine principles, including justice, grace, and a principle of expansion. Jesus saw God's realm as already present and God as Father of humankind. Jesus challenged conventional moral ideas and Mosaic Laws.

Now it is time to look at some of the words attributed to Jesus that he probably did *not* say. We will not look at every such saying, but instead look at examples of sayings which typify the perspectives of the different Gospel authors. These are sayings most likely invented by the gospel authors to tell their story and express their interpretation of Jesus.

Understand that in making the distinction between "authentic" and "attributed" sayings, we are dealing with probabilities rather than certainties. For the purpose of making the case that Jesus was a healer-philosopher, we do not need to look at every saying in the Gospels. The "authentic sayings" are sufficient to discern Jesus' philosophy and understand, at least in part, how Jesus healed.

Sayings attributed to Jesus that express the idea of God's realm and rule as distant in space and future in time contrast with the unique perspective and voice of Jesus – the authentic philosophy of Jesus. Sayings attributed to Jesus strictly supporting all Mosaic Law contrast with other sayings in his authentic philosophy. Condemnatory sayings attributed to Jesus contradict his idea of an unconditionally loving Father-God and the forgiving heart of his philosophy. As an ordinary human being, Jesus might have contradicted himself from time to time. Yet if Jesus was truly an enlightened human being, his message would more likely be self-consistent than self-contradictory.

Sayings which quote Hebrew Scriptures and rephrase views commonly held in Jesus' culture before he was born tell us nothing about him and so cannot securely be ascribed to him. Therefore we cannot know if Jesus believed in a Messiah coming from the sky, a resurrection or final judgment, let alone if he believed he was that Messiah. Beliefs in a resurrection and final judgment were commonly held by Zoroastrians and Jews long *before* Jesus. He may have believed them but he may also have *not* believed them.

In any case, although Paul and other early Christians adopted conventional Messianic ideas and expected Jesus would come in the clouds during their lifetimes ushering in the resurrection and final judgment, those events did not happen. If Jesus believed as Paul and the others did, he was mistaken on those points.

Some thirty-five years after the crucifixion, the Romans destroyed Jerusalem and the Temple. This was a traumatic event for Jews and Christians alike. The Pharisaic rabbis and local synagogues salvaged Judaism, replacing the central Temple with many centers for Judaism. The early Christians interpreted the destruction of Jerusalem as a sign that soon Jesus would come in the clouds with the final judgment. As the return (the "parousia") was delayed, followers of Jesus wrote their Gospels.

All the passages below are from the NRSV translation.

## Mark

With the destruction of the Temple fresh in the minds of Jews and Christians and the delay of the Parousia of Jesus, one ingenious Christian wrote a narrative of Jesus' life, stitching together remembered sayings and stories about Jesus into a relatively coherent "gospel" ("good news"). That narrative is known to us as the *Gospel of Mark*. Most biblical scholars have concluded that the Gospels were not written by the individuals they were attributed to, but for simplicity's sake I use the traditional names when referring to the authors of the Gospels.

Mark's primary theme was that Jesus was the Messiah (Christ), but that this truth was kept secret during his life.

Mark used the Greek words "εὐθέως" (eutheos) and "εὐθύς" (euthus) at least thirty-seven times. "Eutheos" and "euthus" both mean "immediately" or "straightway." From this repetitive use of words meaning "immediately" we can gather that Mark felt great urgency in presenting his message. He still expected Jesus to return soon. From various scriptures (especially Daniel) and events from the war between Rome and Judea, Mark also composed an "apocalyptic" sermon for Jesus. The so-called "little apocalypse of Mark" is in line with the urgency of Mark's message, especially in the use of descriptions of events during the siege by Romans against Jerusalem.

An analysis of the "little apocalypse" indicates that it was written near the time of the Temple's destruction (over 30 years after Jesus' earthly life) and relies heavily on passages from the Hebrew Scriptures. The references to events long after Jesus' life indicate that such passages were probably written after the events occurred, rather than described by Jesus beforehand. The reliance of the "little apocalypse" on Hebrew

Scriptures means the thoughts there did not *originate* with Jesus and so those thoughts do not provide us with words that originated with Jesus. The little apocalypse's description of post-crucifixion events could more easily have originated with Mark than Jesus, and so does not provide reliable accounts of Jesus' words. It seems probable therefore that the whole section originated with the author of *Mark* rather than with Jesus.

What follows is an analysis of part of the "little apocalypse" of *Mark*, which formed the basis of similar passages in Matthew and Luke.

> *"Many will come in my name, saying, `I am he!'*
> *and they will lead many astray.  And when you hear of*
> *wars and rumors of wars, do not be alarmed; this must*
> *take place, but the end is not yet.  For nation will rise*
> *against nation, and kingdom against kingdom; there will*
> *be earthquakes in various places, there will be famines;*
> *this is but the beginning of the birth-pangs." (Mark 13:*
> *6-8)*

During most times in history there have been wars and earthquakes, so that "prediction" is not particularly telling.  During the Judean-Roman war (66-70 C.E.), there was a great famine in Jerusalem,[177] several "false prophets" arose,[178] and it was rumored that an earthquake occurred in the Temple.[179]

> *"But take heed to yourselves; for they will deliver you up to*
> *councils; and you will be beaten in synagogues; and you will stand*
> *before governors and kings for my sake, to bear testimony before them.*
> *And the gospel must first be preached to all nations.  And when they*
> *bring you to trial and deliver you up, do not be anxious beforehand what*
> *you are to say; but say whatever is given you in that hour, for it is not*
> *you who speak, but the Holy Spirit."(Mark 13: 9-11)*

Jesus' followers were persecuted periodically after the crucifixion, by both Roman and Jewish leaders.  Paul's letters make reference to the persecutions of early Christians.  Again, the persecutions happened after Jesus was crucified and so more likely were written by his followers than spoken by him.  The above passage expresses concerns of the early church, not things that happened while Jesus was alive.

> *"And brother will deliver up brother to death, and the father his*
> *child, and children will rise against parents and have them put to death*

*and you will be hated by all for my name's sake. But he who endures to the end will be saved." (Mark 13: 12-13)*

Josephus describes how the famine in Jerusalem led to family members turning against each other in desperation for food.[180]

> *"But when you see the desolating sacrilege set up where it ought not to be (let the reader understand), then let those who are in Judea flee to the mountains; let him who is on the housetop not go down, nor enter his house, to take anything away; and let him who is in the field not turn back to take his mantle. And alas for those who are with child and for those who give suck in those days!" (Mark 13: 14-17)*

The imagery here is drawn from Daniel and 1 Maccabees 2: 28: *". . . and upon the wing of abominations shall come one who makes desolation." (Dan 9: 27) ". . . and they shall set up the abomination that makes desolation." (Dan 11: 31) "And he and his sons fled to the hills and left all that they had in the city." (1 Macc 2: 28)*

> *"Pray that it may not happen in winter. For in those days there will be such tribulation as has not been from the beginning of the creation which God created until now, and never will be. And if the Lord had not shortened the days, no human being would be saved; but for the sake of the elect, whom he chose, he shortened the days." (Mark 13: 18-20)*

The language in this passage is drawn from Daniel 12: 1: *"And there shall be a time of trouble, such as never has been since there was a nation till that time; but at that time your people shall be delivered, every one whose name shall be found written in the book."*

Mark originally ended his Gospel with women running from an empty tomb, afraid to convey the message given them by a young man at the tomb: "Do not be amazed; you seek Jesus of Nazareth, who was crucified. He has risen, he is not here. . . . go tell his disciples and Peter that he is going before you to Galilee; there you will see him, as he told you." (Mark 16: 6, 7) Since the women were afraid to convey the message, one wonders how Mark found out about the message.

Some years later, two other writers used Mark's Gospel as the primary source for their own narratives. Those two writers are known to us as Matthew and Luke. Matthew and Luke also very probably had a second source for their Gospels: a list of sayings of Jesus (the hypothetical *Q* document). Matthew and Luke each had access to some sayings not available to the other. Matthew and Luke also had somewhat different theological agendas and so used *Mark* and *Q* in somewhat different ways.

## *M a t t h e w*

Matthew was concerned to portray Jesus as the fulfillment of the "Law and the Prophets." At every opportunity Matthew points to an event as a fulfillment of some prophecy, even though some of the "prophecies" are just phrases from the *Psalms* or reference to a time in Israel's past. Matthew ingeniously wove together his own thoughts with scripturally influenced sayings, and sayings of Jesus to produce "the Sermon on the Mount" as we know it today. To Jesus' original sayings Matthew added "beatitudes" drawn from Hebrew Scriptures, commentaries on Mosaic Law, and thoughts on fasting and prayer. The Sermon on the Mount is powerful and influential, but in some ways more reflective of Matthew's agenda than Jesus' original philosophy.

Here are a few "Sermon on the Mount" sayings added by Matthew to the words of Jesus, presenting Jesus as being stricter about the Law than the Pharisees:

> *"Think not that I have come to abolish the law and the prophets; I have come not to abolish them but to fulfill them. For truly, I say to you, till heaven and earth pass away, not an iota, not a dot will pass from the law until all is accomplished. Whoever then relaxes one of the least of these commandments and teaches men so, shall be called least in the kingdom of heaven; but he who does them and teaches them shall be called great in the kingdom of heaven. For I tell you, unless your righteousness exceeds that of the scribes and Pharisees, you will never enter the kingdom of heaven.*
>
> *You have heard that it was said to the men of old, 'You shall not kill; and whoever kills shall be liable to judgment.' But I say to you that everyone who is angry with his brother shall be liable to judgment;*

*whoever insults his brother shall be liable to the council, and whoever says, 'You fool!' shall be liable to the hell of fire."* (Matt 5: 17-22)

*"You have heard that it was said, 'You shall not commit adultery.' But I say to you that everyone who looks at a woman lustfully has already committed adultery with her in his heart. If your right eye causes you to sin, pluck it out and throw it away; it is better that you lose one of your members than that your whole body be thrown into hell. And if your right hand causes you to sin, cut it off and throw it away; it is better that you lose one of your members than that your whole body go into hell."* (Matt 5: 27-30)

In Chapter 6, Jesus' unorthodox positions on the Law were discussed and it was seen that he did *not* have a strict view of the Mosaic Law. You may recall that Jesus said regarding the Sabbath commandment that it was made for man and not man for the commandment. Matthew was undoubtedly concerned about Jesus' reputation as being "relaxed" about the Law and so attempted to portray Jesus as "more righteous than the Pharisees," thereby reflecting the beliefs of some of the more conservative Jewish followers of Jesus.

Matthew indicated his dualistic perspective on the cosmos in the opening chapters by having Magi visit the birth of Jesus. Magi were dualistic Zoroastrian priests, who believed in resurrection, final judgment, and an Evil One opposed to the Good Spirit. The Zoroastrian religion was widespread and influential for hundreds of years before the Gospels were written. Zoroastrians had a religion that emphasized works more than faith or grace; that is the position Matthew held to as seen in the following example:

*"Not everyone who says to me, 'Lord, Lord,' shall enter the kingdom of heaven, but he who does the will of my Father who is in heaven. On that day many will say to me, 'Lord, Lord, did we not prophesy in your name, and cast out demons in your name, and do many mighty works in your name? And then will I declare to them, 'I never knew you; depart from me, you evildoers.'"* (Matt 7: 21-23)

## *L u k e*

Luke was probably the best educated of the Gospel writers and he opens his book asserting that he had done research. In other words, Luke saw himself as a historian and his Gospel (and *Acts*) as a history. Yet it is important to understand that historians of Luke's era felt free to invent speeches, conversations, and events to tell their stories, so even books written for historical purposes were not thoroughly documented and contained "convenient fictions." It is important to recognize that the standards for history in Luke's era were not as rigorous as modern standards. We cannot take every statement in Luke as accurate history.

Luke incorporated much of *Mark* and of *Q*; his version of the Gospels reflects those two sources, but without Matthew's legalistic emphasis. Luke included some authentic parables of Jesus which are not found in other Gospels but which reflect Jesus' style and ideas. Luke, like other Gospel authors, also undoubtedly attributed some of his own ideas and words to Jesus.

Luke had special empathy for the poor, as did Jesus. However, Luke also had a stronger antipathy toward the Pharisees and the wealthy than did Jesus. Those biases can be seen in words Luke attributed to Jesus, such as:

> *"Woe to you that are rich, for you have received your consolation. Woe to you that are full now, for you shall hunger. Woe to you that laugh now, for you shall mourn and weep. Woe to you, when all men speak well of you, for so their fathers did to the false prophets."* (Luke 6:24-26)
>
> *"Woe to you Pharisees! For you tithe mint and rue and every herb, and neglect justice and the love of God; these you ought to have done, without neglecting the others. Woe to you Pharisees! For you love the best seat in the synagogues and salutations in the market places. Woe to you! For you are like graves which are not seen, and men walk over them without knowing it.*
>
> *Woe to you lawyers also! For you load men with burdens hard to bear, and you yourselves do not touch the burdens with one of your fingers. Woe to you! For you build the tombs of the prophets whom your fathers killed. So you are witnesses and consent to the*

*deeds of your fathers; for they killed them, and you build their tombs."* (Luke 11: 42-48)

To the original blessings of Jesus, Matthew added Beatitudes drawn from Hebrew Scriptures, such as "Blessed are the meek, for they shall inherit the earth." In his "sermon on the plain," Luke instead added "woes" which were complementary to Jesus' blessings. Jesus blessed the poor; Luke damned the rich. Jesus challenged strict legalism; Luke damned the legalists.

## John

The *Gospel of John* was written 20 to 30 years after the other Gospels, yet it is likely that John did not have access to the earlier Gospels. John had access to many of the same stories found in *Mark*, which suggests that some collection of stories about Jesus existed before *Mark* and *John* were written. The words ascribed to Jesus in the *Gospel of John* are very different from the other three Gospels (and from *The Gospel of Thomas*). It is highly probable that John was concerned primarily to express his own "revelations" and what his community had come to believe about Jesus. It has also been argued by Elaine Pagels and other scholars that the *Gospel of John* was written as an oppositional response to the earlier *Gospel of Thomas*.[181]

Many of the words ascribed to Jesus by John reflect the spirit of Jesus' philosophy, if not the letter. In the synoptic Gospels Jesus advocates having faith in the Father God; in *John* Jesus also advocates having faith in the Christ (i.e. Jesus himself). The *Gospel of John* has the same spirit of love as expressed in the philosophy of Jesus. However, Jesus' style of speech is very different in *John* than in the other Gospels. In the synoptic Gospels and in *Thomas*, Jesus speaks in short witty aphorisms and stories; in *John* Jesus speaks primarily in long discourses and self affirmations ("I am" discourses).

One passage of Jesus' sayings from *John* is sufficient to illustrate the obvious difference between *John* and the Jesus of the synoptic Gospels:

*I am the true vine, and my Father is the vinedresser. Every branch of mine that bears no fruit, he takes away, and every branch that does bear fruit he prunes, that it may bear more fruit. You are already*

*made clean by the word which I have spoken to you.
Abide in me, and I in you. As the branch cannot bear
fruit by itself, unless it abides in the vine, neither can
you, unless you abide in me.*

*I am the vine, you are the branches. He who
abides in me, and I in him, he it is that bears much fruit,
for apart from me you can do nothing. If a man does not
abide in me, he is cast forth as a branch and withers;
and the branches are gathered, thrown into the fire and
burned. If you abide in me, and my words abide in you,
ask whatever you will, and it shall be done for you.*

*By this my Father is glorified, that you bear
much fruit, and so prove to be my disciples. As the
Father has loved me, so have I loved you; abide in my
love. If you keep my commandments, you will abide in
my love, just as I have kept my Father's commandments
and abide in his love. These things I have spoken to you,
that my joy may be in you, and that your joy may be full.*

*This is my commandment, that you love one
another as I have loved you. (John 14: 1- 15: 12)*

This is a beautiful passage, but it probably originated with John
and not with Jesus. The style is long and discursive rather than
consisting of the short aphorisms and parables as found in the other
Gospels. The central focus of the passage is Jesus in contrast to the
"kingdom of God" focus in the other Gospels. The passage reflects the
ideas of love and faith found in the philosophy of Jesus; however it
doesn't have the style of Jesus and has an emphasis on faith in *Jesus* that
is not found in the authentic sayings.

## Thomas

Since the 19th century most New Testament scholars have agreed
that the Gospels of *Matthew* and *Luke* each independently used a list of
sayings of Jesus as a source for their Gospels. This Gospel is referred to
as the *"Q" Gospel* and even though no copy of *Q* has ever been
discovered, the internal comparative evidence found in *Matthew* and
*Luke* is so strong that almost all scholars today accept the *Q* theory.

The rediscovery of *The Gospel of Thomas* in 1945 proved that there were sayings Gospels similar to *Q*. Like the hypothetical *Q*, *Thomas* consists almost entirely of sayings of Jesus; contains no narrative of Jesus' life; makes no mention of his crucifixion and resurrection; and contains many of the sayings hypothesized to be in *Q*, along with other sayings found in the synoptic Gospels. In addition, *Thomas* contains a few sayings which were previously lost yet probably originated with Jesus, according to the criteria of the Jesus Seminar.

Undoubtedly all the authors of the Gospels believed they were being true to the message and spirit of Jesus. Modern Christians, like previous generations, will emphasize the sayings that are most meaningful to them, regardless of whether the sayings originated with Jesus or with the authors of the Gospels. Nevertheless, the true story and authentic philosophy of the historical Jesus is worth seeking, not only for the sake of historical accuracy but also for understanding how he healed.

## A 21st Century Study of Jesus' Philosophy and Altered States of Consciousness

Is there any practical difference between listening to the philosophy of the historical Jesus and words attributed to him by others? In an attempt to answer this question, I did an exploratory research project on the possible psychosomatic effects of Jesus' philosophy on modern listeners. I wanted to see if listening to Jesus' parables and aphorisms would affect people in a therapeutic way. I wanted to check for immediate short term effects. I also wanted to see if there was any difference in effect between listening to sayings thought by scholars to be "authentic" and those thought to be attributable to the Gospel authors rather than to Jesus.

The design of the experiment was approved by an Independent Review Board and the means of statistical analysis was approved by a professional statistician.

In the experiment, thirty participants listened to an approximately 30 minute recording of "authentic" sayings of Jesus and thirty listened to an approximately 30 minute recording of "attributed" sayings. The "authentic" list consisted of most of the sayings discussed in previous chapters. The "attributed" list consisted of the sayings from the canonical Gospels discussed in this chapter, plus: Matthew 13: 47-50; 25: 31-46; Luke 7: 41-42; 10: 19-20; 12: 4-5; 12: 42-48; 14: 12-14; Mark 7: 8-13, 20-23; 13: 21-36; and John 5: 19-29; 10: 1-5,7-18; 12: 44-50;

13:34-35; 17: 5-7, 20-26.

I used the State-Trait Anxiety Inventory (STAI) as one of the instruments in my research. Participants filled out the inventory before listening to the recordings and then a second time after listening. The STAI is known to be a reliable instrument as the result of its use in psychological practice and research.

Some research using the STAI has indicated measurable reduction of anxiety in meditators, e.g. a 1976 study by Richard J. Davidson, Daniel J. Goleman and Gary E. Schwartz published in *Journal of Abnormal Psychology*. [182] Another study indicated that STAI measured anxiety reduction equally from 20 minutes of three methods: non-cultic meditation, quietly resting in a recliner, and acute physical activity. [183] That study encouraged me to use STAI for my research since my study did not involve any training and the STAI attained measurable results for those only briefly trained in meditation and even for those who were simply resting in a recliner.

The participants in my study sat in straight-back chairs and were listening to a voice recording with no relaxing background music. Consequently, any effects of the experiment would not be attributable to resting in a recliner while listening to relaxing music.

Participants also filled out the Profile in Mood States (POMS) instrument before and after listening to the recording. POMS measures shifts in various "moods": tension, anxiety, depression, dejection, anger, hostility, fatigue, inertia, confusion, bewilderment, vigor, and activity. POMS is used extensively as a measurement of patient responses to mental health therapeutic interventions.

The third aspect of my research was use of peripheral skin temperature (PST) as a way to detect a relaxed meditative state in the participants. The logic of using peripheral skin temperature to detect a meditative state is as follows:

(1) Scientific research indicates that meditation reduces stress. [18] Biofeedback studies have shown that a common indicator of people in meditative states is the increase of alpha brain-wave amplitude.

(2) One physiological indicator of relaxation and stress reduction is peripheral skin temperature increase, which in biofeedback studies is usually measured as finger temperature. For example, a study by Patrick A. Boudewyns in *Behavior Therapy* concluded: "Finger temperature decreased under assumed stress conditions and increased under assumed relaxation conditions." [185]

(3) Relaxed states in general (including hypnotic states) have

been shown to be associated with higher amplitude alpha and theta waves.[186] In *"Fundamentals of EEG Measurement"* M. Teplan notes: "Alpha activity is induced by closing the eyes and by relaxation."[187] I should note here that my participants were not instructed to relax and close their eyes, but were told that they could close their eyes if they wanted to.

(4) Since increased finger temperature indicates a relaxed state and a relaxed state is accompanied by increased alpha amplitude, it follows that increased finger temperature would be accompanied by increased alpha amplitude. At least in terms of increased alpha amplitude, a relaxed state is physiologically equivalent to a meditative state.

(5) Of the physiological effects of meditation and hypnosis, the simplest measure is peripheral skin temperature. Increase in peripheral skin temperature usually indicates a physiological state of relaxation, which in turn usually indicates an altered state of consciousness such as those produced during meditation and hypnosis.

The participants in my experiment experienced increased peripheral skin temperature to a statistically significant degree while listening to recordings of both Jesus' authentic sayings and the attributed sayings. The increased PST indicated that, on average, participants had relaxation responses while listening. There was no significant difference in PST between the two groups of listeners; both groups had, on average, significant response and some individuals within each group had increases in PST of over seven degrees Fahrenheit. Those who had increases of 7 degrees or more almost certainly also had meditative experiences.

From these results it appears that listening to a recording of sacred writings for 30 minutes tends to be relaxing, regardless of difference in content. However, this experiment is not sufficient to prove that point; proof would require further research using different lists of quotations.

Even though there was apparently little difference in relaxation between the two groups, there was a significant difference between them in reported *anxiety* after listening to the recordings. Self-reported anxiety traits as measured by STAI decreased significantly after listening to recordings, significantly more so for those who listened to the recording of "authentic sayings of Jesus." In fact, the change in the "authentic" group was responsible for the statistical significance. The "authentic sayings" group scores decreased by an average of 2.56 points.

The "attributed" group scores averaged only a 0.73 decrease. This was a surprising result because "anxiety *traits*" are generally stable – they do not tend to fluctuate. The results indicate that participants perceived their *general* anxiety as lower after listening to the authentic sayings of Jesus.

Self-reported anxiety *states* and other negative emotions (POMS) similarly decreased after listening to recordings, but not to a statistically significant degree. In both tests, the decrease in anxiety and negative moods was greater for the "authentic" group than for the "attributed" group. The anxiety state scores of the "authentic" group decreased an average of 4.4 points; the "attributed" group decreased an average of 0.1 points. On the POMS scores, total mood disturbance (TMD) for the *attributed* group actually averaged an *increase* of 1.34 points, while the *authentic* group TMD *decreased* an average of 2.3 points.

I did an additional preliminary investigation to see what might result from a recording designed to be more conducive to meditation. I asked a few extra volunteers to listen to a meditation recording which consisted of a few words of instruction followed by selected passages from the authentic sayings of Jesus. I did not have enough volunteers for statistically significant comparison, but I was curious to see if a recording designed for meditation rather than a reading might result in greater relaxation and decrease of anxiety. The main difference between the recording for the extra experiment and the original "authentic sayings" recording was there were fewer sayings and more silence for contemplation. In the additional experiment, the volunteers were asked to take the STAI questionnaire before and after listening to the recording. Their PST was measured while listening to the recording.

The average difference between base and peak temperatures in the "extra" experiment was 2.98 degrees Celsius, which was about 1.0 degree (1.8 F) higher than the average of the original "attributed" group and 1.28 degrees (2.3 F) higher than the "authentic" group. Two of the seven participants (29%) in the extra experiment had temperature increases of 4 or more degrees Celsius (7 degrees F), compared with the 4 of 28 (14%) participants in each of the original two groups. In other words, the preliminary results indicate that *100% more participants* had significant relaxation responses when the recording was designed to be a meditation than when the recording was designed as a "reading."

The mean decrease in anxiety-state scores for this experimental group was 7 compared to the 0.1 and 4.4 decreases for the original experimental "attributed" and "authentic" groups, respectively. The mean decrease in anxiety-trait scores was 4.57 compared to the decreases of 1 and 2.56 for "attributed" and "authentic" groups respectively. (See Appendices A – C for more details.)

While the sampling from the extra experiment was too small to have statistical significance, the results suggest that designed meditations using Jesus' authentic sayings could produce meditative experiences and anxiety reduction for those who are open to such experiences. The experiments also indicate that those who originally heard Jesus might have had meditative experiences and stress reduction as a result of hearing and contemplating his sayings.

## A Brief Digression on History, Mythology & Reality

Biblical scholarship, my analysis of Jesus' philosophy, and my experiment convince me that much of the Gospels' contents are non-historical. Nevertheless, I believe that even some of the non-historical content has spiritual value.

History deals with evidence of momentary events and probabilities. History is useful because, like science, it can liberate us from the superstitions and false concepts of our ancestors. Accepting that our scriptures may not be literally true in every detail can help us have the humility to allow others to have different unverifiable beliefs. Having some humility about our beliefs can make us less insistent on our own way: *"Love does not insist on its own way."* (1 Corinthians 13: 5)

The study of history can also bring us fresh and useful insights from the past. It can tell us where we came from, suggest where we are going, and help us learn about what works and what doesn't. History includes inspiring, enlightening, and fascinating stories that are part of what we ourselves are. For all these reasons and more, historical studies can bring light and delight to our experience.

When historical study casts doubt upon writings generally deemed sacred, historians encounter resistance from those who resist questioning their scriptures and beliefs. But such resistance is unnecessary. When we let go of the need to have our sacred scriptures be entirely and literally infallible, we are ready to draw upon the empowering depths of spiritual and mythological meaning. Only by letting go of pride in our opinions can we have the necessary humility to find the truth. Only when we let go of the need to be right, can we truly find spiritual light.

The historical Jesus and his philosophy as proposed in this book open up possibilities for healing and spiritual enlightenment. His philosophy can be contemplated to induce meditation, reduce anxiety, strengthen faith, and release unconscious potentialities within us. His ethic remains highly idealistic, yet is also practical in many ways. Sorting through and analyzing the evidence, we can glimpse the life of Jesus and the very beginning of the Christian religion.

Even so, the *non*-historical Jesus is also valuable.

The Gospel authors created a "mythology of Jesus." By "mythology" I do not mean "fiction" or "falsehood." A myth, like fiction, can be developed from facts of history, as when a movie is said to be "based upon a true story." The purpose of a mythology is to *represent* the origins, values, and traditions of a tribe, nation, or religious community. The purpose is to find meaning and share insights.

The myth of George Washington cutting down a cherry tree and confessing it to his father is pure imagined invention; yet George Washington was a real person and the story was told to represent his basic honesty. The story is part of American mythology, like stories about Davy Crockett (an actual person) and Paul Bunyan (a fictional character). Likewise, invented stories told about Jesus can still stand as representations of what he was or at least what his followers believed him to be. Many of the mythologies of the ancient world can be seen as "historical fiction," to be read for the ideas or feelings behind the stories rather than as accurate records of actual events.

The stories of Jesus' birth are almost certainly mythological rather than factual. Yet the beauty and power of the nativity stories do not depend upon their being factual. Their value lies in their symbolism and the feelings they evoke. Among other things, the Nativity stories symbolize the truth that any child born into this world, whether visited by kings or in the humblest circumstances, has the potential to achieve greatness and enlightenment.

Likewise the stories of miracles, inspired no doubt by Jesus healing works, need not be taken as literal eyewitness reports to be meaningful. Miracle stories inspire us to stretch beyond our apparent limitations and symbolize the greatest miracle: the existence of the Universe.

The stories of Jesus' final days and resurrection appearances symbolize archetypal ideas found in Mystery Religions and popular literature: ideas of the "hero's journey" leading to a new way of being.

If the moral and spiritual ideas in Matthew's "Sermon on the Mount" do not all originate with Jesus, what does it matter? Either the ideas are valuable or they are not, regardless of *whose* words they are. Every moral idea must be evaluated to determine whether or not it is of value for individuals and society. An anonymous proverb or poem can be just as illuminating and morally valid as one with a known source.

The cosmic "Word" of John's Gospel is a profound metaphysical and mystical idea with parallels in Stoic philosophy and world mysticism. The words of Jesus in *John* may be taken as affirmations of a light and life that is within us all: "in him was life, and the life was the light of humankind." (John 1: 4)

The mythologies of the world symbolize eternal concerns and archetypes of the collective unconscious (if Jung was correct, which I believe he was). The mythologies of the world have value for psychological theory, therapy, understanding of cultures, and self-knowledge. Freud saw in ancient myths the pathologies he discovered in modern humans. Jung saw in the mythologies of the world keys to understanding the depths and potentialities of all humankind. Transpersonal and Integral psychology use those "Jungian archetypes" to help clients plumb their spiritual depths, heal their neuroses, and become empowered to live a life of greater meaning and fulfillment.

The mythological Jesus embodies the archetypes of the Self, the Hero and the Healer. That in his case the mythology is constructed upon an actual life just makes the "mythological Christ" a more powerful representation of human spiritual potential. Rather than insisting that the Gospels are historically infallible, which position is clearly false, Christians would be better served by a two-fold strategy: (1) continue the quest for the historical Jesus to discover what can be learned about and from him and (2) utilize the Gospels' "mythological Jesus" as an archetypal representation of human spiritual potential.

Reality is more than history and science can tell us; mythology can help us discover that "more." History and science can tell us what has been and how the cosmos and humanity got where we are now. History and science can even give us a glimpse of what will be. Mythology can help us discover our inner hidden psychological and spiritual depths, which are also a part of reality; ultimately, for us, the most important part.

# Chapter  Fourteen:   Conclusion

Almost all reputable New Testament scholars agree on a few basic "facts" about the historical Jesus. He was born in Nazareth to Mary and Joseph. He was a poor laborer. He was baptized by John. Jesus taught in parables and memorable aphorisms. Some of his disciples were women. He performed exorcisms. He entered Jerusalem on a donkey, caused a disturbance in the Temple, was arrested and crucified by Pontius Pilate. Jesus' followers claimed he was resurrected and would return for the resurrection and final judgment.

I believe the story about Jesus' entering Jerusalem could have been constructed from a passage in *Zechariah*. I believe the story about Jesus in the Temple could have been based upon something Jesus said rather than something he did. I am not convinced that Jesus "performed exorcisms," but I am convinced he was a healer. Other than those three points, I believe the rest of the facts generally accepted by scholars are well established. In addition, I believe Jesus was an unorthodox Jew, a philosopher, and a mystic.

Biblical scholarship has led to identification of parables, aphorisms and witticisms in the four canonical Gospels and the *Gospel of Thomas* which reflect ideas and a style that can only be attributed to the historical Jesus. No one else in his era expressed in quite the same way or had quite the same combination of ideas.

The eschatological ideas attributed to Jesus in the canonical Gospels reflect ideas and styles common by the time of his era and are unlike and even contradictory to his other sayings. Consequently, it is not probable that such sayings originated with Jesus; it is more likely that the Gospel authors constructed such sayings on the basis of previous Jewish writings to express their own eschatological views.

Even though Jesus' style and ideas can be identified as unique some of the ideas and forms of expression found in Cynic, Stoic Pythagorean, and some Eastern philosophies are similar to the sayings of the historical Jesus. The similarities are not strong enough to assert that Jesus borrowed from those philosophies, but are strong enough to assert that Jesus was in the stream of the Hellenistic philosophical thought of his time. When the sayings are arranged by themes, Jesus' philosophy becomes fairly clear.

## Jesus the Therapist

The only clues we have to what lies in any individual's consciousness are that individual's words and behavior. If we would understand the impact Jesus had on world culture, we must understand his beliefs, attitudes and feelings. The primary practical reason to focus on his philosophy is to understand his consciousness.

By understanding Jesus' consciousness we may learn something about fuller expression of human potential and new ways to maintain physical health and heal illness. Since behind all words and actions there is causation in consciousness, it must be the case that behind his touch and words Jesus had *inner states of consciousness* from which healing flowed.

Consciousness is understood to be primary in the modern "metaphysical movements" such as Unity, Religious Science and Christian Science; in those movements touch and even the spoken word are thought to be supplementary and perhaps even unnecessary. There is ample anecdotal evidence of healing through prayer in those metaphysical movements to support their theory. William James also provided such anecdotes in his classic work *The Varieties of Religious Experience*. There are also modern scientific studies indicating that silent prayer has some therapeutic effect. [188] The metaphysical movements - which emphasize optimism, faith, metaphysical law, love, forgiveness, prayer, and meditation as in the philosophy of Jesus - provide important clues for understanding the healing consciousness of the historical Jesus.

It is a historical fact that Jesus' *consciousness* affected his contemporaries in such a way as to create his *reputation* as a great spiritual healer. He inspired faith in his followers which most likely affected at least psychosomatic healing. Examination of the words of the historical Jesus reveals therapeutic elements in his philosophy. Jesus' radical optimism could have had therapeutic effects. He used illustrations from nature to urge his listeners to let go of worry; letting go of worry relieves stress, which is one of the leading causes of illness. His sense of humor could also have helped his listeners release stress. His parables and aphorisms could have induced altered states of consciousness which, like the hypnotherapy of Milton Erickson, would have helped some of his followers experience healing and their own potential to be healers.

Beyond understanding his healing and transformational impact on his contemporaries, reflection upon the philosophy of Jesus can lead us to better self-understanding, ways to harmonize society, and even insight into the way the universe works.

The combination of all the elements of Jesus' philosophy is likely to have been more powerful than any of those elements considered separately. It is probable that Jesus' effect on his contemporaries was at least as powerful as any "psychic," "faith healer," or "spiritual" healer today. The evidence from analysis of Jesus' philosophy correlated with modern research strongly indicates that he was an effective healer in his time, which conclusion is in alignment with the way he is portrayed in the Gospels.

Any illnesses cured by Jesus could have been psychological and psychosomatic rather than purely somatic in nature. On the other hand, it might also be the case that he healed all manner of illness, including physically caused illness; after all, the same could be said of even the humble placebo.

More important than whatever happened historically with regard to Jesus and healing, clearly the elements of his philosophy, *if conscientiously applied*, are beneficial to general well-being of individual humans and humanity as a whole. Jesus' philosophy has positive relevance to and bearing upon human health and society.

## The Original Philosophy of Jesus

Jesus' thought and practice was very similar to the thought and practice of Cynic philosophers. Some of his ideas were like those of the Stoic philosophers. Some of his practices were like those of the Pythagoreans. He gave reasons for not abiding by Jewish practices. His thought is comparable to ideas in Chinese philosophies. His methods of teaching were the same as some methods used in the philosophy of his era. He clearly participated in the philosophical tradition and so *was a* philosopher.

The fact that a religion developed on the basis of his life shows that his *followers* were religious, not that *he* was. The fact that he spoke of God does not place him outside philosophical tradition, nor does it necessarily make him a preacher of religion. Jesus probably did participate in the Jewish traditions such as attending synagogue meetings, even though he challenged some Jewish traditions.

As shown in the discussion of the philosophy of the historical

Jesus, the elements of his philosophy have no requirement to accept Christian dogma. One may think of Jesus as a great philosopher without adopting the view that he was the biblically prophesied "Messiah" or "Christ." One may adopt his philosophy without believing in "Judgment Day," "resurrection," "Virgin birth," "transubstantiation," or any other dogmas created by his followers. While his philosophy was not "secular" in a modern sense, it can still be adopted as a spiritual philosophy in the modern era without adopting any particular *religious* affiliation.

Health research indicates that *the universe is so structured that optimism, faith, love, forgiveness, humor, meditation and prayer are beneficial to human beings.* Was the universe so structured as a result of random accident of material forces? That would be more amazing and "miraculous" than if the universe was so structured as the result of Benign Intelligent design. Based on the fact that the universe supports optimism, faith, love and other spiritual attitudes and practices, it is no more irrational to believe in a good Supreme Being than to disbelieve.

Jesus' philosophy can be abstracted from the religion about him and explored critically as other philosophies are explored critically. Because that is so, the philosophy of Jesus of Nazareth belongs in philosophy curriculums as much as Stoic, Cynic, Pythagorean, Platonic, Aristotelian, and Neo-Platonic philosophers. The historical Jesus, as a philosopher, still has some important things to teach us about healing, ourselves, ethics, and the nature of the universe.

The wisdom of any age, no matter how distant in the past, is precious and worthy of consideration; for all generations of humans, though their conditions change, have their humanity in common and have faced similar trials of existence. There is still much to be discovered and understood in the universe. "God's Realm" is an inexhaustible treasure, a gift and discovery that can bring us great joy.

# APPENDIX A – ABSTRACT

## The Therapeutic Psychosomatic Effects of The Philosophy of the Historical Jesus

**Objectives**: (1) To explore the possibility that Jesus could be classified as a philosopher by comparing "authentic sayings" of Jesus to philosophies of his era. (2) To test for effects of listening to sayings attributed to Jesus on peripheral skin temperature and self-reported emotional states.

**Design and setting**: Jesus' "authentic sayings" were compared in content and style with the Greek philosophical schools of Cynics, Stoics, and Pythagoreans, as well as with the Chinese philosophies of Taoism and Moism. Jesus' philosophy was examined for elements related to research in holistic health methods. The study recorded peripheral skin temperature while participants listened to recordings in church office spaces and used a pre-test and post-test administration of the State-Trait Anxiety Inventory and Profile of Mood States (Brief form).

**Participants**: Adult volunteers (N = 68) from two Unity Churches, 64% females and 36% males.

**Results**: Clear similarities in content and style were found between Jesus' philosophy and the philosophies of Cynicism, Stoicism, Pythagoreanism, Taoism and Moism. Parallels were found between Jesus' philosophy and holistic therapy methodologies. Peripheral skin temperature of participants increased significantly ($p < .01$) while listening to recordings, indicating some had relaxation responses. Self-reported anxiety traits decreased significantly ($p < .01$) after listening to recordings, especially for those who listened to the recording of "authentic sayings" of Jesus. Self-reported anxiety states and other negative emotions similarly decreased after listening to recordings, but not to a statistically significant degree.

**Conclusions**: Preliminary evidence suggests that (1) Jesus could be classified as a philosopher whose philosophy had therapeutic effects and (2) listening to the "authentic sayings" of Jesus and possibly other types of literature can help reduce anxiety states and induce stress relieving meditation states. Results indicate that research into effects of listening to different types of wisdom literature could produce methods beneficial to emotional and physical health.

# APPENDIX B – Study of Effects of Sayings of Jesus

*HYPOTHESES*

Scientific research has indicated that meditation reduces stress.[189] Biofeedback studies have shown that a common indicator that an individual is in a meditative state is "the relaxation response." One of the simplest measurements of the relaxation response is peripheral skin temperature. When peripheral skin temperature increases, the increase indicates that the person is relaxing.[190] The relaxation response is also accompanied by increased amplitude of alpha brain-wave frequencies.[191]

If listening to Jesus' sayings results in the increase of peripheral skin temperature that would be an indication that those sayings could be used to induce meditative states. Insofar as contemplation of Jesus' philosophy induces meditative states, a meditation method based on his philosophy could be therapeutic in the ways other forms of meditation can be therapeutic.

For comparison purposes I made a distinction between "authentic sayings" and "attributed sayings" of Jesus. The reasons for this distinction are explained in Chapter 2. In my experimental research those listening to "authentic sayings" were the experimental group and those listening to "attributed sayings" were the comparison group.

If both type sayings showed significant increase of peripheral skin temperature, that would indicate both types of sayings could be used for meditation method. If neither type saying resulted in meditative states, the experiment will fail to reject the null hypotheses regarding inducing meditative states.

If the experimental group contemplating the sayings showed no significant difference from the comparison group in increasing peripheral skin temperature, the hypothesis regarding the distinction between "authentic" and "attributed sayings" would not be supported by that aspect of the research.

The participants were also tested using the "Profile of Mood States" (POMS) and "State Trait Anxiety Inventory" (STAI), before and after listening to the sayings. The POMS and STAI instruments were used to investigate whether or not contemplating Jesus' sayings contributes to diminishing stressful states and moods such as anxiety and anger. If contemplation of Jesus' sayings diminished stressful emotions, that would indicate that such contemplation has a therapeutic value.

The hypotheses tested by my dissertation research and experiment were as follows:

**Hypothesis 1:**

The sayings and ideas of the historical Jesus are similar to the sayings and ideas of philosophers of his era (500 BCE to 200 CE) and therefore he was a philosopher.

**Null Hypothesis 1:**

The sayings and ideas of the historical Jesus are not similar to the sayings and ideas of philosophers of his era and therefore he was not a philosopher.

**Hypothesis 2:**

Listening to the "authentic sayings" of Jesus has the effect of producing the lowered sympathetic nervous system arousal in participants as measured by an increase in peripheral skin temperature.

**Null Hypothesis 2:**

There is no significant statistical change in peripheral skin temperature while listening to the "authentic sayings" of Jesus.

**Hypothesis 3:**

Listening to the "authentic sayings" of Jesus increases the peripheral skin temperature significantly more than listening to the "attributed sayings" of Jesus.

**Null Hypothesis 3:**

There is no significant difference in peripheral skin temperature increase from listening to the "authentic sayings" of Jesus compared to listening to the "attributed sayings" of Jesus.

**Hypothesis 4:**

Listening to the "authentic sayings" of Jesus results in significant reduction of health-counterproductive emotions (e.g. tension-anxiety, depression-dejection, anger-hostility, fatigue-inertia, and confusion-bewilderment).

**Null Hypothesis 4:**

Listening to the "authentic sayings" of Jesus has no significant effect on health-counterproductive emotions.

**Hypothesis 5:**

Listening to the "authentic sayings" of Jesus results in significantly greater reduction of heath-counterproductive emotions than listening to the "attributed sayings" of Jesus.

**Null Hypothesis 5:**

There is no significant difference in effect on reduction of health-counterproductive emotions between listening to authentic sayings of Jesus and "attributed sayings" of Jesus.

If the null hypotheses 1, 2 and 3 and/or 1, 4 and 5 are rejected, then the hypothesis that Jesus can be classified historically as a therapeutic philosopher is adequately demonstrated.

Null hypotheses 1, 2, 4, and 5 were rejected by the research and experiment. Therefore the hypothesis that Jesus can be classified historically as a therapeutic philosopher is adequately demonstrated.

# APPENDIX C – RESEARCH & METHODOLOGY

## Research Design

I tested the hypothesis that the philosophy of the historical Jesus had (and can still have) therapeutic effects by means of an experiment utilizing three instruments of measurement. I tested the effects of listening to Jesus' words on the Peripheral Skin Temperatures (PST) of participants, to measure for physical relaxation. In addition, the experiment used two psychological instruments: the "State-Trait Anxiety Inventory" (STAI) and the "Profile of Mood States" (POMS) instrument. The STAI was used to measure any shifts in temporary anxiety state and the more stable trait anxiety. Self-reported anxiety indicates how "stressed" a person feels. The POMS was used to test for any shifts in moods that could be beneficial to the overall well-being of the individual. The feelings measured by POMS are related to psycho-physiological moods such as anxiety, depression, and anger that may affect health and healing. The STAI and POMS instruments were used to investigate whether or not contemplating Jesus' sayings contributes to diminishing anxiety and stressful moods.

If contemplation of Jesus' sayings increased relaxation and diminished anxiety and stressful emotions that would indicate that such contemplation has a therapeutic value. It would further indicate that a meditation method based upon the sayings of the historical Jesus could provide an alternative and therapeutic form of meditation for those who do not relate to Eastern traditions and whose spirituality is connected to Christian traditions. Such a method might also have appeal beyond those who identify themselves as Christians, since the method would not require membership in a Christian church, acceptance of Christian creeds, or participation in Christian rituals.

### Population:

The participants consisted of 60 English speaking volunteers aged 21 or older from the Kansas City, Missouri area without regard to race, gender, or religious beliefs. Participants in this study were recruited from the Unity Village Chapel in Unity Village, MO and Unity

Church of Overland Park in Overland Park, KS. Volunteers were solicited to participate in this study by church announcements through Unity organizations in the Kansas City, Missouri area and were asked to contact the Principal Investigator (PI).

Unity is a Christian organization whose publications, prayer ministry, retreats, and classes are also used by people affiliated with other Christian denominations, non-Christian faiths, and also people not affiliated with any faith. The inter-denominational and inter-faith appeal of Unity publications and programs indicates that most religious beliefs of Unity students are within the mainstream of the general population.

In terms of self-description, a higher percentage of Unity congregants (90%) than non-Unity people (58%) see themselves as honoring all paths to God and as open-minded (93% to 69%) about spiritual development and growth.

Attendees of Unity programs are diverse in terms of age, gender, and ethnicity. They tend to be somewhat older with higher levels of education than the general population. There is a higher percentage of female Unity students than is found in the general population. The percentage of attendees who are members of non-white ethnic groups is somewhat lower than the general population.[192]

The PI welcomed volunteers who heard of the research through Unity friends but who were not themselves involved in Unity.

The participants in this experiment consisted of 64% females and 36% males recruited through Unity Churches in Unity Village, MO and Overland Park, KS. The age group percentages of the participants were: between 21 and 29 years, 2%; 30 to 60 years, 49%; 61 to 70 years, 36%; and over 70 years, 13%. The ethnicity of participants was varied, but deemed irrelevant and so not included in statistical analysis

Due to some technical difficulties with temperature logger and computer recording at a few points during my research, the PST data for a few participants was lost. Data did not record for 2 participants in the "authentic sayings" group and for 3 participants in the "attributed group." In order to balance the number of participants in each group, PST was recorded for one more volunteer for the "attributed group," making a total of 28 measurements in each group. In the end, there was PST data for 56 volunteers and STAI and POMS data for 60 volunteers.

One participant told me at the beginning of her session that she had "hot flashes" which might affect her PST during the session. I decided to do the session anyway, in case she did not have "hot flashes" during the session. After the participant listened to the recording, she told me she had a "hot flash" toward the end and where the recording was when she had it (it was about 18 minutes into the 26 minute recording). There was a dramatic temperature increase at the point described by the participant after a steady temperature during the first part of the recording. Since I was testing for relaxation, I did not use the temperature increase from that participant in the study, but used only the data from the first 18 minutes. The PST data from all other participants was used starting at 2 minutes and ending with the end of the recording. I used the 2 minute mark to be sure that the temperatures of participants had reached a normative point and was not rising or falling as a result of the difference between their temperature and the temperature of the thermometer before it was attached.

Volunteers were asked if they were 21 years or older and any who were under 21 were thanked for their interest and told they were not eligible for the study. They were also asked if they have been diagnosed with ADD, schizophrenia, post-traumatic stress disorder, dementia hearing impairment, or bipolar disorder. If the prospective participant had been diagnosed with any of those disorders, they were excluded from the study.

**Inclusion Criteria:** 21 years or older, literate in English, and participants showed willingness to participate by signing a voluntary informed consent form.

**Exclusion Criteria:** Self reported ADD or other impairment that would inhibit ability to listen to recordings and sustain normal focus of thought for the 30 minute experimental periods; diagnosed with schizophrenia, post-traumatic stress disorder, dementia, hearing impairment, or bipolar disorder.

**Protection of the authentic responses and contamination prevention:** Participants were asked to refrain from discussing their experience with anyone until the research project is complete participants were asked if they had heard other participants discuss their experience; those who heard discussions by other participants were excluded from the study.

The 60 volunteer participants were randomly assigned to the experimental or comparison group. Those whose last names had an even number of letters were assigned to the experimental group and those whose names had an odd number of letters were assigned to the comparison group. Once one group had 30 participants the remainder of volunteers was assigned to the other group.

Individuals in the experimental group and comparison group

made appointments for 1 hour at times amenable to both the participants and the PI. At the beginning of the sessions, participants were asked not to discuss their experience with others until after they had been contacted and told the research is complete. What they would be doing during the session was briefly described.

### Confidentiality Statement

The following statement of confidentiality was included as part of the informed consent form:

"Your participation in this study and any forms generated will be held in strict confidence. Your name will not in any way be associated with the research findings. The information will be identified only by a code number. There is no financial cost to you to participate in this study. Your participation is solicited, although strictly voluntary."

### Procedure

Both groups were asked to participate for a one hour session. All participants were told that they were part of a study of effects on finger temperature and emotions in subjects who sit and listen to readings for periods of 30 minutes. Both groups were asked to take the STAI and POMS before and after participation in the listening part of the study. Once they completed the STAI and POMS forms, participants were provided with a comfortable chair and instructed to listen to a 30 minute recording. They were told that they could, if they chose, close their eyes at any time during the session. They were then connected to the finger temperature monitor and the recording was played for them.

The experimental group listened to a recording of the sayings of the historical Jesus and the comparison group listened to a recording of sayings attributed to Jesus by Gospel authors. After filling out the STAI and POMS instruments the second time, both the experimental and comparison group were asked to write comments describing their experience and any insights or feelings they may have had.

### Recordings

The scripts used for the recordings consisted of words attributed to Jesus, selected from the four canonical Gospels and the *Gospel of Thomas*. The recording of "attributed (Gospel) sayings" heard by the comparison group (A1) consisted of sayings which scholars contend did not originate with Jesus. The recording of "authentic (Jesus) sayings" heard by the experimental group (A2) consisted of sayings which the same scholars contend originated with Jesus.

Selected passages for the "attributed" recording were selected from each of four canonical Gospels to reflect ideas specific to each Gospel writer. The sayings were arranged in the traditional order of the Gospels: Matthew, Mark, Luke and John.

A central part of Matthew's agenda was to present Jesus as the Messiah, who was upholder of Mosaic Law, so selections reflecting that agenda were in the script.

Mark's agenda was to present Jesus as the Messiah who would return at final judgment and resurrection, so selections reflecting that agenda were used from Mark.

Luke was an advocate for the poor and engaged in polemics against establishment figures, so passages reflecting his opposition to the rich and the Pharisees were used.

John was concerned to present Jesus as Word of God or "Cosmic Christ." Consequently, John attributes many sayings to Jesus claiming his divinity in the form of "I am" statements. John also emphasized love, oneness and peace. Therefore the script contained many "I am" statements from John.

Passages in the "attributed" recording were taken from a traditional translation (NRSV) to reflect the "liturgical" quality and purposes of the canonical Gospels.

The "attributed sayings" were selected to reflect the depiction of Jesus found in the different Gospels, including his statements about Jewish Law and the "final days." On the other hand, it seemed to me that sayings about judgment and the "end of the world" in those Gospels could evoke adverse reactions in listeners. Since I did not want to intentionally produce a negative effect with the "attributed sayings," chose to end the recording on a relatively positive note with the "gentler" sayings from John. Based upon comments of the participants, John's sayings proved in fact to be better received and more comforting to participants than the apocalyptic and moral commandments in the earlier passages of the script.

Here are a few examples of comments from participants on the moral law and eschatological sections at the beginning of the recording:

I became very *relaxed due to Jim's voice – not the Biblical passages chosen.* Most of those were somewhat *negative* in content, at least *in the beginning*."

"Interesting passage from the Bible, full of hell and brimstone (whatever that is?). The *part of Christianity I do not like*; believe like me or you are condemned to hell."

"All of the quotes in the beginning seemed to be *bad/judgmental/negative*. As they went on they *started to be more positive*, but all seemed to say that Jesus was the only way."

"My general observation is that *the bible readings were progressing from a negative tone to a positive tone* as they progressed."

15 out of 23 participants in the "attributed" group who commented on the experience explicitly mentioned having a negative reaction to the first part of the "attributed sayings" recording.

"Authentic sayings" were selected and arranged in a way to present the whole of Jesus' philosophy. For the most part the sayings were organized in a way that reflected my discussion of Jesus' philosophy in the first part of this paper. I attempted to arrange the sayings in such a way that the early passages laid out foundational ideas relatively clearly. It was my hope that the context provided by the early passages would make later passages more easily understood.

The sayings and parables of Jesus can be confusing and even with the relatively straightforward passages at the beginning, a few participants commented on the surprising and confusing nature of some of the sayings. For example:

"I found some of the *passages unfamiliar and cryptic* and that surprised me."

"Occasionally, his parables leave me a little *confused* as to their interpretations in our daily lives."

"Some Bible verses are *difficult to understand* (what they mean) and I felt cut off by them."

A few of the "authentic sayings" were taken from the *Gospel of Thomas*, so technically those sayings were not "Bible passages," but the sayings did originate with the historical Jesus, according to scholars. I used the Jesus Seminar's "Scholars Version" (SV) translation which sought to reflect the informal language of the Greek used in the Gospels. The Greek used in Jesus' sayings in the Bible is informal and conversational rather than polished, formal and liturgical.

For the recordings I read the passages myself and attempted to read them in a way appropriate to the content. Since I have no way of knowing the tone, pitch, or pace of Jesus' speech patterns, I chose to read at a moderate pace in calm tones and my normal pitch. I read the parables as if telling a story, rather than in a preaching tone. I read the aphorisms as if citing proverbs. I chose to read the preaching and prophetic sections of the attributed sayings in a moderate tone rather than a fervent "preachy" tone; my intention was to simply convey the meaning, not to emotionally manipulate and evangelize. While I am not a professional actor or "recording artist," I am confident that my voice and readings were adequate to the task. My confidence was verified by comments from seven participants who commented that my voice was soothing or pleasant, which indicated that my readings did not detract from experiencing the ideas in the sayings. None of the participants complained about how the passages were read.

## Measurement Tools

Peter A. Parks, PhD, a psychologist, counselor and biofeedback trainer, graciously provided the equipment and guidance for the peripheral skin temperature (PST) aspect of the research. An RC-30B Temperature Data Logger was used to measure peripheral skin temperatures of participants. The thermometer was taped to participants' index fingers on their dominant hands. The Data Logger recorded temperatures in degrees Celsius to 0.1 of a degree. The Logger was set to record a reading every 10 seconds. The Celsius measurements were used in the statistical evaluation. Biofeedback monitors are non-invasive and have no side-effects.

To measure participants' psychological responses to the recordings, two instruments were used: the State-Trait Anxiety Inventory (STAI) and the Profile of Mood States (POMS) Brief assessment. The STAI measures temporary *states* of anxiety and the more stable anxiety *traits*. POMS measures transient fluctuating mood states in six categories: tension-anxiety, depression-dejection, anger-hostility, fatigue-inertia, vigor-activity, and confusion-bewilderment.

The STAI consists of a series of 40 statements: 20 ask for self report regarding "how respondents feel '*right now*, at this moment," and 20 ask for "how people *generally* feel." [193] The "feel right now" statements evaluate *state* of anxiety (S-Anxiety scale) and the "generally" feel" statements evaluate *trait* anxiety (T-Anxiety scale).

The S-Anxiety scale measures "feelings of apprehension, tension, nervousness, and worry." Scores on the S-Anxiety scale have been used to measure decreases in stress resulting from relaxation training and changes in anxiety experienced by patients in counseling.[194] That is the primary reason for my using the STAI, since I was testing to see if listening to "Jesus sayings" measurably decreases stress.

"More than 2,000 studies using the STAI have appeared in the research literature since the *STAI Test Manual* was published" in 1970, according to the *STAI Test Manual*.[195] The STAI has been used in medicine, dentistry, education, psychology, and other social sciences.[196]

Each statement on the S-Anxiety scale asks respondent to identify the *intensity* of their feelings regarding their agreement with the statement in terms of: (1) not at all; (2) somewhat; (3) moderately so; and (4) very much so. The T-Anxiety scale questions have responses to measure the *frequency* of their feelings: (1) almost never; (2) sometimes; (3) often; (4) almost always.[197]

POMS is a widely used instrument for measuring patient responses to therapeutic intervention. According to the POMS technical manual, "By the end of 1992 there were almost 2,000 citations of the POMS, and by the end of 2002 the number approached 3,000. . . . In the past decade, approximately 3,800 authors cited the POMS in 1,000 reports published in about 400 journals."[198] In addition, "seven areas of research have provided evidence of the predictive and construct reliability of the POMS. These seven areas are: (1) brief psychotherapy studies; (2) controlled outpatient drug trials; (3) cancer research; (4) drug abuse and addiction research; (5) studies of response to emotion-inducing conditions; (6) research on sports and athletes; (7) studies of concurrent validity coefficients and other POMS correlates."[199]

The POMS Brief consists of 30 words describing different psycho-physiological feelings, by which participants rate their identification with those feelings in terms of "not at all," "a little," "moderately," "quite a bit," or "extremely." My research was not technically a therapeutic intervention, but since the POMS can measure short term shifts in moods related to mental and physical health, I thought it might provide useful data for measuring mood shifts induced by listening to the recordings used in my experiment. I used the POMS Brief form since the longer form is used for more extensive psychological analysis.

I was especially interested in the POMS scores for "Depression-

Dejection" and the "Total Mood Disturbance" (TMD). The "Depression-Dejection" category scores correlate with sense of personal inadequacy, feelings of unworthiness, emotional isolation and guilt.[200] I theorized that since Jesus' philosophy emphasized the value of humans as children of God, hearing those ideas might help somewhat uplift the listener's sense of self-worth. The TMD is used to identify "a single global estimate of affective state."[201] I analyzed the TMD to see if any shift occurred toward a health enhancing affective state in listeners.

**Results**

**Analysis**

The results of this study were analyzed using the mixed design ANOVA test. The mixed design ANOVA test is used where there is a combination of one independent measures factor and one repeated measures factor. The mixed design ANOVA analyzes variance using degrees of freedom, sums of squares, and mean squares to calculate variance ratios (F values) and is appropriate for measurements under different conditions over time. Calculating the F value measures the variability of the scores from the mean of the sample using the sums of the squares of the differences between the mean and individual scores. Dividing the sums of the squares by degrees of freedom produces an average variability of a score in the sample.

The mixed design ANOVA method allows measurement of variability produced by random error and systematic differences, within conditions and between conditions. The F value is the variance ratio of between conditions variance to error variance, which can also be expressed as the ratio of systematic differences plus error variance to error variance. When the null hypothesis of an experiment is false, the ratio of F is expected to be greater than 1 because the systematic differences should be greater than the error variance. The larger the systematic differences, the larger the F value. What amounts to a significant F value will vary according to sample size degrees of freedom and the number of conditions degrees of freedom.

I chose to use the ANOVA statistical test because it is best suited to my research, which involved measurement of one independent factor and one repeated measures factor. The independent factor consisted of the participants listening to sayings of the historical Jesus and the participants listening to sayings attributed to Jesus which probably did not originate with him. The repeated measure factor consisted of measurements done before and after the listening sessions.

The scores used for analysis of the STAI and POMS were the standard scores used for those instruments. The scores for the finger temperature measurement were the difference between the participants' base finger temperatures (2 minutes after beginning) and their peak finger temperatures while listening to the recordings. The results from the STAI, POMS, and finger temperature measurements were analyzed using the mixed design ANOVA test.

## Results of Peripheral Skin Temperature (PST) Test

**Hypothesis 2:** Listening to the "authentic sayings" of Jesus has the effect of producing the lowered sympathetic nervous system arousal in participants as measured by an increase in peripheral skin temperature.

**Null Hypothesis 2:** There is no significant statistical change in peripheral skin temperature while listening to the authentic sayings of Jesus.

**Hypothesis 3:** Listening to the "authentic sayings" of Jesus increases the peripheral skin temperature significantly more than listening to the "attributed sayings" of Jesus.

**Null Hypothesis 3:** There is no significant difference in peripheral skin temperature increase from listening to the "authentic sayings" of Jesus compared to listening to the "attributed sayings" of Jesus.

The experiment investigated the question of whether or not listening to sayings of Jesus ("authentic" or "attributed") would produce spontaneous relaxation responses in listeners similar to relaxation responses observed in people practicing meditation, using relaxation exercises and being hypnotized. Peripheral skin temperature (PST) is a good measure of relaxation, since increased PST often accompanies a relaxation. In previous experimentation and during this experiment I have observed that different individuals have different "normal" PST and that the PST normally fluctuates moment to moment. For a person in a stable temperature environment, PST normally increases and decreases in a range of 1 to 3 degrees Celsius. If a participant's PST fluctuated in that fairly narrow range, it would not necessarily indicate a relaxation response. If within a stable temperature environment a participant's PST increased by 4 or more degrees Celsius (7.2 degrees Farenheit), there is a good chance that participant had a relaxation response. For purposes of statistical analysis, base PST was compared to peak PST during the listening session. Comparison of those scores for all participants provides a picture of average temperature increase of the study population during the sessions. However, looking at individual PST measurements also provides a valid picture of relaxation responses, since one can see whether or not an *individual's* PST rose 4 or more degrees during the session.

ANOVA mixed design variance ratios for Factor A ("attributed" v "authentic sayings") were $F (1, 28) = 4.20$; for Factor B (before and after listening), $F (1, 58) = 4.00$. The results of the analysis rejected null hypothesis 2 with regard to factor B: listening to a recording of sayings of Jesus, *both* "attributed" and "authentic," was associated with significant variance of PST with respect to a rise in temperature. Therefore hypothesis 2 that listening to sayings of Jesus produces a relaxation response is supported.

However, there was no significant difference in relaxation response between listening to "attributed" and "authentic sayings" (factor A). The experiment failed to reject the null hypothesis 3 that "listening to the "authentic sayings" of Jesus increases the peripheral skin temperature significantly more than listening to the "attributed sayings' of Jesus.

In both groups there was, on average, a significant increase in PST. The mean scores for base temperature were: 30.475 degrees for the "attributed sayings" group and 31.31 degrees for the "authentic sayings' group. The mean scores for peak temperatures were: 32.47 degrees for the "attributed sayings" group and 33.01 degrees for the "authentic sayings" group. The difference between base and peak temperatures were: 2 degrees for the "attributed sayings" group and 1.7 degrees for the "authentic sayings" group.

14.29 % (4 out of 28) participants in each group experienced marked relaxation responses above 4 degrees Celsius (7.2 degrees Fahrenheit). It is interesting to note that on average participants in the "attributed sayings" group had a slightly greater difference between base and peak temperatures than did the "authentic sayings" group. On average the "authentic sayings" group had slightly higher base and peak temperatures. Again, those differences were not statistically significant. Those relatively equal scores indicate that simply sitting and listening for 30 minutes to passages from revered texts *could* produce relaxation responses in listeners, even if listeners disagree with much of the content (as in the "attributed" group) or find the content somewhat confusing (a in the "authentic" group).

While there was no significant difference between "attributed" and "authentic sayings" with regard to relaxation response/meditative experience, there was a difference in *comments* upon the two recordings. The difference in responses to the different content was indicated not only by comments but also by results measured by the STAI and POMS instruments.

### Self-Evaluation Instruments: STAI and POMS

**Hypothesis 4:** Listening to the "authentic sayings" of Jesus results in significant reduction of health-counterproductive emotions (tension-anxiety, depression-dejection, anger-hostility, fatigue-inertia, and confusion-bewilderment).

**Null Hypothesis 4:** Listening to the "authentic sayings" of Jesus has no significant effect on health-counterproductive emotions.

**Hypothesis 5:** Listening to the "authentic sayings" of Jesus results in significantly greater reduction of heath-counterproductive emotions than listening to the "attributed sayings" of Jesus.

**Null Hypothesis 5:** There is no significant difference in effect on reduction of health-counterproductive emotions between listening to "authentic sayings" of Jesus and "attributed sayings" of Jesus.

### STAI

According to analysis using the ANOVA mixed design variance ratios, the results of the experiment failed to reject the Null Hypothesis with regard to Anxiety State as measured by STAI. For variance ratios $F_{(1, 28)}$ and $F_{(1, 58)}$, Factor B (listening) was 0.32 lower than critical value of F distribution.

Participants in this research had noticeably lower anxiety states (as measured by STAI) than adult norms. The mean for working adults in the 50 to 69 age group (the age group from which most of the present experiment drew) is 33.355. The pre-test mean for participants in this research was 29.55. It may be that the relatively low pre-test anxiety level affected the outcome in terms of how much their anxiety state *could* decrease.

While the decrease in anxiety state was not statistically significant, the mean scores indicate that the "authentic" group had a noticeable decrease in anxiety state: from 29.3 to 24.9; a decrease of 4.4 points compared to the 0.1 decrease in the "attributed" group. The decreased anxiety state of the "authentic" group, considered in light of participants' comments, suggests that listening to "authentic sayings" was more effective at reducing anxiety than listening to the "attributed sayings."

Surprisingly, while the STAI state measurements failed to reject null hypotheses 4 and 5, the STAI trait measurements *did* reject those null hypotheses. This was a surprising result because the trait scores are generally more stable than the state scores. The STAI trait scores supported the hypothesis that listening to "authentic sayings" more effectively reduced anxiety than listening to "attributed sayings."

The ANOVA mixed design analysis of variance ratios rejected the Null Hypotheses 4 and 5. Listening to recordings significantly affected participants' perceptions of how they generally felt. Examining the mean scores we can see that the difference in pre-test and post-test scores was primarily affected by the scores of those in the "authentic" group. The scores of the "authentic" group showed a 2.56 average decrease in trait anxiety, compared to only a 0.73 decrease in the "attributed" group.

> Means: before recording
> > Attributed group (A-1): 32.4
> > Authentic group (A-2): 33.03
> Means: after recording
> > Attributed: 31.67 (down 0.73)
> > Authentic: 30.47 (down 2.56)

### POMS

The results of the ANOVA mixed design variance ratios analysis of the POMS scores failed to reject the Null Hypotheses 4 and 5. The POMS TMD scores are calculated by adding the scores for: Tension Anxiety (T), Depression-Dejection (D), Anger-Hostility (A), Fatigue Inertia (F), and Confusion-Bewilderment (C), and subtracting the Vigor Activity (V) scores. The TMD raw scores were sometimes negative numbers when the sum of the T, D, A, F and C scores was less than the sum of the V scores. In analyzing the TMD, I used raw scores in one analysis and raw scores plus 20 in a second analysis. I did the second analysis to check and see if results from using some negative score would produce different results than using all positive scores. The results from both analyses were the same. In both analyses, the TMD failed to reject the Null Hypotheses.

I also did an analysis of D scores using "T-scores" provided on the POMS Brief score sheet; the variance ratio on D scores was higher than that of the TMD scores, but still not significant. I would note however that the mean scores on the POMS indicated decreased Depression-Dejection and the "authentic group" decrease in D was greater than the decrease for the "attributed group."

Mean scores for Depression-Dejection:
  Attributed: 35.43 to 34.97 (down 0.46)
  Authentic: 34.27 to 33.2 (down 1.07)

The Total Mood Disturbance mean scores increased for the "attributed group" and decreased for the "authentic group."

Mean scores for TMD:
  Attributed: 18.03 to 19.37 (up 1.34)
  Authentic: 17.83 to 15.53 (down 2.3)

While the differences on the POMS scores were not statistically significant, the differences were in the same direction as the results of the STAI, viz. listening to "authentic sayings" of Jesus tended to decrease health counterproductive emotional states more than listening to "attributed sayings." In one test (Total Mood Disturbance), the "attributed sayings" seemed to slightly *increase* health counterproductive emotions.

**Conclusion regarding effect on moods of listening to recordings**

Null hypotheses 4 and 5 can be rejected based upon STAI-T results. Furthermore, there were differences in other scores (STAI-S, POMS-D and POMS-TMD) which all "leaned" in the direction of the STAI-T results, i.e. listening to recordings reduced anxiety and negative moods, "authentic sayings" more effectively than "attributed" ones. By rejecting null hypotheses 4 and 5, the STAI-T results supported hypotheses 4 and 5: (4) listening to the "authentic sayings" of Jesus results in significant reduction of health-counterproductive emotions and (5) listening to the "authentic sayings" of Jesus results in significantly greater reduction of heath-counterproductive emotions than listening to the "attributed sayings" of Jesus. The results that were not statistically significant for STAI-S, POMS-D, and POMS-TMD also indicated support for the hypotheses 4 and 5.

# BIBLIOGRAPHY

[NOTE: A few of the sources below were used in sections of my dissertation that were not included in this book. I have retained the sources in my bibliography because the dissertation was, in effect, the "first draft" of this book. My 2013 dissertation can be seen on the holosuniversity.org website.]

Anand, B. K.; G. S. Chhina, and Baldev Singh. "Some Aspects of Electroencephalographic Studies in Yogis," *Electroencephalography and Clinical Neurophysiology*, Vol.13 (3), June 1961.

Anderson, J. A. D; M. A. Basker and R. Dalton. "Migraine and Hypnotherapy," *International Journal of Clinical And Experimental Hypnosis*, Vol. 23 (1), 1975, pp. 48-58.

Aristotle. *The Basic Works of Aristotle*, Richard McKeon, ed. New York: Random House, Inc., 1941.

Aslan, Reza. *Zealot: The Life and Times of Jesus of Nazareth.* Random House Publishing Group, 2013-07-16, Kindle Edition.

Astin, John A PhD, Elaine Harkness BSc, Edzard Ernst MD PhD. "The Efficacy of 'Distant Healing': A Systematic Review of Randomization Trials," *Annals of Internal Medicine*, Vol.132 (11), June 6, 2000, pp. 903-910.

Bahrke, Michael S. and William P. Morgan. "Anxiety Reduction Following Exercise and Meditation," *Cognitive Therapy and Research*, Vol. 2 (4), December 1978, pp. 323- 333.

Banquet, J. P. "Spectral analysis of the EEG in Meditation," *Electroencephalography and Clinical Neurophysiology*, Vol. 35 (2), August 1973.

Barber, Theodore X. PhD. "Hypnosis, Suggestions, & Psychosomatic Phenomena: A New Look from the Standpoint of Recent Experimental Studies," *American Journal of Clinical Hypnosis*, Vol. 21 (1), 1978.

Barnstone, Willis and Marvin Meyer, editors. *The Gnostic Bible.* Boston: Shambhala Publications, Inc., 2003.

Batey, Richard A. *Jesus and the Forgotten City.* Grand Rapids, MI: Baker Book House Company, 1991.

Benson, Herbert and Richard Friedman. "Harnessing the Power of the Placebo Effect and Renaming it 'Remembered Wellness,'" *Annual Review of Medicine,* Vol. 47, 1996, pp. 193-199.

Blasi, Anthony J., Jean Duhaime and Paul-Andre Turcotte, ed. *Handbook of Early Christianity: Social Science Approaches.* Walnut Creek, CA: Alta Mira Press, 2002.

Boehm, JK and LD Kubzansky. "The Heart's Content: the Association between Positive Psychological Well-Being and Cardiovascular Health," *Psychological Bulletin,* 2012 July Vol. 138 (4), pp. 655-691.

Borg, Marcus. "A Renaissance in Jesus Studies," *Theology Today,* Vol. 45, (3), October 1988.

Boudewyns, Patrick A. "A Comparison of the Effects of Stress vs. Relaxation Instruction on the Finger Temperature Response," *Behavior Therapy* vol. 7 (1) January 1976, pp. 54-67.

Branham, R. Bracht and Marie-Odile Goulet-Cazé, ed. *The Cynics: The Cynic Movement in Antiquity and Its Legacy.* Berkeley: University of California Press, 1996.

Chan, Wing-Tsi, ed. & tr. *A Source Book in Chinese Philosophy.* Princeton: Princeton University Press, 1963.

Clark, L. Verdelle. "Effect of Mental Practice on the Development of a Certain Motor Skill," *Research Quarterly of the American Association for Health, Physical Education, and Recreation,* Vol 31, 1960, pp. 560-569.

Cogan, Rosemary, Dennis Cogan, William Waltz and Melissa McCue. "Effects of Laughter and Relaxation on Discomfort Thresholds"

*Journal of Behavioral Medicine,* Vol. 10 #2, 1987, pp. 139-144.

Collison, D. R. "Which Asthmatic Patients Should Be Treated by Hypnotherapy?" *The Medical Journal of Australia,* Vol. 1 (25), 1975, pp. 776-781.

Cousins, Norman. *Anatomy of an Illness.* New York: Bantam Books, 1981.

Crossan, John Dominic. *The Historical Jesus: The Life of a Mediterranean Jewish Peasant.* San Francisco: HarperCollins, 1991.

Daly, Lloyd W. *Aesop without Morals; the Famous Fables, and a Life of Aesop.* New York: Thomas Yoseloff, 1961.

Davidson, Donald. "Radical Interpretation," *Dialectica,* (27) 1973, pp. 313-328.

Davidson, Karina W., Elizabeth Mostofsky and William Whang. "Don't Worry, Be Happy: Positive Affect and Reduced 10-Year Incident Coronary Heart Disease: The Canadian Nova Scotia Health Survey," *European Heart Journal,* Vol. 31 (9), 2010, pp. 1065-1070.

Davidson, Richard J.; Daniel J. Goleman and Gary E. Schwartz. "Attentional and Affective Concomitants of Meditation: A Cross-sectional Study," *Journal of Abnormal Psychology,* Vol. 85 (2), April 1976.

Davies, Stevan. *Jesus the Healer: Possession, Trance, and the Origins of Christianity.* New York: The Continuum Publishing Co., 1995.

Dossey, Larry M.D. *Healing Words: The Power of Prayer and the Practice of Medicine.* San Francisco: HarperSanFrancisco, 1993.

Downing F. Gerald. *Cynics and Christian Origins.* Edinburgh: T. & T. Clark, 1992.

Emerson, Ralph Waldo. *Emerson's Essays*. New York: Harper and Row, Publishers, 1926.

Erickson, Milton and Ernest L. Rossi. "Autohypnotic Experiences of Milton H. Erickson," *The American Journal of Clinical Hypnosis*, Vol. 20, July, 1977, pp. 36-54.

Ewin, Dabney M. "Hypnotherapy for Warts (Verruc Vulgaris): 41 Consecutive Cases with 33 Cures," *American Journal of Clinical Hypnosis*, Vol. 35 (1), 1992, pp. 1-10.

Fletcher, Joseph. *Situation Ethics: The New Morality*. Philadelphia: Westminster, 1966.

Fox, Paul A.; Donald C. Henderson; Simon E. Barton; Andrew J. Champion; Matthew S. H. Rollin; Jose Catalan; Sheena M. G. McCormack and John Gruzelier. "Immunological Markers of Frequently Recurrent Genital Herpes Simplex Virus and Their Response to Hypnotherapy: A Pilot Study," *International Journal of STD and AIDS*, Vol. 10 (11), November 1999, pp. 730-734.

Freedman, Suzanne R. and Robert D. Enright. "Forgiveness as an Intervention Goal with Incest Survivors," *Journal of Consulting and Clinical Psychology*, Vol. 64 (5), pp. 983-992.

Funk, Robert W., Roy W. Hoover and the Jesus Seminar. *The Five Gospels: The Search for the Authentic Words of Jesus.* New York: Macmillan Publishing Company, 1993.

Greenleaf, Eric, PhD. "The Red House: Hypnotherapy of Hysterical Blindness," *American Journal of Clinical Hypnosis*, Vol. 13 (3), 1971.

Gutherie, Kenneth Sylvan, ed. & tr. *The Pythagorean Sourcebook and Library*. Grand Rapids, MI: Phanes Press, 1987.

Hawking, Stephen. *A Brief History of Time: From the Big Bang to Black Holes*. New York: Bantam Books, 1988.

Hegedus, Carol and Roger Nelson. *Alternative Medicine: Expanding Medical Horizons: A Report to the National Institutes of Health on Alternative Medical Systems and Practices in the United States.* Honolulu: University Press of the Pacific, 2002.

Higgenson, Thomas Wentworth (tr.). *Epictetus: Discourses and Enchiridion.* Roslyn, NY: Walter J. Black, Inc., 1944.

Ievleva, Lydia, Terry Orlick. "Mental Links to Enhanced Healing: An Exploratory Study" *The Sport Psychologist*, Vol. 5 (1), Mar 1991, pp. 25-40.

James, William. *The Varieties of Religious Experience.* New York: The American Library, 1958.
_____ *Pragmatism: A new name for some old ways of thinking.* New York: Longman Green and Co, 1907.

Johnson, Luke Timothy. *The Real Jesus: The Misguided Quest for the Historical Jesus and the Truth of the Traditional Gospels.* San Francisco: HarperCollins, 1996.

Kasamatsu, Akira M.D. and Tomio Hirai, M.D. "An Electroencephalographic Study on the Zen Meditation (Zazen)," *Psychiatry and Clinical Neurosciences*, Vol. 20 (4), December 1966.

Kaushik Rajeev Mohan, Reshema Kaushik, Sukhdev Krishan Mahajan and Vevreddi Rajesh. "Effects of Mental Relaxation and Slow Breathing in Essential Hypertension," *Complementary Therapies in Medicine*, Vol. 14 (2), June 2006.

Lane, James D. PhD; Jon E. Seskevich, RN, BSN, BA; and Carl F. Pieper, DrPH. "Brief Meditation Training Can Improve Perceived Stress and Negative Mood," Alternative *Therapies*, Vol 13 (1), 2007.

Lefebvre, R.; Anne Abbott and Charles S. Carver. "Dispositional optimism and recovery from coronary artery bypass surgery: The beneficial effects on physical and psychological well-being," *Journal of Personality and Social Psychology*, Vol. 57 (6), Dec 1989, pp.1024-1040.

Levy, Becca R; Martin D. Slade; Suzanne R. Kunkel; Stanislav V. Kasl. "Longevity Increased by Positive Self-Perceptions of Aging," *Journal of Personality and Social Psychology*, Vol. 83 (2), August 2002, pp. 261-270.

Lin, Wei-Fen, David Mack, Robert D. Enright, Dean Krahn, Thomas W. Baskin. "Effects of Forgiveness Therapy on Anger, Mood and Vulnerability to Substance Use Among Inpatient Substance-Dependent Clients," *Journal of Consulting and Clinical Psychology*, Vol. 72 (6), Dec 2004, 1114-1121.

Mack, Burton. *The Lost Gospel of Q: The Book of Christian Origins.* San Francisco: HarperSanFrancisco, 1993.

Malherbe, Abraham J. *The Cynic Epistles: A Study Edition.* Atlanta: Society of Biblical Literature, 1986.

Maltz, Maxwell M.D. *Psycho-Cybernetics: A New Technique for Using Your Subconscious Power.* Englewood Cliffs, N.J.: Prentice-Hall, Inc., 1960.

Manusov, Eron G. "Clinical Applications of Hypnotherapy," *The Journal of Family Practice*, Vol. 31 (2), August 1990, pp. 180-184.

Mead, G. R. S. *Apollonius of Tyana.* Kila, MT: Kessinger Publishing Company, 1901.

Meier, John P. *A Marginal Jew: Rethinking the Historical Jesus, Vol. 1.* New Haven, CT: Anchor Yale Bible Reference Library, 1991.
_____ *A Marginal Jew: Rethinking the historical Jesus; Vol. 3: Companions and Competitors.* New York: Doubleday, 2001.

Miller, Robert J. *The Jesus Seminar and Its Critics.* Santa Rosa, CA: Polebridge Press, 1999.
_____ (ed.) *The Complete Gospels, Annotated Scholars Version.* San Francisco: HarperSanFrancisco, 1994.

Moody, Raymond, Jr., M.D.  *Life After Life*.  Covington, GA: Mockingbird Books, 1975.

Morse, DR, JS Martin, ML Furst & LL Dubin.  "A physiological and subjective evaluation of meditation, hypnosis, and relaxation," *Psychosomatic Medicine*, Vol. 39 (5), 1977, pp. 304-324.

Norris, Patricia A. and Garrett Porter.  *Why Me? – Harnessing the Healing Power of the Human Spirit*.  Walpole, NH:  Stillpoint Publishing, 1985.

O'Connor, Anahad.  "Well: Really?  Optimism Reduces the Risk of Heart Disease," *New York Times archives*: April 23, 2012. http://well.blogs.nytimes.com/2012/04/23/really-optimism-reduces-the-risk-of-heart-disease.

Pagels, Elaine.  *Beyond Belief: The Secret Gospel of Thomas*. New York: Random House, 2003.

Pelikan, Jaroslav.  *Jesus through the Centuries*.  New Haven, CT: Yale University Press, 1985.

Pelletier, Kenneth R.  *Mind as Healer, Mind as Slayer*. New York: Dell Publishing Co., Inc., 1977.

Plutarch. *The Parallel Lives, Loeb Classical Library, Vol. 10,* Bernadotte Perrin, tr.  Cambridge, MA: Harvard University Press, 1921.

Rammohan, Gowri.  *New Frontiers of Human Science*. Jefferson, North Carolina: McFarland and Company, Inc., 2002.

Rein, Glen, Mike Atkinson and Rollin McCraty.  "The Physiological and Psychological Effects of Compassion and Anger," *Journal of Advancement in Medicine*, Vol. 8 (2), Summer 1995.

Rorty, Richard.  *Consequences of Pragmatism*.  Minneapolis: University of Minnesota Press, 1982.

Rossi, Ernest, Sheila Rossi and Milton Erickson.  *Hypnotic Realities*.

New York: Irvington, 1976.

Rubin, Norman A. "Origin of the Word Talent," www.helium.com/items/1050703-origin-of-the-wordtalent.

Russell, Bertrand. *A History of Western Philosophy*. New York: Simon & Schuster, 1945.

Scheier, Michael F., Karen A. Matthews, Jane F.Owens, George J. Magovern, R. Craig Lefebvre, R. Anne Abbott and Charles S. Carver, "Dispositional optimism and recovery from coronary artery bypass surgery: The beneficial effects on physical and psychological well-being," *Journal of Personality and Social Psychology*, Vol 57(6), Dec 1989, 1024-1040.

Albert Schweitzer (William Montgomery, tr.). *The Quest of the Historical Jesus*. New York: The MacMillan Company, 1950.

Shapiro, Shauna L., Roger Walsh, and Willoughby B. Britton. "An Analysis of Recent Meditation Research and Suggestions for Future Directions," *Journal for Meditation and Meditation Research*, 2003, Vol. 3, pp. 69-90.

Siegel, Bernie S., M.D. *Love, Medicine and Miracles*. New York: Harper and Row, 1986.

Spiegel, David and Joan R. Bloom. "Group Therapy and Hypnosis Reduce Metastatic Breast Carcinoma Pain," *Psychosomatic Medicine*, Vol. 45 (4), August 1983, pp. 333-339.

Steward, A. C. and S. E. Thomas. "Hypnotherapy as a Treatment for Atopic Dermatitis in Adults and Children," *British Journal of Dermatology*, Vol.132 (5), May 1995, pp. 778-783.

Strong, James. *The New Strong's Exhaustive Concordance of the Bible: New Strong's Concise Dictionary of the Words in the Greek Testament*. Nashville: Thomas Nelson Publishers, Inc. 1995.

Teplan, M. "Fundamentals of EEG Measurement," *Measurement Science*

*Review*, Vol. 2, Section 2, 2002.

*The Holy Bible, New International Version.* Grand Rapids, MI: Zondervan, 1978.

*The New Oxford Annotated Bible with The Apocrypha.* New York: Oxford University Press, 1977.

Toda, M., S. Kusakabe, S. Nagasawa, K. Kitamura and K. Morimoto. "Effect of Laughter on Salivary Endrocrinological Stress Marker Chromogranin A," *Biomedical Research* (Tokyo, Japan), Vol. 28 (2), 2007, pp. 115-118.

Travis, Frederick; Theresa Olson, Thomas Egenes and Hemant K. Gupta. "Physiological Patterns During Practice of the Transcendental Meditation Technique Compared with Patterns While Reading Sanskrit and a Modern Language," *International Journal of Neuroscience*, Vol. 109, No 1-2, 2001, pp. 71-80.

Trueblood, Elton. *The Humor of Christ.* San Francisco: Harper and Row, 1975.

Vandell, R.A., R. A. Davis and H. A. Clugston, "The Function of Mental Practice in the Acquisition of Motor Skills," *Journal of General Psychology*, Vol. 29, 1943, pp. 243-250.

VanItallie, Theodore B. "Stress: A Risk Factor for Serious Illness," *Metabolism*, Vol. 51, No. 6, Suppl 1, June, 2002.

Ventgodt, Soren; Mohammed Morad, Eytan Hyam and Joav Merrick. "Clinical Holistic Medicine: Induction of Spontaneous Remission of Cancer by Recovery of the Human Character and the Purpose of Life (Life Mission)," *The Scientific World Journal* (4) 2004.

Verbin, John S. Kloppenborg. *Excavating Q: The History and Setting of the Sayings Gospel.* Minneapolis: Fortress Press, 2000.

Walker, Williston, Richard A. Norris, David W. Lotz, and Robert T. Handy. *A History of the Christian Church (4ᵗʰ ed.)*. New York: Charles Scribner's Sons, 1985.

West, Michael A. "Meditation and the EEG," *Psychological Medicine*, 1980, pp. 369-375.

Whiston, William, tr. *The Works of Josephus, Complete and Unabridged*. Peabody, MA: Hendrickson Publishers, Inc., 1987.

Whitehead, Alfred North. *Process and Reality*. New York: The Free Press, 1978.

Wilbur, Ken. *Integral Psychology: Consciousness, Spirit, Psychology, Therapy*. Boston: Shambhala Publications, Inc., 2000.
_____ *Quantum Questions: Mystical Writings of the World's Great Physicists*. Boston: Shambhala Publications, Inc., 2001.

Williams, John D. and John H. Gruzelier. "Differentiation of Hypnosis and Relaxation by Analysis of Narrow Band Theta and Alpha Frequencies," *International Journal of Clinical and Experimental Hypnosis*, Vol. 49 (3), 2001, pp. 185-206.

Yonge, Charles Duke, tr. *The Works of Philo Judaeus*. London: H. G. Bohm, 1854-1855.

# Endnotes

## Introduction

[1] Soren Ventgodt, Mohammed Morad, Eytan Hyam and Joav Merrick, "Clinical Holistic Medicine: Induction of Spontaneous Remission of Cancer by Recovery of the Human Character and the Purpose of Life (Life Mission)," (*The Scientific World Journal* (4), 2004), pp. 368-369.

[2] *Ibid.* pp. 365-366.

[3] *Ibid.* pp. 371-372.

[4] *Ibid.* p. 367.

[5] Kenneth Sylvan Gutherie, ed. & tr., *The Pythagorean Sourcebook and Library* (Grand Rapids, MI: Phanes Press, 1987), p. 72.

[6] Charles Duke Yonge, tr., *The Works of Philo Judaeus*, Vol. 4 (London: H. G. Bohm, 1855), p. 1.

[7] Bertrand Russell, *A History of Western Philosophy* (New York: Simon & Schuster, 1945), pp. 53, 55.

[8] G. R. S. Mead, *Apollonius of Tyana* (Kila, MT: Kessinger Publishing Company, 1901), p. 111.

[9] *Love, Medicine and Miracles*, (New York: Harper and Row, Publishers, Inc., 1986), p. 178.

## Chapter One

[10] Robert J. Miller, ed (San Francisco: HarperSanFrancisco, 1994).

[11] Williston Walker, *A History of the Christian Church* (New York: Scribner, 1985), p. 624.

[12] Jefferson wrote *The Life and Morals of Jesus of Nazareth, Extracted textually from the Gospels in Greek, Latin, French and English*, which was not published until 1904. Cited in *Jesus through the Centuries* by Jaroslav Pelikan (New Haven, CT: Yale University Press, 1985), p. 192.

[13] Jaroslav Pelikan, *Jesus through the Centuries* (New Haven, CT: Yale University Press, 1985), p. 187.

[14] Albert Schweitzer (William Montgomery, tr.), *The Quest of the Historical Jesus* (New York: The MacMillan Company, 1950), pp. 122-125.

[15] Burton Mack, *The Lost Gospel of Q: The Book of Christian Origins* (San Francisco: HarperSanFrancisco, 1993), p. 21.

[16] *Op. cit.*

[17] Albert Schweitzer, *Op. cit.*, p. 238.

[18] *A Marginal Jew: Rethinking the historical Jesus; vol. 3: Companions and Competitors* (New York: Doubleday, 2001), p, 47.

[19] Robert W. Funk, Roy W. Hoover and the Jesus Seminar, *The Five Gospels: The Search for the Authentic Words of Jesus* (New York: Macmillan Publishing Company, 1993), pp. 533-537.

[20] *Ibid*, pp. 19-28.

[21] P. 284, "A Renaissance in Jesus Studies," *Theology Today, vol. 45, no. 3* (October 1988).

### Chapter Two

[22] *The Works of Josephus, Complete and Unabridged*, William Whiston, tr. (Peabody, MA: Hendrickson Publishers, Inc., 1987), p. 484.

[23] Robert Funk and the Jesus Seminar, *The Acts of Jesus: What Did Jesus Really Do?* (San Francisco: HarperSanFrancisco, 1998), p. 62.

### Chapter Three

[24] Bertrand Russell, *A History of Western Philosophy* (New York: Simon and Schuster, Inc., 1945), pp. 48-49.

[25] *Ibid*, p. 263.

[26] Aristotle, *The Basic Works of Aristotle*, Richard McKeon ed. & tr. (New York: Random House, 1941), p.885.

[27] James Strong, *The New Strong's Exhaustive Concordance of the Bible, Concise Dictionary of the Words in the Greek Testament* (Nashville: Thomas Nelson Publishers, Inc., 1995), p. 17.

[28] *Epictetus: Discourses and Enchiridion*, Thomas Wentworth Higgenson, tr. (Roslyn, NY: Walter J. Black, Inc., 1944), p.226.

[29] Stephen Hawking's description of the "big bang," *A Brief History of Time: From the Big Bang to Black Holes* (New York: Bantam Books, 1988), p. 117.

[30] "Harnessing the Power of the Placebo Effect and Renaming it 'Remembered Wellness,' *Annual Review of Medicine*, Vol. 47, 1996, pp. 193-199.

[31] Carol Hegedus and Roger Nelson, *Alternative Medicine: Expanding Medical Horizons: A Report to the National Institutes of Health on Alternative Medical Systems and Practices in the United States* (Honolulu: University Press of the Pacific, 2002), p. 7.

[32] *Ibid.*

[33] Quoted by Patricia A. Norris, PhD in *Why Me?* (Walpole, NH: Stillpoint Publishing, 1985), pp. 130-131.

[34] "Harnessing the Power of the Placebo Effect and Renaming it 'Remembered Wellness,'" *Annual Review of Medicine*, Vol. 47, 1996, pp. 193-199.

[35] Lydia Ievleva and Terry Orlick, "Mental Links to Enhanced Healing: An Exploratory Study," *The Sport Psychologist*, Vol. 5 (1), Mar 1991, pp. 25-40.

[36] (New York: Harper and Row, Publishers, Inc., 1986), p. 175.

[37] *Varieties of Religious Experience* (New York: The New American Library, Inc., 1958), pp. 106-111.

[38] *Ibid*, p. 88.

[39] William James quoted Dresser a few times in his lecture on "healthy mindedness." Besides writing about metaphysical healing, Dresser published on more conventional philosophical topics.

### Chapter Four

[40] Becca R Levy, Martin D. Slade, Suzanne R. Kunkel, Stanislav V. Kasl, "Longevity Increased by Positive Self-Perceptions of Aging," *Journal of Personality and Social Psychology*, Vol. 83 (2), August 2002, pp. 261-270.

[41] James Strong, *Op. cit*, p. 24.

[42] See Maxwell Maltz, *Psychocybernetics: A New Technique for Using Your Subconscious Power* (Englewood Cliffs, NJ: Prentice-Hall, Inc., 1960), pp. 31-36.

[43] Kenneth R. Pelletier, *Mind as Healer, Mind as Slayer* (New York: Dell Publishing Co., Inc., 1977), pp. 252-259.

[44] Anahad O'Connor, "Well: Really? Optimism Reduces the Risk of Heart Disease," *New York Times archives*: April 23, 2012, http://well.blogs.nytimes.com/2012/04/23/really-optimism-reduces-the-risk-of-heart-disease.

[45] JK Boehm, and LD Kubzansky, "The Heart's Content: the Association between Positive Psychological Well-Being and Cardiovascular Health," *Psychological Bulletin*, 2012 July Vol. 138 (4), p. 655.

[46] Michael F. Scheier, Karen A. Matthews, Jane F. Owens, George J. Magovern, R. Craig Lefebvre, R. Anne Abbott and Charles S. Carver, "Dispositional optimism and recovery from coronary artery bypass surgery: The beneficial effects on physical and psychological well-being," *Journal of Personality and Social Psychology*, Vol 57(6), Dec 1989, pp. 1024-1040.

[47] See *Psycho-Cybernetics* by Maxwell Maltz, M.D. (Englewood Cliffs, N.J.: Prentice-Hall, Inc., 1960).

[48] *Ibid*, p. 31-32.

[49] R. A. Vandell, R. A. Davis and H. A. Clugston, "The Function of Mental Practice in the Acquisition of Motor Skills," (Vol 29, 1943), pp. 243-250.

[50] L. Verdelle Clark, "Effect of Mental Practice on the Development of a Certain Motor Skill," *Research Quarterly of the American Association for Health, Physical Education, and Recreation*, Vol 31, 1960, pp. 560-569.

[51] See "What Oprah Learned from Jim Carrey," https://www.youtube.com/watch?v=nPU5bjzLZX0.

### Chapter Five

[52] Glen Rein, Mike Atkinson and Rollin McCraty, "The Physiological and Psychological Effects of Compassion and Anger" (*Journal of Advancement in Medicine*, Vol. 8 no.2, Summer 1995), pp. 87-89.

[53] *A History of Western Philosophy* (New York: Simon and Schuster, Inc., 1945), p.710.

[54] *Emerson's Essays* (New York: Harper and Row, Publishers, 1926), pp. 73-74

[55] *Ibid*, p. 74.

[56] *Ibid*, p. 90.

[57] *Ibid*, p. 88.

[58] *Ibid*. p.89.

[59] *Situation Ethics: The New Morality* (Philadelphia: Westminster, 1966).

[60] James Strong, *Op. cit*, p.90.

[61] Richard A. Batey, *Jesus and the Forgotten City* (Grand Rapids, MI: Baker Book House Company, 1991), pp. 90-91.

[62] See e.g. the works of Menander, Plautus, and Terrence, most of which can be accessed online.

[63] *The Basic Works of Aristotle*, Richard McKeon, ed. (New York: Random House, Inc., 1941), p. 1460.

[64] Batey, *op. cit*, p 99.

[65] Suzanne R. Freedman and Robert D. Enright. "Forgiveness as an Intervention Goal with Incest Survivors," (*Journal of Consulting and Clinical Psychology*, Vol. 64, no. 5), pp. 985-986.

[66] *Ibid*, p. 983.

[67] Wei-Fen Lin, David Mack, Robert D. Enright, Dean Krahn, Thomas W. Baskin, "Effects of Forgiveness Therapy on Anger, Mood and Vulnerability to Substance Use Among Inpatient Substance-Dependent Clients" (*Journal of Consulting and Clinical Psychology*, Vol. 72, no. 6, Dec 2004), pp. 1114-1121.

[68] Freedman and Enright, *op. cit.*, p. 83.

**Chapter Six**

[69] Stevan L. Davies, *Jesus the Healer* (New York: The Continuum Publishing Co., 1995), pp. 107-108,

[70] *The Works of Philo Judaeus*, C. D. Yonge, tr. (London: H. G. Bohn, 1855), p. 164.

[71] *Ibid*.

[72] *Ibid*, p. 155.

**Chapter Seven**

[73] *Jesus the Healer: Possession, Trance, and the Origins of Christianity* (New York: The Continuum Publishing Company, 1995), pp. 121-128.

[74] Ernest Rossi, Sheila Rossi and Milton Erickson, *Hypnotic Realities* (New York: Irvington, 1976), pp. 20, 226.

[75] Milton Erickson and Ernest L. Rossi, "Autohypnotic Experiences of Milton H. Erickson," (*The American Journal of Clinical Hypnosis*, Vol. 20, July, 1977), pp. 36-54.

[76] Davies, *op. cit.*, p. 129.

[77] *Ibid*, p. 130.

[78] *Ibid*.

[79] *Ibid*, p. 131.

[80] Rossi, Rossi, and Erickson, *op cit.*, pp. 304 and 312.

[81] *Ibid*, p. 205.

[82] Wing-Tsi Chan, ed. & tr., *A Source Book in Chinese Philosophy* (Princeton: Princeton University Press, 1963), p. 151.

[83] Bertrand Russell, *A History of Western Philosophy* (New York: Simon and Schuster, 1945), pp. 41-45.

[84] Kenneth Sylvan Guthrie, ed. & tr., *The Pythagorean Sourcebook and Library* (Grand Rapids, MI: Phanes Press, 1987), p. 116.

[85] See *Aesop without Morals; the Famous Fables, and a Life of Aesop* by Lloyd W Daly (New York: Thomas Yoseloff, 1961).

[86] Kenneth R. Pelletier, *Mind as Healer, Mind as Slayer* (New York: Dell Publishing Co., Inc., 1977), p. 229.

[87] *Ibid*, p. 238.

[88] Plutarch, *The Parallel Lives, Loeb Classical Library, Vol. 10,* Bernadotte Perrin, tr. (Cambridge, MA: Harvard University Press, 1921), p. 167.

**Chapter Eight**

[89] Larry Dossey, M.D, *Healing Words: The Power of Prayer and the Practice of Medicine* (San Francisco: HarperSanFrancisco, 1993), p. 98.

[90] *Ibid.* (For descriptions of the Spindrift's history and experiments, go to www.spindriftresearch.org.)

[91] Article "Prayer and Healing" by Larry Dossey in Gowri Rammohan, *New Frontiers of Human Science* (Jefferson, North Carolina: McFarland and Company, Inc., 2002), pp. 22-23.

[92] John A. Astin, Elaine Harkness, Edzard Ernst, "The Efficacy of 'Distant Healing': A Systematic Review of Randomization Trials" (*Annals of Internal Medicine* Vol 132 no. 11, June 6, 2000), pp. 903-910

[93] Theodore B. VanItallie, "Stress: A Risk Factor for Serious Illness" (*Metabolism*, Vol. 51, No. 6, Suppl 1, June 2002), p. 40.

[94] *Ibid*, p. 40-42.

[95] Karina W. Davidson, Elizabeth Mostofsky and William Whang, "Don't Worry, Be Happy: Positive Affect and Reduced 10-Year Incident Coronary Heart Disease: The Canadian Nova Scotia Health Survey" (*European Heart Journal*, Vol. 31, no. 9, 2010), p. 1065.

[96] *Ibid.*

[97] D. R. Morse, J. S. Martin, M. L. Furst and L. L. Dubin, "A physiological & subjective evaluation of meditation, hypnosis, & relaxation" (*Psychosomatic Medicine*, Vol. 39 no. 5, 1977), pp. 304-324.

[98] See e.g. Eric Greenleaf, PhD, "The Red House: Hypnotherapy of Hysterical Blindness" (*American Journal of Clinical Hypnosis*, Vol. 13 (3), 1971), pp. 155 161.

[99] www.mayoclinic.com/health/conversion-disorder/DS00877, accessed 8/23/2013.

[100] Eron G.Manusov, "Clinical Applications of Hypnotherapy," (*The Journal of Family Practice*, Vol. 31 (2), August 1990), pp. 180-184.

[101] David Spiegel and Joan R. Bloom, "Group Therapy and Hypnosis Reduce Metastatic Breast Carcinoma Pain" (*Psychosomatic Medicine*, Vol. 45, no. 4, August 1983), pp. 333-339.

[102] A. C. Steward and S. E. Thomas, "Hypnotherapy as a Treatment for Atopic Dermatitis in Adults and Children" (*British Journal of Dermatology*, Vol.132 no. 5, May 1995), pp. 778-783.

[103] D. R. Collison, "Which Asthmatic Patients Should Be Treated by Hypnotherapy?" (*The Medical Journal of Australia*, Vol. 1 no. 25, 1975), pp. 776-781.

[104] J. A. D. Anderson, M. A. Basker and R. Dalton, "Migraine and Hypnotherapy" (*International Journal of Clinical and Experimental Hypnosis*, Vol. 23 no. 1, 1975), pp. 48-58.

[105] Dabney M. Ewin, "Hypnotherapy for Warts (Verruc Vulgaris): 41 Consecutive Cases with 33 Cures" (*American Journal of Clinical Hypnosis*, Vol. 35 no.1, 1992), pp. 1-10.

[106] Paul A. Fox, Donald C. Henderson, Simon E. Barton, Andrew J. Champion, Matthew S. H. Rollin, Jose Catalan, Sheena M. G. McCormack and John Gruzelier, "Immunological Markers of Frequently Recurrent Genital Herpes Simplex Virus and Their Response to Hypnotherapy: A Pilot Study" (*International Journal of STD and AIDS*, Vol. 10 no.11, November 1999), pp. 730-734.

[107] Theodore X. Barber, PhD, "Hypnosis, Suggestions, & Psychosomatic Phenomena: A New Look from the Standpoint of Recent Experimental Studies," (*American Journal of Clinical Hypnosis*, Vol. 21, 1978).

[108] Shauna L. Shapiro, Roger Walsh, and Willoughby B. Britton, "An Analysis of Recent Meditation Research and Suggestions for Future Directions," (*Journal for Meditation and Meditation Research*, 2003, Vol. 3), pp. 70-71.

[109] *Ibid*, p. 71.

[110] *Ibid*, pp. 71-72.

[111] *Ibid*, pp. 78-79.

[112] Some studies showing the effects of meditation on alpha waves include: "Spectral analysis of the EEG in Meditation" by J. P. Banquet in *Electroencephalography and Clinical Neurophysiology*, Vol. 35 (2), August 1973, pp. 143-151; "Meditation and the EEG," by Michael A. West in *Psychological Medicine*, 1980, pp. 369-375; "Some Aspects of Electroencephalographic Studies in Yogis" by B. K. Anand, G. S. Chhina, and Baldev Singh in *Electroencephalography and Clinical Neurophysiology*, Vol. 13

(3), June 1961, pp. 452-546; and "An Electroencephalographic Study on the Zen Meditation (Zazen)" by Akira Kasamatsu, M.D. and Tomio Hirai, M.D. in *Psychiatry and Clinical Neurosciences*, Vol. 20 (4), December 1966, pp. 315-336.

## Chapter Nine

[113] For a helpful discussion see *Psycho-Cybernetics* by Maxwell Maltz, M.D. (Englewood Cliffs, N.J.: Prentice-Hall, Inc., 1960).

[114] Philip A. Harland, "The Economy of First-Century Palestine: State of the Scholarly Discussion" in *Handbook of Early Christianity: Social Science Approaches*, Anthony J. Blasi, Jean Duhaime & Paul-Andre Turcotte, ed. (Walnut Creek, CA: Alta Mira Press, 2002), p. 515.

[115] Abraham J. Malherbe, *The Cynic Epistles: A Study Edition* (Atlanta: Society of Biblical Literature, 1986), p. 49.

[116] Norman A. Rubin, "Origin of the Word Talent," www.helium.com/items/1050703-origin-of-the-word-talent.

## Chapter Ten

[117] *The Complete Gospels Annotated Scholars Version*, Robert J. Miller, ed. (San Francisco: HarperSanFrancisco, 1994), p. 431.

## Chapter Eleven

[118] William Whiston, translator, *The Works of Josephus, Complete and Unabridged* (Peabody, MA: Hendrickson Publishers, Inc. 1987), p. 477.

[119] Charles Duke Yonge, translator, *The Works of Philo Judaeus, Vol. 1* (London: H. G. Bohm, 1854), p. 2.

[120] Charles Duke Yonge, tr., *The Works of Philo Judaeus, Vol. 3* (London: H. G. Bohm, 1855), p. 140.

[121] Willis Barnstone and Marvin Meyer, editors, *The Gnostic Bible* (Boston: Shambhala Publications, Inc., 2003), 48.

[122] Anthony A. Long, "The Socratic Tradition: Diogenes, Crates, and Hellenistic Ethics," *The Cynics: The Cynic Movement in Antiquity and Its Legacy*, R. Bracht Branham and Marie-Odile Goulet-Cazé, ed. (Berkeley: University of California Press, 1996), p. 32.

[123] See e.g. *The Historical Jesus: The Life of a Mediterranean Jewish Peasant* by John Dominic Crossan (San Francisco: HarperCollins, 1991).

[124] M.-O. Goulet-Cazé (translated by Michael Chase), "Introduction," *The Cynics: The Cynic Movement in Antiquity and Its Legacy*, R. Bracht Branham and Marie-Odile Goulet-Cazé, ed. (Berkeley: University of California Press, 1996), p. 8-9.

[125] See Matthew 6: 25-30.

[126] See Luke 10: 7 regarding kosher and Mk. 2: 27, 28 regarding Sabbath rules.

[127] Robert W. Funk., Roy W. Hoover, and The Jesus Seminar, *The Five Gospels: The Search for the Authentic Words of Jesus* (New York: Macmillan Publishing Co., 1993), p. 31.

[128] *The Cynics: The Cynic Movement in Antiquity and Its Legacy*, R. Bracht Branham and Marie-Odile Goulet-Cazé, ed. (Berkeley: University of California Press, 1996), p. 27.

[129] Mt 8: 30, SV.

[130] Mk 6: 8, NIV.

[131] Mt 10: 10, NIV.

[132] Lu 9: 3, NIV.

[133] M.-O. Goulet-Cazé, *op cit.*, p. 16.

[134] *Ibid.*

[135] Thom. 97:1-4, SV.

[136] Abraham J. Malherbe, ed., *The Cynic Epistles: A Study Edition* (Atlanta: Society of Biblical Literature, 1986), p.49.

[137] Long, *op cit.* p. 42.

[138] *Ibid*, p. 44.

[139] Mark 10: 29-30, NIV.

[140] John L. Moles, "Cynic Cosmopolitanism," *The Cynics: The Cynic Movement in Antiquity and Its Legacy*, R. Bracht Branham and Marie-Odile Goulet-Cazé, ed. (Berkeley: University of California Press, 1996), p. 113.

[141] M.-O. Goulet-Cazé, "Religion and the Early Cynics," *The Cynics: The Cynic Movement in Antiquity and Its Legacy*, R. Bracht Branham and Marie-Odile Goulet-Cazé, ed. (Berkeley: University of California Press, 1996), p. 72.

[142] Moles, *op. cit.,* p. 107.

[143] Bertrand Russell, A *History of Western Philosophy* (New York: Simon and Schuster, 1945), p. 253.

[144] *Ibid*, p. 263.

[145] *Ibid*, p. 264.

[146] *Ibid*, p. 254.

[147] *Ibid.*

[148] *Ibid.*

[149] *Ibid*, p. 256.

[150] *Ibid*, p. 257.

[151] Kenneth Sylvan Guthrie, ed. & tr., *The Pythagorean Sourcebook and Library* (Grand Rapids, MI: Phanes Press, 1987), p. 32.

[152] *Ibid*, p. 116.

[153] *Ibid*, p. 131.

[154] Wing-Tsi Chan, ed. & tr., *A Source Book in Chinese Philosophy* (Princeton: Princeton University Press, 1963), p. 144.

[155] *Ibid*, p. 165.

[156] *Ibid*, p. 149.

[157] *Ibid*, p. 150.

[158] *Ibid*, p. 164-165.

[159] *Ibid*, p. 151.

[160] *Ibid*, p. 157.

[161] *Ibid*, p. 162.

[162] *Ibid*, p. 176.

[163] *Ibid*, p. 220.

[164] *Ibid*, p. 214.

[165] *Ibid*, p. 217.

[166] "Defacing the Currency: Diogenes' Rhetoric and the Invention of Cynicism," *The Cynics: The Cynic Movement in Antiquity and Its Legacy,* R. Bracht and Marie-Odile Goulet-Cazé, ed., (Berkeley: University of California Press, 1996), pp. 92-93.

[167] San Francisco: Harper and Row.

[168] *Anatomy of an Illness* (New York: Bantam Books, 1981).

[169] http://news.cancerconnect.com/laughter-may-boost-immune-system/ Reference cited was MP Bennett, JM Zeller, L Rosenberg, et al. "The effect of mirthful laughter on stress and natural killer cell activity" (*Alternative Therapies In Health And Medicine*, 2003;9), pp. 38-45.

[170] Rosemary Cogan, Dennis Cogan, William Waltz and Melissa McCue, "Effects of Laughter and Relaxation on Discomfort Thresholds" (*Journal of Behavioral Medicine,* Vol. 10 #2, 1987), pp. 139-144.

[171] M. Toda, S. Kusakabe, S. Nagasawa, K. Kitamura and K. Morimoto, "Effect of Laughter on Salivary Endrocrinological Stress Marker Chromogranin A" (*Biomedical Research,* Vol. 28 #2, 2007), pp. 115-118.

## Chapter Twelve

[172] *The Works of Josephus, Complete and Unabridged*, William Whiston, tr. (Peabody, MA: Hendrickson Publishers, Inc., 1987), p. 480.

[173] Aslan, Reza (2013-07-16). *Zealot: The Life and Times of Jesus of Nazareth* (Kindle Locations 1336-1339). Random House Publishing Group. Kindle Edition.

[174] *Ibid*, p. 480.

[175] *Ibid*, p. 538.

[176] For examples, see *Life After Life* by Raymond Moody, Jr., M.D. (Covington, GA: Mockingbird Books, 1975).

## Chapter Thirteen

[177] *The Works of Josephus, Complete and Unabridged*, William Whiston, tr. (Peabody, MA: Hendrickson Publishers, Inc., 1987), pp. 722, 727.

[178] *Ibid*, pp. 741-742.

[179] *Ibid*, p. 742.

[180] *Ibid*, p. 719.

[181] *Beyond Belief: The Secret Gospel of Thomas* (New York: Random House, 2003).

[182] "Attentional and Affective Concomitants of Meditation: A Cross-sectional Study" (*Journal of Abnormal Psychology*, Vol. 85 (2), April 1976), pp. 235-238.

[183] Michael S. Bahrke and William P. Morgan, "Anxiety Reduction Following Exercise and Meditation" (*Cognitive Therapy and Research*, Vol. 2 (4), December 1978), pp. 323-333.

[184] E.g. see James D. Lane, PhD; Jon E. Seskevich, RN, BSN, BA; and Carl F. Pieper, DrPH. "Brief Meditation Training Can Improve Perceived Stress and Negative Mood" (*Alternative Therapies*, Vol 13 (1), pp. 38-44, 2007) and Richard J. Davidson, Daniel J. Goleman and Gary E. Schwartz, "Attentional and Affective Concomitants of Meditation: A Cross-sectional Study" (*Journal of Abnormal Psychology*, Vol. 85 (2), April 1976, pp. 235-238).

[185] "A comparison of the effects of stress vs. relaxation instruction on the finger temperature response" (*Behavior Therapy* vol. 7 (1) January 1976), pp. 54-67.

[186] For example see John D. Williams and John H. Gruzelier, "Differentiation of hypnosis and relaxation by analysis of narrow band theta and alpha frequencies" (*International Journal of Clinical and Experimental Hypnosis*, Vol. 49 (3), 2001), pp. 185-206.

[187] *Measurement Science Review*, Vol. 2, Section 2, 2002.

## Chapter Fourteen

[188] For a helpful review of scientific studies on prayer, see *Healing Words: The Power of Prayer and the Practice of Medicine* by Larry Dossey, M.D. (San Francisco: HarperSanFrancisco, 1993).

## Appendix B

[189] E.g. see James D. Lane, PhD; Jon E. Seskevich, RN, BSN, BA; and Carl F. Pieper, DrPH. "Brief Meditation Training Can Improve Perceived Stress and Negative Mood" (*Alternative Therapies*, Vol 13 (1), pp. 38-44, 2007) and Richard J. Davidson, Daniel J. Goleman and Gary E. Schwartz "Attentional and Affective Concomitants of Meditation: A Cross-sectional Study" (*Journal of Abnormal Psychology*, Vol. 85 (2), April 1976, pp. 235-238).

[190] E.g. "Effects of Mental Relaxation and Slow Breathing in Essential Hypertension" by Rajeev Mohan Kaushik, Reshema Kaushik, Sukhdev Krishan Mahajan and Vevreddi Rajesh in Complementary Therapies in Medicine, Vol. 14 (2), June 2006, pp. 120-126.

[191] Some studies showing the effects of meditation on alpha waves include: "Spectral analysis of the EEG in Meditation" by J. P. Banquet in *Electroencephalography and Clinical Neurophysiology*, Vol. 35 (2), August 1973, pp. 143-151; "Meditation and the EEG," by Michael A. West in *Psychological Medicine*, 1980, pp. 369-375; "Some Aspects of

Electroencephalographic Studies in Yogis" by B. K. Anand, G. S. Chhina, and Baldev Singh in *Electroencephalography and Clinical Neurophysiology*, Vol. 13 (3), June 1961, pp. 452-546; and "An Electroencephalographic Study on the Zen Meditation (Zazen)" by Akira Kasamatsu, M.D. and Tomio Hirai, M.D. in *Psychiatry and Clinical Neurosciences*, Vol. 20 (4), December 1966, pp. 315-336.

## Appendix C

[192] The characterizations of Unity congregants are based upon research by the "Branding Solutions" firm which can be accessed on unityonline.org.

[193] Charles D. Spielberger, *State-Trait Anxiety Inventory for Adults Manual and Sample* (Washington, DC: Consulting Psychologists Press, Inc., 1983), p. 7.

[194] *Ibid.*

[195] *Ibid*, p. 9.

[196] *Ibid.*

[197] *Ibid*, p. 12.

[198] Douglas M. McNair, PhD. And JW P. Heuchert, PhD, *Profile of Mood States Technical Update* (Toronto: Multi-Health Systems, Inc., 2012), p.1.

[199] *Ibid*, p. 9.

[200] *Ibid*, p. 6.

[201] *Ibid*, p. 8.

51989070R00159

Made in the USA
Charleston, SC
08 February 2016